The Fiction of E. M. Forster

The Fiction of E. M. Forster

by George H. Thomson

Wayne State University Press, Detroit, 1967

George H. Thomson is a graduate in English of the University of Western Ontario. He received the M.A. and Ph.D. degrees from the University of Toronto.

The manuscript was edited by Robert H. Tennenhouse. The book was designed by Joanne E. Colman. The jacket was designed by Paul Schawinsky. The type used for the text is Linotype Granjon, redesigned by George W. Jones from a face cut by Claude Garamond. The display face is Legend designed by F. H. E. Schneidler in 1937.

The book is printed on S. D. Warren's Olde Style Antique paper and bound in Columbia Mills' Fictionette cloth. Manufactured in the United States of America.

To
my mother and father
and
Miss M. L. Brock
(1877–1967)

Contents

Acknowledgments   *9*

Editions of Forster   *11*

Introduction   *13*

1   E. M. Forster   *23*

       Mythology and Symbolism   *31*

2   Romance Moralities   *45*

       The Short Stories   *56*

3   Narrator as Archetype   *91*

       The Italian Romances   *100*

4   Hero as Archetype   *125*

       The Longest Journey   *134*

5   Object as Archetype   *161*

       Howards End   *170*

6   Novel as Archetype   *201*

       A Passage to India   *220*

Appendixes

A: Forster and the Nineteenth-Century View of Nature
and Symbol   *251*

B: The Manuscripts of *A Passage to India*   *261*

Notes   *273*

Index   *294*

Acknowledgments

I wish to thank the following: Murray Tolmie and Keith Hollingsworth for advice, encouragement, and friendship; Frederick P. W. McDowell for his generous interest and many valuable suggestions; Oliver Stallybrass for unfailing kindness, including permission to use his "Checklist of the Writings of E. M. Forster"; Keith Johnstone, Maurice Beebe, Joyce Measures, and Courtney Johnson for their interest in the manuscript at various stages; Laurie Allison and the staff of the Mount Allison Memorial Library, and the staffs of the London Library, British Museum, University of London Library, and Bodleian for their cheerful assistance; the Marjorie Young Bell Fund and the Regents of Mount Allison for sabbatical leave during 1962–63; and first and last, my wife Dorothy for her devotion to the cause—and to the typewriter.

Acknowledgments are due the following journals for permission to use portions of three articles of mine published in 1961: *Criticism* for "E. M. Forster's Earlier Fiction;" *Modern Fiction Studies* for "Theme and Symbol in *Howards End*;" *Twentieth Century Literature* for "Thematic Symbol in *A Passage to India*." Also the following publishers for permission to quote from the works of E. M. Forster: Edward Arnold Ltd. and Harcourt, Brace and World, Inc. for *Abinger Harvest, Aspects of the Novel, Goldsworthy Lowes Dickinson, The Hill of Devi, Marianne Thornton, A Passage to India, Two Cheers for Democracy;* Edward Arnold Ltd. and Alfred A. Knopf, Inc. for *Howards End, A Room with a View, The Longest Journey, Where Angels Fear to Tread;* Sidgwick and Jackson Ltd. and Alfred A. Knopf, Inc. for *The Collected Tales.* Also the following for permission to quote from copyrighted material: Routledge and Kegan Paul Ltd. for Erwin Rohde, *Psyche,* trans. W. B. Hillis; Robert Ligon Harrison and the University of Texas for "The Manuscripts of *A Passage to India.*"

G.H.T.

Editions of Forster Cited in the Text

The Uniform Pocket Edition of E. M. Forster's Works (London: Edward Arnold), which began in 1947 with the Pocket Edition of all five novels, is not yet complete. In the case of works not included in this edition, the standard American hardcover edition has been cited. The date of first publication is in parentheses.

Abinger Harvest, 1953 (1936).

Aspects of the Novel, 1949 (1927).

The Collected Tales of E. M. Forster. New York: Alfred A. Knopf, 1947. Includes *The Celestial Omnibus and Other Stories* (1911) and *The Eternal Moment and Other Stories* (1928).

Goldsworthy Lowes Dickinson, 1962 (1934).

The Hill of Devi. New York: Harcourt, Brace, 1953.

Howards End, 1947 (1910).

The Longest Journey, 1947 (1907).

Marianne Thornton: A Domestic Biography, 1797–1887. New York: Harcourt, Brace, 1956.

A Passage to India, 1947 (1924).

A Room with a View, 1947 (1908).
Two Cheers for Democracy. New York: Harcourt, Brace, 1951.
Where Angels Fear to Tread, 1947 (1905).

Introduction

*F*our things may be said about the fiction of E. M. Forster: first, that his works are romance rather than novel; second, that symbolism is central to his achievement in the romance form; third, that the principal source of his symbols is ecstatic experience; and fourth, that through the power of ecstatic perception his symbols achieve archetypal significance and mythic wholeness.

During the past hundred years fascination with myth has spread from the confines of anthropology to the ultimate circle of the verbal universe. Yet with some justice Charles Moorman complains that myth critics have neglected to specify the precise function of myth in the individual literary work. He undertakes to rectify this omission by demonstrating that myth imposes order on the fragmented and disoriented experience of twentieth-century man.[1] T. S. Eliot expounded the same belief in a 1923 review of Joyce, entitled "Ulysses, Order and Myth": "In using the myth, in manipulating a continuous parallel between contemporaneity and antiquity, Mr. Joyce is pursuing a method which others must pursue after him. . . . It is simply a way of controlling, of ordering, of giving a shape and a significance to the immense panorama of futility and anarchy which is contemporary history. . . . Instead of narrative method, we may now use the mythical method."[2]

The reader is here offered mythical *materials* and the mythical *method;* he is not offered myth. For this reason he can sympathize with R. P. Blackmur's suggestion "that 'myth' in the lauding sense we use it of Joyce and Kafka can only be a parody, so self-conscious it is, of what we mean by myth in Greek drama." This is not the place to define Blackmur's word "parody," a baggy monster that roams over part of the territory staked out by Northop Frye when he designated the literature of our time as low-mimetic. It will be enough to quote Blackmur's dictum: "Parody emphasizes mechanics, especially pre-scriptive mechanics in executive technique. . . ."[3] No one can doubt the importance of the mythical method in literature of this century; but one may well doubt that the employment of such materials and me-chanics is profound—except in an ironic way. That is to say, the depth emerges not from the mythic but from the low-mimetic character of the contemporary material and from the pointing up of its futility and anarchy.

What is eminently true of Joyce and Eliot, however, is not true of Forster. Forster's mythic or archetypal symbols are the heart of his fiction. They do not add up to a method; rather they constitute the substance and significance of his stories. Everything else exists to en-hance their power and value either by serving positively as a re-enforcement or negatively as a foil. Persons and objects take on arche-typal power and value not because they can be assimilated to a literary or psychological tradition but because within the fiction itself they create an unqualified impression of objective and absolute existence. In the chapters that follow I have argued that they create such an impression because they are seen as objects of mystical or ecstatic vision. Thus it is the manner of their creation and presentation that renders such persons and objects archetypal. In addition, they may and probably will have counterparts in mythic tradition; but they need not, a point readily illustrated by the hay image in *Howards End*. Hay is not a traditional mythic symbol; it is rendered mythic solely by Forster's presentation.

I lack the specialized knowledge to pronounce on the nature of myth as it arises and flourishes among primitive people. But it must be apparent that Forster's practice of showing us the mystical experience of identity with something outside the self and the apprehending of this other-than-self as having an absolute and transcendent existence is much closer to primitive experience than the Joyce-Eliot practice of intellectually imposing a pre-existing pattern on the chaos of experience. When the mythic has its source in ecstatic vision, the myth is a striving for an adequate mode of representation, a way of figuring forth the experience of an intuitive or transcendent pattern. Here myth, far from imposing order, seeks to embody a pre-existent order of experience. This contrast in the role of order strongly underlines Forster's radical apartness from the Joyce-Eliot tradition. In this Forster is not alone. Joseph Conrad, D. H. Lawrence and—I say it with less confidence—Dylan Thomas likewise stand outside the dominant tradition in their employment of myth.

It is the essence of this employment that the myth is newly created. The archetype is seen to spring Phoenix-like from the writer's experience (for its power lies not in its having existed over and over again but in its being at this moment born or reborn) and it is seen to attain absolute existence through the writer's art. Now it may as well be admitted, if one is to judge from much that passes for myth criticism, that this fresh creating of archetypal symbols is wholly unnecessary, for an author's merest hint or mention of a traditional symbol or story pattern is enough to unleash the most deep-seated reverberations among critics. Possibly they have a Jungian antenna which I lack. But I am more inclined to think they have simply confused two wave lengths. The first is the form and content of the myth, which may be readily exploited for such artistic purposes as order, re-enforcement, contrast, and the sense of the familiar. The second is the quality of experience which first gave rise to the myth and which is afterward reconstituted by participation in the renewal of the myth. This quality of experience is not to be conjured up by memory or gesture or any

15

kind of short cut. It is only to be attained, as I have said, by direct participation in the creation or the renewal of the myth.

Forster allows us this sense of participating. He offers us myth as experienced rather than myth as known. Consequently, this study of his work is not in the main stream of myth criticism—for the reason that Forster's stories and novels do not belong in the dominant tradition of twentieth-century literature characterized by the "mythical method."

Neither do Forster's works belong in the realistic tradition. Consequently, this book is not in the main stream of Forster criticism. That stream numbers among its currents Virginia Woolf, F. R. Leavis, Lionel Trilling, Walter Allen, and Frederick Crews. Its impetus springs from the belief that Forster wrote novels and that, consequently, his works should meet the standards of realism. The present study is wholly devoted to the proposition that Forster wrote romances and that the realistic elements of his fiction are used for other than realistic ends. Nothing further need be said about that now. My task in this place is to describe the realistic expectations brought to Forster's fiction. These may be categorized as physical, social, psychological, and moral.

Physical realism. Is the world of material things represented in an accurate and convincing way? The question has not had much attention from critics, though an affirmative answer seems often to be implied. This is odd because Forster's novels and stories are filled with landscapes, gardens, groves, and houses described with such a wealth of generalization, speculation, and insight that only a blind theorist could imagine the writer's object to be realism.

Social realism. Here critical demand has been more stringent. Forster, so the charge goes, is unfair to the Anglo-Indian ruling class in *A Passage to India;* he is unjust to the Wilcoxes and condescending to Leonard Bast in *Howards End;* and so the catalogue might be extended. I would be the first to admit that, if Forster's object in each novel is to create a balanced and realistic portrait of society, he is indeed unfair in that he gives a limited or biased view.

Far more serious than these complaints is Virginia Woolf's

stricture, echoed time after time in later criticism, that the visionary and the realistic elements in a Forster novel do not fuse. Thus "Mrs. Moore, the nice old lady, and Mrs. Moore, the sibyl" never come together. The prose and the poetry in her character do not unite. This is a serious charge, the more so as it comes from so sensitive a critic. After a careful reading of Virginia Woolf's essay, however, one can only conclude that she came at Forster wrong end to, regarding him as a realist who aspired to vision and couldn't quite bring it off.[4] Had she approached him as a visionary whose aim was to transmute his realistic material she might have reached a different conclusion. Let me illustrate this by going back to Mrs. Moore and to that scene where Adela, accompanied by Ronny Heaslop, returns to her bungalow after partially recovering from the Marabar debacle. One might mention certain remarkable facts: that Mrs. Moore's presence not only cures Adela's echo but somehow suggests to her that Aziz is innocent; and that when pressed she asserts with weary but absolute conviction that of course he is innocent. Here the intuitive genius and the not entirely nice old lady appear in the closest possible conjunction. But what most impresses me in the scene is something else, something simpler.

In a flare-up Ronny has said to his mother, "What do you want?" And she replies "I want my pack of patience cards" (p. 210).[5] This seems to me one of the fine moments of the novel, and its fineness hinges on the way the statement utterly fulfills and then absolutely transcends the obviousness of the pun. Mrs. Moore's reply is a bitter comment on the stupidity, futility, and fuss that inexorably surrounds her; it is a hard-headed request for the only kind of petty consolation that is to be looked for in the human wasteland here represented by her official-minded son and her once-prospective daughter-in-law; and finally it is a profoundly moving appeal not simply for the strength to endure but for another kind of world where patience, rather than serving as a desperate remedy, is a stillness from which understanding and acceptance may grow. If there was ever a separation between the irritable old English woman and the intuitive oriental, this appeal once and for all heals the division. In saying this I do not propose that every reader will find this moment powerful and effective. I think it is a special characteristic of Forster's fiction that there are many such moments and that each reader will find his own. Once he has found it, the gap, which Virginia Woolf could not bridge, will be closed.

Psychological realism. One fact stands out here: a remarkable lack of interest in the psychology of Forster's characters. I am inclined to think this is because they are romance types who do not lend themselves to psychological analysis. It is nonetheless odd that critics who regard Forster as a realist should have had so little to say on the matter.

The deficiency is more than compensated for, however, by the recent development of a back-door approach in which the psychological biography of the author is focused upon. Three books have explored this terrain. Wilfred Stone's *The Cave and the Mountain* is the most substantial and will serve as illustration. Stone believes that "Forster's fiction is essentially an experiment in self-confidence." *The Longest Journey* is Forster's way "of working, mole-like, out of a deep and crushing psychological repression," "it is the record of a rite of passage, a coming-of-age ceremony; and the writer has clearly shown his witnesses that he has a man and an artist locked within him, struggling to be let out."[6]

The objection to this kind of criticism has been underlined by Robert Penn Warren in his injunction: "We must sometimes force ourselves to remember that the act of creation is not simply a projection of temperament, but a criticism and purging of temperament."[7] Forster puts the case more radically in his essay on "Anonymity": "Imagination is our only guide into the world created by words. Whether those words are signed or unsigned becomes, as soon as the imagination redeems us, a matter of no importance, because we have approximated to the state in which they were written, and there are no names down there, no personality as we understand personality, no marrying or giving in marriage."[8] Not a thousand pages of biographia psychologica can shake my confidence in the quiet authenticity of this statement. However, the main point to be made here is not that Stone does less than justice to Forster as creative artist, but that his approach is a species of realist criticism. Both the failures and the triumphs of the writer's art are viewed as reflections of the author. Even the most fantastic and improbable aspects of his fiction are seen to be the real products of his experience and his psychic processes. In this way psychological realism enters into Forster criticism via the back door.

It may be confessed at this point that in speaking of realist critics I have very ungraciously neglected the many sound analyses and insights which have placed every reader of Forster in their debt. And I have, especially in what is to follow, unfairly isolated their most extreme statements and positions. I have done so not to ridicule them (for I have deliberately named critics who command respect) but to expose through their extreme statements the underlying premises of their criticism. My object is to make the reader aware of the radical divergence between the realist position and the one maintained in this book.

Moral realism. From first to last this has been the supreme theme of Forster studies. Here the place of honor may be given to F. R. Leavis. Our example comes from that scene in which Fielding and Hamidullah learn of Mrs Moore's death. They are saddened but not much exercised by the news. Forster represents not their thoughts but the *tone* of their response: "How indeed is it possible for one human being to be sorry for all the sadness that meets him on the face of the earth, for the pain that is endured not only by men, but by animals and plants, and perhaps by the stones?" (p. 257) This comment is prelude to a later event. Every reader will recall Professor Godbole's attempt during the Mau festival to impel to that place where completeness can be found an old lady from Chandrapore days, a wasp resting on a stone, and the stone itself. In the last endeavor he fails. His desire to bring the stone within the circle of salvation was the product of conscious effort rather than love. The stone on which Professor Godbole stubs his spiritual toe proves even more recalcitrant when encountered by Professor Leavis's moral toe. But whereas the Hindu Professor knows why he has been defeated by the stone, the English Professor does not even know he has been defeated. Instead he is morally distressed by those stones. It is not reasonable that stones should be objects of sympathy, let alone of salvation. And to make them so is, on Forster's part, lax, self-indulgent, and something less than serious.[9] Anyone who has read Part III of *A Passage to India* with its vision of salvation for all matter and all spirit may think the goal unattainable and the burden too heavy for human frailty to bear, but to call such a vision self-indulgent and less than serious (for we must suppose Leavis was aware of the parallel) is to reveal a certain narrowness and rigidity in one's own values.

Here in extreme and amusing form is the pitfall of all criticism which takes its stand on moral realism. The values the critic finds real (that is to say, acceptable) are *his* values, and if the author's values differ from his, the author is found wanting. In assessing Forster's values, it has been customary to focus the discussion on his liberal humanism. The practice was given much impetus by Lionel Trilling's important book, *E. M. Forster* (New York, 1943) and twenty years later attained its apotheosis in C. B. Cox's *The Free Spirit*. It has been further customary to find Forster's liberal humanism, in one way or another, wanting. In particular, it is thought to lack viability in face of the strenuous realities of the twentieth century. The final absurdity of the viability principle is reached when Cox writes: "Forster, then, has little to say to those whose children are dying of starvation because of social injustice, or to those whose families are decimated by a marauding army."[10]

Such is the judgment of the moment. But in the long perspective it will matter very little whether or not Forster's liberal humanism and moral philosophy were specifically applicable to his own time. What will matter is that with splendid narrative and symbolic evocation he has expressed the polarities of man's experience of the universe from his encounter with absolute negation to his entry into ultimate affirmation. In the course of time the debate over liberal humanism will be, like Jeremy Taylor's dying man, of a departing interest; but *A Passage to India* (to take but one example) will assert its relevance, because "Caves" and "Temple," the Marabar and the Mau festival, have been structured by art and informed by experience which can never be, so long as we are human, of a departing interest.

Allegories stalk in the background, not always upon all fours. The contrast between the material and the immaterial, the contrast between pleasure and action, the nature of wedded joy . . . *Chitra* symbolizes all three ideas in turn. It is true that the play is not the least spoilt by the symbolism. . . . Indeed, one's enjoyment is increased by the sense of half-audible stirrings in the midst of the jasmine bowers. But to drag the allegory from its retirement, and proclaim it has importance in itself is to brutalize the atmosphere and pay no real honour to the author.

—Abinger Harvest

Moby Dick is full of meanings: its meaning is a different problem. It is wrong to turn the Delight or the coffin into symbols, because even if the symbolism is correct, it silences the book. Nothing can be stated about *Moby Dick* except that it is a contest. The rest is song.

—Aspects of the Novel

As an insider, long initiated and thereby a shaman in the art of fiction, Forster is out of sympathy with those who would explore, define, and —as they hope—clarify. But as an outsider in the art of painting, he says a different thing and speaks for all of us who are not initiated: "Then the friend I was with . . . set to work on my behalf, and cautiously underlined the themes. There is a wave. There is a half-wave. The wave starts up on the left, with the head of the painter, and curves down and up through the heads of the three girls. The half-wave starts with the head of Isabel de Velasco, and sinks out of the canvas through the dwarfs. Responding to these great curves, or inverting them, are smaller ones on the women's dresses or elsewhere. . . . I put it more crudely than did Charles Mauron, nor do I suppose that his account would have been Velasquez's, or that Velasquez would have given any account at all. But it is an example of the way in which pictures should be tackled for the benefit of us outsiders: coolly and patiently, as if they were designs, so that we are helped at last to the appreciation of something non-mathematical."

1
E. M. Forster

E. M. Forster was a great grandson of Henry Thornton, a leading member of the Clapham sect.[1] In other words he was born into that intellectual aristocracy which played so important a part in nineteenth-century English life. As a result of social ties and marriage, this aristocracy of brains and bourgeois principles formed itself into a whole series of constellations during the reign of Victoria. Bloomsbury, with which Forster had close ties, was the last of that series. In comparison with earlier groupings it may be distinguished by its greater emphasis on art and personal relations. It began to take shape quite spontaneously at the end of the last century when a group of remarkable young men found themselves members of an intimate society. This society and the Bloomsbury Group which grew out of it deserve a place in any account of Forster's background.

The most authoritative and convincing assessment of the membership of Bloomsbury is provided by Leonard Woolf in the third volume of his autobiography. His list for the original Bloomsbury is: The three Stephens—Vanessa, Virginia, and Adrian (Thoby died in 1906)—Lytton Strachey,[2] Clive Bell, Leonard Woolf, Maynard Keynes, Duncan Grant, E. M. Forster, Saxon Sydney-Turner, Roger Fry, and Desmond and Molly MacCarthy. Of the ten men in this group, nine had been at Cambridge (Duncan Grant is the exception) and eight had been more or less contemporary at King's and Trinity (Roger Fry is the further exception). Moreover, of the nine Cambridge men, seven (Clive Bell and Adrian Stephen are the exceptions) were members of a small, select, and intimate society called The Apostles.[3]

It would be grossly misleading to suggest that these young men thought alike, but it would be fair to say that Cambridge, "that great modern focus of free thought,"[4] helped to unite them in a spirit of revolt against the Victorian heritage of materialism, Grundyism, and ponderous skepticism.[5] Cambridge helped also to form their ideal of a life intelligent, humane, lively, and productive. G. E. Moore's *Principia Ethica* (Cambridge, 1903), with its philosophical emphasis on intuition as a path to the direct apprehension of unanalyzable but objective properties of the real world, was especially timely and influential. It was through Moore and Cambridge that the future Bloomsberries came to value, above all else, and with varying degrees of emphasis, intuition, intellect, and personal relations.[6] Intuition saved them from abstractness, intellect saved them from sloppiness, and personal relations saved them from being inhuman. Along with Moore as their philosopher, one should also mention Lowes Dickinson, whom they embraced as their guardian angel. After graduation they remained in contact with both men, and indeed with all those whom they valued in the university.

Then, as now, London dominated England's financial, political, and social life. And within London, Bloomsbury, with its squares of substantial houses next door to the British Museum, provided an admirable locale for the intelligentsia. During the early years of the century when only a minority of those who came to be associated with Bloomsbury lived there, the most important residents were the Stephens at 46 Gordon Square. Leslie Stephen's two sons, Adrian and Thoby, were impressive young men and his two daughters, Virginia and Vanessa, were even more beautiful than they were intelligent. During the formative years, 46 Gordon Square was especially important to the development and holding together of this society which was to become Bloomsbury. For of course Leonard Woolf is correct when he insists that the Bloomsbury Group only came into existence between 1911 and 1914 when all its members except Desmond and Molly MacCarthy had come to live in that one area of London. But the special and intimate relations of its members go back much further and have their foundations in Cambridge and the Cambridge Apostles.[7]

Cambridge, London, Bloomsbury, and a tradition of close association among the intelligentsia, all these centripetal forces are at work in shaping the society of Bloomsbury. They do not, however, explain the dynamic of the group nor how that dynamic remained viable despite marriages, children, separations, and diverging interests. Keith Johnstone has made a valuable initial study with emphasis on the intellectual and esthetic, but anything like a full history of the Bloomsbury group has not yet been written for the good reason that some of the more personal documents are not yet available and some of the passions and prejudices aroused by Bloomsbury are not yet allayed.[8] For the present it may be safest to accept Leonard Woolf's summing up: "We were and always remained primarily and fundamentally a group of friends. Our roots and the roots of our friendship were in the University of Cambridge."[9]

Forster has said in a letter, as reported by K. W. Gransden, "that he does not regard himself as belonging or having belonged to Bloomsbury, but that critics like putting people into groups."[10] Forster attended Cambridge, was an Apostle, lived for a time in Brunswick Square, and numbered among his close friends most of those on Woolf's list. Moreover, Woolf asserts that the thirteen persons on his list were also the original thirteen members of the Memoir Club which met from time to time to hear one or another of the group read an autobiographical paper.[11] Though Forster is free to regard himself as not belonging, the unbiased observer must settle the matter on the basis of evidence rather than opinion. The evidence suggests that, if Bloomsbury existed at all, Forster belonged.

There is, however, some justice in his negative attitude, for the truth would seem to be that he was never a fully participating member of Bloomsbury. His habit of withdrawing into the country, like his habit of withdrawing into himself, signified his detachment. No group could hold him.

Later in this chapter, after discussing mythology and symbolism, it will be possible to say with some precision how Forster's temperament and intellectual stance set him apart from Bloomsbury. For the present I want only to make the point that Forster cultivated a certain detachment. Besides, one guesses that he found this society of furiously brilliant young people rather too sophisticated for his taste. Yet the Bloomsberries were important to him. They were, after all, his friends, and their acceptance of him must have enhanced his confidence as a young writer. It must have helped him to the conviction that what was within—about which he always felt a kind of certitude —was worth launching into the world outside.

Forster's detachment had other implications. It was capacious enough to group in one vision all the erudition of his time. The nineteenth century was a period of swift and pervasive change. Nowhere was this more obvious than in the monumental advances of scientific and social studies. Massive and learned volumes crowded one upon another and controversy raged ponderously, the more so as the century progressed and studies in classical literature, archeology, anthropology, philology, mythology, religion, biology, geology, psychology, history, and philosophy became increasingly interdependent. Forster appears to have read little of this vast array of erudition. He did not even read Moore's *Principia Ethica* which caused such a stir among his Bloomsbury friends. Yet far from being behind the times he was one of the sensitive and profound who listen, observe, and—within their range of interest—grasp with intuitive clarity the essential issues of the age.

For Forster, there was just one great issue: the survival and full development of the individual personality in face of a civilization increasingly urbanized, industrialized, and routinized. The Romantics were alive to the problem. It was most incisively stated by William Blake:

> I wander thro' each charter'd street
> Near where the charter'd Thames does flow
> And mark in every face I meet
> Marks of weakness, marks of woe.

But so long as millions simply survived in poverty and ignorance like Egyptian slaves building a vast pyramid, it could never be a central issue. The great achievement of the nineteenth century was that it built not a pyramid but a mighty machine which spewed out wealth in such abundance that even the slaves of the machine began to foresee their freedom. By the turn of the century it was possible to believe in a time when most men would have education and wealth sufficient to permit the cultivation of their individual natures. But could the personality grow and flourish in the chartered civilization of the machine? Though dictators and bombs have filled the headlines and obscured the issues, this has remained a central question in our century. No novelist has explored it more sensitively and deeply than Forster and, so far as I know, the only writer outside the novel who has overreached him is Carl Jung.

Forster has said he could not read either Freud or Jung.[12] That he could not read Freud is understandable. The emphasis on sex, the persistent analysis back to infantile origins, and Freud's somewhat Jehovah-like attitude to his patients, all these would be alien and offensive to Forster.

Jung, on the other hand, would appear eminently congenial. His emphasis on what he called individuation, the self-realization of the personality through the integration of the ego and the unconscious, his wide interest in myth and symbol, his conception of the therapeutic situation as the man in the doctor confronting the man in the patient on fundamentally equal terms, and, generally, his regard for the dignity and freedom of the individual, all these would be in harmony with Forster's outlook. However, Forster may have been put off by the detailed technical matter necessary to Jung's discipline. And anyway, he thinks it most undesirable to leave so important a matter to experts. "But man is an odd, sad creature as yet, intent on pilfering the earth and heedless of the growths within himself. He cannot be bored about psychology. He leaves it to the specialist, which is as if he should leave his dinner to be eaten by a steam-engine. He cannot be bothered to digest his own soul."[13] It need not surprise us, then, that what might have interested Forster most in Jung's work he had already arrived at in his own way. Thus Mrs. Wilcox is a splendid example of an individuated personality, though *Howards End* was published in 1911 before Jung had elaborated his theory.

One feature of Jung's development is especially instructive. The more deeply he probed the human psyche the more decisively he found himself committed to the representation of his findings by means of myth and symbol; and this for two reasons: first, the unconscious when it emerges into consciousness expresses itself in symbols; second and quite apart from this, myth and symbol are the best means of *effectively representing* psychic processes.

Jung (born 1875 in Switzerland) and Forster (born 1879 in England) came from settled middle-class backgrounds, they saw the central issue of the twentieth century as modern man in search of a soul, they agreed at first that the search should be directed toward the full development of the personality and later that it should be directed toward a more impersonal and universal goal which each called the spirit (*A Passage to India* and Jung's works on religion and alchemy), and they early recognized that myth and symbol were the most effective way of expressing their understanding. Though he was the younger, Forster in every case arrived at these positions before Jung.

The comparison should be pushed no further, for its validity applies only to essentials. But it is worth making for three reasons. One, it is frequently said that Forster is old-fashioned and, what is more slighting, Edwardian. In the sense intended this is nonsense. He did, of course, belong to his time; but as the comparison with Jung shows he was ahead of his time, confronting a problem which we must still confront. Two, his use of myth and symbol was neither a return to romantic convention nor indulgence in the esthetic and symbolist modes of the nineties, but a bold and original response to the psychological demands of the twentieth century. Three, his preceding Jung in the use of myth and symbol as the appropriate means of expressing the modern dilemma suggests that we should investigate the background to this usage.

That background is not to be found in the literature or symbolism of the late nineteenth century. The literature of the nineties was woven of three strands, the new or "shameless" realism, sentimental romanticism, and estheticism inherited from the previous decades.[14]

Its distinctly moribund condition did nothing to relieve the barrenness of the previous decade. Indeed, during the quarter century between 1879 when Forster was born and 1904 when he was writing his first novel not a single major poet established himself on the English literary scene—though Hopkins was working off stage and Yeats was on stage playing a familiar part with all the poetic stances characteristic of the late eighties and nineties. Except for Conrad who established himself with *The Nigger of the Narcissus* (1898) and *Lord Jim* (1900), the same is true of fiction. The best England could offer were the romances of Stevenson and Moore, the realistic narratives of Gissing, the short stories of Kipling, and the fantastic and imaginative romances of H. G. Wells.

The young men of Forster's generation, when they looked for the best in contemporary English fiction, found it in the works of the older masters, Meredith, Hardy, and James. Moreover, if they had strong roots in the intellectual aristocracy, they did not regard French realism and naturalism with favor. These sturdy plants were rejected all round, by a complacent middle class, by leading esthetes like Oscar Wilde, and by the intelligentsia. Typical of the latter group is Jane Harrison who in 1885 speaks of "warily shunning the rank unwholesome pastures of modern realism"—a remark all the more significant for its being an aside.[15] Bloomsbury modified this earlier attitude by stressing the drabness of realism rather than its unwholesomeness.

John Addington Symonds gives us a summary of the situation in 1890: "Up to the present moment there are but few signs of any vital resurrection of the spirit. Not only in Europe, but in America also, culture continues to be mainly reproductive and imitative. The conflict of romanticism with classicism liberated taste; yet artists still handle worn-out themes in the old formal ways, without the earlier grasp upon them, without fervour of conviction, and without power to awake popular enthusiasm." Had Symonds lived another ten years it is unlikely he would have revised his judgment.[16]

In view of this situation, I do not propose to investigate what the esthetes or symbolists were doing with the Romantic Image during the nineties. Rather, I propose to investigate what the experts were

29

saying about mythology and symbolism before and shortly after the turn of the century. This will give some notion of the most advanced ideas of the time. It will be safe to assume that Forster read few of the books discussed. His attitude in 1905 is nicely indicated by a comment on the survival of the Greek gods during the Middle Ages. The gods in their immortality, he says, "could endure the philosophy of that day, just as they will endure the archaeology of this."[17] He rejected the ponderous analytical soullessness of scholarship; yet he participated in the spirit animating some of the boldest humanistic research of the time.

Mythology and Symbolism

But the artist appeals to that part of our being which is not dependent on wisdom: to that in us which is a gift and not an acquisition—and, therefore, more permanently enduring. He speaks . . . to the latent feeling of fellow-ship with all creation—and to the subtle but invincible conviction of solidarity . . . which binds together all humanity—the dead to the living and the living to the unborn.

—Joseph Conrad

The biological century was so named not because biology in its own right was an overwhelming preoccupation, but because it had provided the analogy for an organic concept of mind and because it was the first to establish with massive and irrefutable proof the theory of evolution. This theory, which Charles Lyell propounded for geology and Charles Darwin for biology, was applied by Thomas Henry Huxley to every branch of knowledge. The more widely the concept of evolution was applied the more urgent became the problem of its implications. In a strictly biological and geological context it was tempting to give the theory an apparently simple mechanistic interpretation. Writers like Samuel Butler resented such an interpretation because it appeared to banish mind from the universe.[18] Though Darwin never committed himself to the theory of a mindless universe, many of his followers did. This may explain—on the principle of reaction—the remarkable fact that during the 1870's no less than three writers, Eduard Hering, Thomas Laycock, and Butler, working independently, developed theories of unconscious organic memory.[19]

In Butler's view, the difficulty with mechanistically conceived evolution was twofold: it did not explain the emergence of the animate out of the inanimate; and it did not explain the emergence of

31

mind or spirit out of the animate. Professor Tyndall in his celebrated article in *Nineteenth Century* (November 1878) wrote: "It is generally conceded (and seems to be a necessary inference from the lessons of science) that spontaneous generation must at one time have taken place." "No inference" replied Butler "can well be more unnecessary or unscientific. I suppose spontaneous generation ceases to be objectionable if it was 'only a very little one,' and came off a long time ago in a foreign country. The proper inference is, that there is a low kind of livingness in every atom of matter. Life eternal is as inevitable a conclusion as matter eternal."[20] And mind eternal is as inevitable a conclusion as life eternal.[21]

Of the two loose ends in the theory of biological evolution, the emergence of mind or spirit out of the animate was the one that gave rise to by far the greatest mass of investigation and speculation. Most of the investigation was carried forward in anthropology and psychology and these, in turn, came together in the study of mythology. It will prove most helpful if we take up these subjects in the order in which they have been listed. We begin, so to speak, at the lowest level with biology and must after that pass through anthropology and psychology to arrive at the highest level, the mythic symbol and the literary symbol.

The great stimulus to anthropology during the latter half of the nineteenth century was the result of a convergence of interests. The higher criticism of the Bible could not be separated from comparative religion; comparative religion could not be separated from comparative mythology; and comparative mythology was obviously best served by anthropology's cross-cultural study of ancient and modern primitive societies. Thus anthropology and mythology took on immense interest because they offered a scientific approach to the question which most obsessed the nineteenth century: religion, true or false.

For an understanding of the state of anthropological and mythological studies in the latter part of the century, we cannot do better than begin with Andrew Lang's *Myth, Ritual, and Religion* published in 1887. Lang was a prolific writer, his interests were wide, and his style was sufficiently lively and clear to appeal to the intelligent and interested general reader. What is more important for our purposes, he expounds the theory of myth which was the most respected in his day, yet always he is on the verge of breaking through to a more revolutionary and modern theory. Thus he points us in the right direction. His book begins with a brief history of mythological studies from early Greek speculation to the rise of comparative philology in the nineteenth century. He then turns to comparative anthropology: "It is inevitable that this science should also try its hand on mythology. Our purpose is to employ the anthropological method—the study of the evolution of ideas, from the savage to the barbarous, and thence to the civilized stage—in the province of myth, ritual, and religion. . . ."[22]

This "evolution of ideas" apparent in human history, this "development of the imagination"[23] is seen by Lang as analogous to Darwin's evolution of the physical organism: "As the anomalies and apparently useless and accidental features in the human or in other animal organisms may be explained as stunted or rudimentary survivals of organs useful in a previous stage of life, so the anomalous and irrational myths of civilized races may be explained as survivals of stories which, in an earlier stage of thought and knowledge, seemed natural enough"[24]

For Lang, then, myth is irrational and barbaric or, when it persists among highly civilized peoples, a series of anomalous but interesting stories the original significance of which has been lost. There is not much advance here on the view expressed by Darwin that rituals and strange superstitions and customs are among the "miserable and indirect consequences of our highest faculties."[25] This so-called ethnological approach is reductive, seeking explanation in origins. It is the method which a few years later Freud was to apply to the study of the psychology of the individual.

The narrowness of the ethnological approach of Lang, Jane Harrison, J. G. Fraser,[26] and others, an approach which "would hunt an Aryan myth or custom back to a state of pre-existent savagery, discover its germs in similar beliefs or practices prevalent among Red Indians or Andaman Islanders," did not go unobserved.[27] As early as 1890 Symonds expressed a deeply felt need to extend the psychological significance of primitive myth. "At a distant period, myths were certainly ways of explaining the spiritual essence of the world and man to the imagination. That essence must, except in symbol and parable, remain for ever inscrutable and incognisable for the human mind. It is therefore by no means proved that the intuitions embodied in the myths of races like the Greek are even now devoid of actuality."[28]

Lang could not have agreed with such a proposition. Nevertheless he made a beginning at developing a more significant and revolutionary conception of myth. He simplified and universalized his theory of the origins of myth by proposing that the "*diffusion* of stories practically identical in every quarter of the globe may be (provisionally) regarded as the result of the prevalence in every quarter, at one time or another, of similar mental habits and ideas."[29] Quite apart from this general statement, the whole of *Myth, Ritual, and Religion*, like the books that came before it and after it, demonstrates that from Australia to Greece and from India to Peru the human mind has been alike at like stages of civilization. This emphasis on the universal character of the products of the mind, accompanied as it is by a belief in psychological, imaginative, or spiritual evolution points toward a deeper understanding of the nature of myth. This deeper understanding will be better appreciated if we approach it by way of psychology.

At the end of the eighteenth century Friedrich Mesmer stimulated a new interest in psychology. His doctrine of human magnetism pointed to a scientific bridging of the gap between mind and body. At the same time, his demonstration of the exciting and mysterious character of psychic influence, as manifested in hypnotism, prepared the way for bolder speculation about mental and spiritual evolution. During the nineteenth century much of this speculation centered round the possibility of establishing scientifically the existence of soul and spirit. But by no means all the speculation was restricted to a scientific approach. Arthur Waite, writing of alchemy in 1888, gives us a vivid idea of the kind of spiritual ferment at work among those with esoteric interests: "In the facts and possibilities of mesmerism and in the phenomena of ecstatic clairvoyance, in ancient magic and modern spiritualism, in the doctrines and experiences of religious regeneration, we must seek the *raison d'être* of the sublime dream of psychochemistry—that, namely, there is a change, a transmutation, or a new birth, possible to embodied man which shall manifestly develop the esoteric potencies of his spiritual being, so that the flesh itself shall be purged, clarified, glorified, and clothed upon by the essential light of the divine pneuma."[30] The more mature the century grew, the more riotous grew the fair images of transcendent hope. Thus we find the eighties and nineties canvassing the whole spectrum of spiritual possibilities from ritual and alchemy to psychical research and Madame Blavatsky.

In all areas, the main preoccupation of the initiate was the hope of spiritual survival. But that hope was not shared by some of those who took an interest in such speculations. J. A. Symonds, for instance, was a friend and admirer of Henry Sidgwick, one of the leaders in psychical research. Like Sidgwick he was a firm believer in man's spiritual evolution and spiritual progress, yet unlike him, he neither hoped for nor desired survival after death. Symonds grasped the spirit that underlay psychical research and, especially in his essays in evolution, gave eloquent expression to it.

Probably the most important student of psychical research at this time was Frederic Myers whose massive two-volume study *Human Personality,* running to over 700,000 words, was published in February 1903 and reprinted in March. Though Oscar Wilde found Myers' earlier work and the Transactions of the Psychical Society "the most depressing things" he had ever read,[31] many of the intelligent thought otherwise. It was investigators like Myers and William James, "rather than Freudian psychology, which at the turn of the century and for some time afterwards were evoking appreciable interest among educated people."[32] The following passage demonstrates Myers' evocative power:

> ... the time is ripe for a study of unseen things as strenuous and sincere as that which science has made familiar for the problems of earth. . . . The scheme of knowledge which can commend itself . . . must be a scheme which, while it *transcends* our present knowledge, steadily *continues* it;—a scheme not catastrophic, but evolutionary. . . . *Spiritual evolution:*—that, then, is our destiny, in this and other worlds. . . . Nay, in the infinite Universe man may now feel, for the first time, at home.

35

The worst fear is over; the true security is won. The worst fear was the fear of spiritual extinction or spiritual solitude; the true security is in the telepathic law.[33]

We have already seen how Symonds, accepting the idea of a life-penetrated and mind-penetrated universe, was confronted by the spiritual essence of the world forever inscrutable and incognizable except insofar as it could be expressed in symbol and parable. In the same way he says that "poetry and art may be destined, on a far more elevated platform and with far profounder assurance of the truth, to use [nature myths and allegories] again for the illumination and instruction of mankind."[34] Where Symonds advances with a certain tentativeness, Myers attacks boldly: "The symbolism may be the inevitable language in which one stratum of our personality makes its report to another. The symbolism, in short, may be either the easiest, or the only possible psychical record of actual objective fact; whether that fact be in the first instance discerned by our deeper selves, or be conveyed to us from other minds in this form. . . ."[35] Through psychology, Myers leads us back to myth and symbol, showing them to be far from simply primitive and practical.

He does more: he applies his findings to art. Genius—"that happy mixture of subliminal with supraliminal faculty"—is the true spring of profound symbolism, and art is the most likely place for its manifestation. "The inspiration of Art of all kinds consists in the invention of precisely such a wider symbolism. . . . I am not speaking, of course, of symbolism of a forced and mechanical kind—symbolism designed and elaborated as such—but rather of that pre-existent but hidden concordance between visible and invisible things, between matter and thought, between thought and emotion, which the plastic arts, and music, and poetry, do each in their own special field discover and manifest for human wisdom and joy."[36]

To this list of the arts, Myers might have added the dialogues of Plato. By example as well as precept Plato confirmed that myth was more than primitive and was important to a civilized community. His dialogues were in themselves illustrations of the universal nature of myth and of its power to convey that which could not otherwise be expressed. We will look at three eminent scholars whose understanding of myth was deepened by a study of Plato: Jane Harrison, J. A. Stewart, and B. F. Westcott.

What impresses the reader about Jane Harrison's writings is that when she is dealing strictly with mythology she holds the generally accepted view of Lang and others that myths "have taken their rise . . . in primitive, often savage, and, I think, always *practical* ritual,"[37] but when she approaches art with Plato as guide she is led to a view of the artist as myth-maker. Thus she says: "Such was the passion for form with the Greeks that even to adjectives, to the good, the just, the beautiful, their greatest philosopher was compelled . . . to give some sort of archetypal, transcendental form." Or again, science, she says, "tells us that, by laws as yet rather imagined than understood, the artist comes into the world rich with a wealth of creative impulse, the gift of bygone generations—the poet with an imagination already instinct with centuries of creative impulse."[38]

What Jane Harrison began, John Alexander Stewart in 1905 took to a triumphant conclusion in *The Myths of Plato*. Stewart was the first Englishman of the period to understand the universal nature of Plato's myths and the first to see them as a unique and indispensible way of imparting knowledge.[39] It is impossible in a few brief quotations to convey to the reader Stewart's spirited enthusiasm, but the following passages will at least suggest the quality of his writing. In all of them the idea of dream, dream-image, or dream-state occurs. This is Stewart's graphic way of indicating (to use Myers' terms) the subliminal and supraliminal character of myth. It is his way of saying, with Keats, that the "Imagination may be compared to Adam's dream —he awoke and found it truth."[40]

> In appealing, through the recital of dreams, to that major part of us which feels "values," which wills and acts, Plato indeed goes down to the bedrock of human nature. At that depth man is more at one with Universal Nature—more in her secret, as it were—than he is at the level of his "higher" faculties, where he lives in a conceptual world of his own making which he is always endeavouring to "think."

> The poet's image . . . which began by throwing us into the dream-state, must persist in the state of waking consciousness to which we are now returned, and there, as we look at it in the light of common

37

day, amaze us by its "resemblance" to an archetype seen in the world in which "Time is not."

> This effect may be described as a feeling of having lately been in some divine region, where the true reasons of the things which happen in this world of ordinary experience are laid up; a Place in which one understood the significance of these things, although one cannot now explain what one then understood.[41]

B. F. Westcott in his essay on "The Myths of Plato" says: "The allegory is the conscious work of an individual fashioning the image of a truth which he has seized. The myth is the unconscious growth of a common mind, which witnesses to the fundamental laws by which its development is ruled." In the same essay of 1866 Westcott goes on to say of the myths: "If they are individual and not popular, they are still the individual expression of a universal instinct. Plato speaks not as Plato but as man." They "have yet a meaning which we have not outlived." He asserts, as Harrison was to do later, that "The Myths transcend the domain of pure reason, and their moral power springs out of their concrete form."[42] Agreeing with Westcott, Stewart adds: "I hold that Myth has no *dogmatic* meaning behind its literal sense. Its 'meaning' is, first, its literal sense—the story which is told; and then, beyond this, the *feeling* which it calls up and regulates."[43]

This may look like John Stuart Mill's assertion that poetry embodies "itself in symbols, which are the nearest possible representations of the feeling in the exact shape in which it exists in the poet's mind."[44] But where Mill is talking about the individual poet and the symbols he devises to represent his individual feelings, Stewart is talking about the feelings of those who receive the myth, and he is saying that the myth which calls up and regulates these feelings is the unconscious growth of a common mind. Thus Westcott and Stewart, like Symonds, Harrison, and Myers, have deepened and universalized Mill's notion of subjective feeling and its symbolization, and have shown how the symbol may be an archetype. For the present, we may define an archetype as a symbol which, in the area of its reference, embodies a content that seems to be total in a form that seems to be universal. So defined, as I will explain in the introductory section of Chapter 3, an archetype is a mythic symbol.

It must be obvious, even from the brief excerpts quoted here, that this deeper and more universal conception of symbol is dependent on another conception—that of the unconscious. Indeed, for these writers the idea of the unconscious would appear to be at least as important as the idea of the evolving mind. We may in a few sentences recapitulate the development of the idea. At the beginning of the nineteenth century, German critics working from an organic concept of art came to hold that artistic creation was an unconscious process of mind.[45] This idea spread slowly during the century, as did the general idea of the unconscious, until by the seventies the unconscious was a European commonplace.[46] It was not until the nineties, however, that the extraordinary implications of the concept began to have a wide influence.

The theorists we have been looking at have little of a direct nature to say about the unconscious, but it is everywhere implicit in their thinking. They sought after that which was below normal consciousness and that which was above, they plunged and soared into the subliminal and the supraliminal, and they intuitively reconciled the two because as non-rational experiences they were not readily separable and because they attained a unified and harmonious embodiment in myth. Myth was at once the appropriate language and the appropriate form for expressing man's deepest insights and highest aspirations.

And so it is that myth, or what Myers calls symbol, becomes the means of embodying and expressing the paradox inherent in the thought of all these writers. On the one hand they believe in that which is permanent, in universal nature, universal mind, a collective unconscious, and the continuing expressiveness of traditional symbols and parables. On the other they believe in that which is changing, in extended powers of perception and more highly developed faculties as a result of mental or spiritual evolution. These contradictory positions are reconciled by assuming that man's higher development has its roots in the unconscious depths of his nature. Thus the subliminal and supraliminal are related. In myth and symbol their relationship can be expressed as a perfect, if paradoxical, union.

These same contradictory positions and the same paradoxical

solution are also to be found in the thinking of Forster. As we should expect, they make their appearance in conjunction with the idea of the unconscious—which he always refers to as the subconscious.

In a 1944 lecture Forster expressed reasonable enthusiasm about the great psychological movement of the twentieth century: "This psychology is not new, but it has newly risen to the surface. Shakespeare was subconsciously aware of the subconscious, so were Emily Brontë, Herman Melville and others. But conscious knowledge of it only comes at the beginning of the century, with Samuel Butler's *The Way of All Flesh.* . . ."[47] In the essay on "Anonymity" (1925) Forster stresses the significance of the subconscious in the creation of literature. There are two personalities, an upper one which writes letters and goes out to dinner, and a lower one which has "something general about it," "something in common with all other deeper personalities." Without this lower personality "there is no literature, because unless a man dips a bucket down into it occasionally he cannot produce first-class work." This brings Forster to the paradox of creation: the lower personality, "As it came from the depths, so it soars to the heights."[48] The paradox is rephrased in a wartime essay in which he says of art: "No violence can destroy it, no sneering can belittle it. Based on an integrity in man's nature which lies deeper than moral integrity, it rises to heights of triumph which give us cause to hope."[49]

These remarks are no more than one might expect from the writer who boldly asserts in *Howards End:* "We are evolving, in ways that Science cannot measure, to ends that Theology dares not contemplate" (p. 254). These words *may* be taken to represent the thought of Margaret Schlegel but the context makes it obvious that the author stands squarely behind them. The same idea is implicit in the nonfiction. Commenting on Lowes Dickinson's long association with the Society of Psychical Research, Forster notes his belief "that there was an unexplained residuum in the phenomena which must be carefully examined, whatever religious orthodoxy may feel or scientific orthodoxy think."[50] More revealing is the conclusion to "Anonymity": "Imagination is our only guide into the world created by words. Whether these words are signed or unsigned becomes, as soon as the imagination redeems us, a matter of no importance, because we have approximated to the state in which they were written, and there are no names down there, no personality as we understand personality. . . . What there is down there—ah, that is another enquiry, and may the clergymen and the scientists pursue it more successfully in the future than they have in the past."[51]

This admirable essay, published a year after *A Passage to India,* is a revealing and impressive document. It sets out Forster's belief that man's imaginative triumph, his spiritual ascent, has its roots in the creative impersonality of the unconscious mind; and that, in view of the backwardness of Science and Theology, art (itself rooted in the unconscious) offers the best insight into man's imaginative and spiritual potentialities. In his 1947 address on "The Raison d'Être of Criticism in the Arts" Forster restates his belief in words which continue to echo the mythic theorists of the turn of the century: "A work of art is a curious object. . . . We . . . undergo a change analogous to creation. We are rapt into a region near to that where the artist worked, and like him when we return to earth we feel surprised. . . . Something has passed. I have been transformed towards his condition, he has called me out of myself, he has thrown me into a subsidiary dream; and when . . . the transformation [is] closed, I too feel surprise."[52]

It would not be profitable to make detailed comparisons between the theories of Symonds, Myers, Harrison, Westcott, and Stewart on the one hand and the theory and practice of Forster on the other. I only wish to suggest that they agree on essentials: on the oneness of man and universal nature, on the importance of a deeper self and its close ties with a higher self, on the necessity of myth to convey the paradox of man's unchanging yet evolving nature, and on the continuing value of life-oriented art as the vehicle of new insights and new myths.

Forster differs from them in emphasis. He sees more clearly than they do that man's higher evolvement must express itself through the higher development of the individual. Man's elemental nature is common to all and is unchanging; his evolving nature is individual and rises like a superstructure from its unalterable foundation. The paradox which runs through the thought of all these writers becomes more explicit in Forster's thought because of his emphasis on individuality.

This intense concern for individuality and the development of the personality is something that Forster shared with Bloomsbury. What he did not share with Bloomsbury was their intellectuality, their supreme self-awareness, and their inclination to be art-oriented. It is for this reason that his emphasis on intuition differs from theirs. Where they, giving pre-eminence to the intellect, value immediacy of insight, he values the direct apprehension of a total experience. In sum then, Forster's distinguishing characteristics are his intuitive grasp of whole experience, his firm acknowledgment of the unconscious, and his intense commitment to life and its individuality. In his art (as in Jung's theories), these three characteristics attain unity of expression in the mythic symbol.

Forster's approach to symbol is inseparable from his approach to nature. This approach, which he shared with the students of myth, entailed a radical departure from the esthetic view of symbol characteristic of the eighties and nineties and from the Romantic view of nature characteristic of the entire nineteenth century. Such a break with the past is of historical and personal interest to the student of Forster, but it would take us further afield than some readers might care to go. For this reason the main discussion has been confined to Appendix A. Here it will be sufficient to indicate how Forster and the mythic theorists in their confrontation with nature short-circuited the self-consciousness of attitude which had prevailed for a hundred years.

Most readers today would agree with Lord Raglan's dictum that there is no such thing as nature worship: "Nobody ever worshipped the sun simply as the sun; it is worshipped only when it is deified, that is to say when a god has been put into it. The same applies to idols of all kinds, including stones and trees, and to human beings."[53] The man who worships nature believes that the spirit is inherent in the external world. So believing, he will experience either conscious identification with nature or unconscious identity with nature. Identification with something or someone is a state in which one is aware of the relationship. Identity with something or someone

is a state in which awareness of relationship is effectively obliterated,
teenth-century writers from Wordsworth to Swinburne. In most cases,
for the self and the object are one.[54]

Identification with nature is characteristic of important nine-
the awareness of relationship is expressed in a thoroughly self-conscious
way. By the 1850's however, this pantheistic awareness is little more
than a pale reflection of the fervid Romantic response to an indwelling
spirit of nature, and by the end of the century it flickers and dies.
Sophisticated, scientific man can no longer believe that nature harbors
a someway kindred spirit. But at the unconscious level he can still
experience a bond with nature. The bond simply is, though as soon as
it emerges into consciousness it takes on the quality of an experience
notable for its givenness. Myth or the mythic image (archetype) is
man's way of expressing the inexpressible, of conveying the experience
of identity with nature or the other-than-self. That is why, for Symonds, it gets at "the spiritual essence of the world and man," and why,
for Stewart, it "goes down to the bedrock of human nature" where
"man is more at one with Universal Nature." Myth and the experience of which it speaks comes to the fore at the end of the nineteenth
century after man has exhausted the possibilities of conscious relationship with nature.

The eternal moment of identity with nature, of union with
the other-than-self, is an impersonal visionary experience. Precisely
this kind of experience is central to Forster's art, and nowhere is it
more central than in the short stories.

If then the mind wishes to apprehend itself as creator, it must recognize in its act of creation an act of annihilation; it must create its very nothingness in order to give itself a being. The "unheard of work" of which Rimbaud speaks, the "marvelous body," the "first time," is possible and visible only if it immediately sets its "innocence" against a time abolished, assassinated, "the time of the assassins." The creative act of time appears first then as a death of time itself: "And do you not understand," writes Gide, "that no instant would ever assume that admirable lustre unless standing, so to speak, against a dark background of death?" "Destroy," says Schwob, "for all creation comes of destruction."

—Georges Poulet, *Studies in Human Time*

This paragraph is torn from a long and closely reasoned analysis of twentieth-century consciousness. I do not propose to go into its many implications. I am interested only in the obvious way it relates to and illuminates E. M. Forster's fiction. In "The Story of a Panic," his first piece, the moment of revelation in which Pan appears is preceded by a death-like stillness and, for the uncomprehending tourists, a blind fear that destroys consciousness. Later the "admirable lustre" of the boy's instant of insight is set against the dark background of the death of the Italian boy Gennaro. The whole body of Forster's fiction may be seen as an exploration of the paradox that "the creative act of time appears first then as a death of time itself."

44

2

Romance Moralities

"The novel . . . is a perpetual quest for reality, the field of its research being always the social world, the material of its analysis being always manners as the indication of the direction of man's soul."[1] Forster would agree with this definition. The traditional novel, he says (speaking of Virginia Woolf's *Night and Day*), "is an exercise in classical realism, and contains all that has characterised English fiction, for good and evil, during the last two hundred years: faith in personal relations, recourse to humorous side-shows, geographical exactitude, insistence on petty social differences."[2]

What then is the nature of the reality so persistently sought by the novelist?

If we examine more closely our ordinary notions of reality, perhaps we should find that we do not consider real what actually happens but a certain manner of happening that is familiar to us. In this vague sense, then, the real is not so much what is seen as foreseen; not so much what we see as what we know. When a series of events takes an unforeseen turn, we say that it seems incredible. That is why our ancestors called the adventure story a fiction. Adventure shatters the oppressive, insistent reality as if it were a piece of glass. It is the unforeseen, the unthought-of, the new. Each adventure is a new birth of the world, a unique process.[3]

45

No better words could be found than these by Ortega y Gasset to take us from the novel to the romance, and so to the writings of E. M. Forster which, though they incorporate elements of the novel, are pre-eminently romance.

Romance arises when man ceases to believe in the cosmology and history of his myths and epics, when the heroic figures of the past no longer grip his imagination. Then he turns to idealized figures of a more subjective mould. The libido, anima, and shadow (Jung) find expression in the hero, heroine, and villain. The story, no longer thought of as literally true, may expand and stretch itself through any number of fabulous adventures. The subject matter, no longer thought of as religiously based, may be handled with a freedom and lightness of touch unthinkable in myth and epic.

With the decline of poetic romance at the end of the Renaissance, we observe romance elements making strong incursions into the prose fiction of Rabelais and Cervantes. But the rise of the novel, by definition realistic and socially oriented, drove romance into a corner from which it has never escaped. For two centuries readers and critics have inclined to the view that romance is acceptable and admirable only so long as it is subordinated to the requirements of realism. Hawthorne, Melville, and the Brontës broke with this predilection and paid for it by being widely misunderstood. The same misunderstanding, which insists on judging romance by standards appropriate only to the novel, has infected most commentary on Forster's fiction and distorted critical evaluation of it.[4]

An appreciation of Forster's work is further complicated by the fact that it combines romance with important elements from the realistic novel. Central to all romance is the archetype of an unfallen world, a golden age in which an idealized hero and heroine experience marvelous adventures in a strange and beautiful landscape. It is a world of innocence and energy. Evil enters this world in the form of wasteland settings, monsters, ogres, and unqualified villains. The remarkable thing about Forster's stories is this: the romance vision of innocence is portrayed with extraordinary purity and directness; but the romance vision of evil or experience is largely excluded from his work. Instead the vision of evil is taken over directly from the Fielding-Austen tradition of the novel where it is exclusively social.

I have put the facts boldly for the sake of clarity; now I must qualify them. There are two kinds of evil in Forster's fiction. The one kind is social and adheres to the characters. The other kind is transcendent and, though it is sometimes expressed through a character, has an existence apart from the characters. It is ominous and inexplicable. The perverted cruelty of Harcourt Worters ("Other Kingdom"), the ultimate horror behind the sham respectability of Michael ("The Point of It"), the terrifying mindlessness of the tentacles of the Mending Apparatus ("The Machine Stops"), and the priest pushing the bride-mother over the cliff ("The Story of the Siren") are like the goblins that walk inexorably over the universe and the Marabar echoes that infect all life: they allow us to glimpse a dark and appalling universe. Elizabeth Bowen has hit upon an image to convey this sense we have of evil, "the sense of conscious life's being built up over a somehow august vault of horror, that rings under the foot, that exhales coldly through cracks."[5] The images associated with this transcendent evil—the monster-like tentacles of the machine, the black figure of the evil priest, the goblins—have parallels with the evil figures of romance. But they do not as in romance have a prominent role to play. They appear only for a moment, just long enough to give us a glimpse of some underlying horror.

Forster's bad characters cannot convey this sense of horror. The point about them is that they are too obtuse even to know it exists. In so portraying them, Forster attempted what he believed to be a true portrait of the average Englishman who is incapable of deliberate wrong, incapable of worshipping the Devil. "His character, which prevents his rising to certain heights, also prevents him from sinking to these depths. Because he doesn't produce mystics he doesn't produce villains either. . . ." His badness is the result of muddle and negation, a kind of moral consumption such as overtakes Jane Austen's Mr. and Mrs. Dashwood during their prolonged deliberations about the appropriate sum to be settled on Mr. Dashwood's sisters.[6]

In exploiting the Fielding-Austen tradition of the novel, however, Forster reinterprets the forces of corruption and gives his socially evil characters a new twist. They became appalling because their destructive power creates an illusion of naturalness; their ignorance, obtuseness, self-righteousness, and egotistical altruism appear as a kind of perverted innocence. In Fielding, Austen and, to take a later example, James, the carriers of social evil are felt to be responsible for their own destinies and for the devastation they bring on others. In Forster, though they are the cause of devastation and are damned on that account, they are not distinguished by the albatross of guilt or responsibility. They are spiritually negative and neither deserve nor justify any further judgment.

We have reached a point now where we can ask how the horror which underlies and overarches Forster's world is related to the bad characters who move on its surface. The answer is that, though they cannot express it, we glimpse the horror through them. In moments of crisis their smooth-functioning worldly surfaces crack and we catch sight of the abyss: "Though they do not generate evil they do, like blocked gutters, receive, store and exhale it."[7] Mr. Bons confronts Achilles in abject suicidal terror ("The Celestial Omnibus"); Henry Wilcox reveals the panic and emptiness adumbrated by the goblins as they walk over the universe from end to end.

Experience-and-evil, with its two levels, is all of a piece and stands as the complete negation of innocence-and-goodness. This brings it into conformity with the romance tradition. The assertion that Forster's people are either saved or damned, are either capable or not capable of vision, is true. The implication that this attitude points to hardness of heart and a kind of arrogance is false. Were Forster a social philosopher his attitude might seem arrogant. Likewise, were Homer a theologian, his treatment of the gods might seem frivolous, or were Tolstoy an historian, his treatment of the past might seem fabricated. We may note that when Forster comes forward as social philosopher or commentator in his nonfictional writing his vision of a sheep-or-goat humanity is severely modified; he is well aware of the dangers of arrogance. But in his fiction the drastic separation of good and evil is essential to the romance tradition in which he works. He does not allow his vision to be narrowed (as Hawthorne did) by "that tiresome little receptacle, a conscience."[8] To complain that he is unjust to the Anglo-Indians, unfair to the Wilcoxes (in fact he tries too hard to give them their due), and overly obvious in the short stories is to condemn an essential characteristic of the romance tradition and to ignore the fact that the conventions taken over from realistic fiction are being used for other than realistic ends.

To the support of this bold confrontation of innocence and experience, good and evil, the saved and the damned, Forster brings a firm moral vision. This is not to deny, of course, that he has always deplored righteousness and dogmatism. Yet his favorite novelist is Jane Austen, who misses being dogmatic only because her truths seem too apparent to need underlining and who misses being righteous only because it does not occur to her that she can be anything but right. At his deepest and most creative level Forster has a cluster of moral convictions almost as assured as Jane Austen's. These convictions admirably support his romance vision and at the same time underpin his satirical thrusts at the wicked. For romance has traditionally depended on the boldness of black and white and "the mountains of Right and Wrong,"[9] and satire has always depended on morality for its bite.

Obviously, Forster chose the romance form because it suited his didactic propensities. But if we ask the *why* of his didactic propensities we are driven to a deeper level at which we observe that the romance form suited the nature of his experience and interests. His experience was visionary. As such it could not be directly described without destroying its quality of transcendence. It had to be symbolized; and for this purpose the greatest possible freedom was needed in selecting images to convey its extraordinary quality. Romance, which has at its disposal a universe of subjectively mediated images, gave him this freedom of selection and allowed him to express the inexpressible.

Forster's psychological interests were equally well-suited to the romance form. He had little interest in exploring the psychological drama of inner conflict; he had a deep interest in externalizing psychological conflict, in rendering it wholly dramatic by expressing the contending forces in separate characters and symbols. This kind of outwardly expressed conflict worked like magic to stimulate his crea-

49

tive powers. Under its spell, evil emerged with sharpness, bite, and remarkable solidity while good emerged with resonant and soaring conviction.

The romance form also suited Forster's satirical bent. An important theme in the more bourgeois novel is the parody of the romance and its ideals: "The tradition established by *Don Quixote* continues in a type of novel which looks at a romantic situation from its own point of view, so that the conventions of the two forms make up an ironic compound instead of a sentimental mixture."[10] Forster reverses this tradition. His type of fiction looks at a novelistic situation from a romance point of view and exposes the situation to ridicule and satirical judgment. Much of his humor and irony stems from this juxtaposing of situation and perspective at odds with each other. Such a procedure fits beautifully into the romance tradition of clearly distinguished worlds of good and evil. At the same time it explains why Forster's evil world is taken over from the tradition of the realistic novel. It is the situations of this evil world which are exposed by being seen through the eyes of romance.

Forster's interest in looking at novelistic situations from the romance point of view also explains why he did not portray his bad people as morally responsible beings. To have done so would have given them too great a stature and spoiled the satire. But a deeper reason is to be found in the nature of his good people. At their most profound they resemble the bad people in this one respect only, that they are not morally responsible beings. And they are not morally responsible because their moments of vision are *given*. Though they are worthy of the revelation that comes to them, they cannot be said quite to have earned it. In so presenting the situation, Forster is true to the essentially subjective world of romance. We do not feel responsible for the goodness of our deepest insights. The goodness is simply given; likewise, the evil is simply present. Romance dramatizes this truth about our subjective experience.

It is not too much to say that Forster's success as a writer depends on this recognition of the limits of moral responsibility. His is not a dark or ominous vision like that of Melville, Conrad, or Faulkner. It allows us only to glimpse the darkness. And though it encroaches on the unimaginable, it creates a sense of luminousness and lucidity. It is a vision which must be taken seriously and at the same time must be handled with lightness of touch. Had Forster taken his bad people overseriously he would almost certainly have lost his urbanity and have succumbed to indignation and righteousness. Had he taken his good people overseriously he would have lost his lightness of touch and succumbed to high-mindedness and sentimentality. His conception of the individual as not morally responsible for either the best or worst in human existence saved him from these dangers.

On the other hand, the sense of a somehow transcendent good and evil, permeating the imagination of the author and his reader, gives rise to a final moral vision as decisive as it is prophetic. The implication is a little surprising, for the reader learns from this vision that man is, after all, a fully responsible moral being. The limitations of responsibility within the fiction were simply devices of the storyteller who found them valuable in constructing his complete image. Because romance is subjective and allegorical in the sense that it pulls apart and externalizes in separate images the elements that make up our inner life, only this complete image can give us a whole vision of man's nature. And only the complete man can in all respects be regarded as a morally responsible being.

I have been generalizing about all of Forster's fiction. The time has now come to distinguish between the novels and short stories. With each novel that Forster wrote he resisted more strenuously the temptation to become a moral legislator of the fallen world or a prophet of the unfallen world. He became more tentative in his moral valuations with the result that his style showed an increase in tension and irony. And these qualities make up one side of his integrity and his personal style. But they are not the dominant note. In the novels, Forster remains prophet and judge despite himself.

Ansell in *The Longest Journey* fails to acknowledge the physical presence of Agnes Pembroke because in the spiritual sense she is not real. Much the same point is made in *Howards End*. The truth is that the people who cannot say "I" for lack of a center within themselves and so go round and round in the social circle of Forster's fallen world are never, in the eyes of their creator, quite alive or real. On the other hand, those characters and scenes which express the vitality and innocence of the unfallen world glow with a beauty and serene passion that lends to them an unforgettable reality. It is within this context that we encounter the eternal moment, the instant of revelation in which tension and irony are resolved and we, with the creator, become one with a world of pristine joy. With each novel that Forster wrote the eternal moment appears with less frequency. This is not because it is absent but because it has been transmuted and is experienced as a subdued and diffused effect rather than as a single moment. Even at its most subdued, however, the sense it gives of revelation is so absolute and is in such decisive contrast to society's sterile habitude that Forster, for all his diffidence and modesty, becomes both judge and prophet.[11]

Now the distinction to be made is this: in the short stories Forster is neither diffident nor modest. In the sharpest possible terms he contrasts the two worlds of innocence and experience. None of the tension or irony comes from tentative valuation. All of it comes from an awareness that the unseeing and unfeeling machinations of society threaten to ensnare the spirit of man. The short stories break with "the demons of Realism and Literal Illusion";[12] they reveal with uncomplicated directness the essential romance pattern of Forster's created world.

The stories (along with four of the five novels) were written in a period of little more than ten years (1902–1912). Forster's opinion of them in 1910 is firmly stated in a letter to Edward Garnett: "I think them better than my long books—the only point of criticism on which I have ever disagreed with you."[13] Why should he think them better? And thinking so, why within two years should he give up writing them? For that matter why, with four novels to his credit at the age of thirty-two, should he have published only one more and that fourteen years later?[14] These questions are related and can in part be answered by considering the nature of Forster's inspiration.

He is an artist of vision. And according to his own description of such artists, they have one salient characteristic: "Everything comes to them in a rush, their arms are filled at once with material for a life's work, and their task is to sort and re-sort what they have rather than to seek fresh experiences." As a consequence the artist of

52

vision does not, "like Shakespeare or Goethe, pick up something and then something more." "He does not care for fresh people or problems. . . . He is always harking back to some lonely garden or sombre grove, to some deserted house whose entrance is indeed narrow but whose passages stretch to infinity. . . ." It should be noted that sometimes the vision "only yields its inmost meaning to the touch of memory," it reveals significant depths only after years of sorting and re-sorting.[15]

In thus speaking of Forrest Reid, Forster speaks of himself. As an artist of vision, his range of characters is limited. Many of them are based on relatives and on those he came to know during his undergraduate years at Cambridge. "In no book have I got down more than the people I like, the person I think I am, and the people who irritate me. This puts me among the large body of authors who are not really novelists, and have to get on as best they can with these three categories. We have not the power of observing the variety of life and describing it dispassionately."[16]

The importance of youthful experience is one of Forster's main themes. In 1906 he had this to say about childhood: "We saw the Tritons and the Sirens with our spiritual eye, though we did not know their names. The stars sang tunes to each other, and our spiritual ears listened."[17] The point of the short story "The Point of It" is that man's salvation depends on the vision of youth and the memory of that vision. Or to take another example, old Mr. Lucas, on the road from Colonus, regains his kingdom by regaining his youth. In 1923 Forster makes the point again in discussing the difficulties of comprehending and making contact with the East: "Only in youth or through memories of youth, only in the joyous light of the morning, can the lines of the Oriental landscape be seen, and the salutation accomplished."[18]

There is one characteristic of the artist of vision which is not discussed by Forster. The insights and revelations of youth will be associated with specific experiences, specific persons and places. But for a certain number of years—which will vary from artist to artist— they may flow into and illuminate some new locality or situation. In this way the vision finds a new body of imagery in which to express itself. Such imagery may be the means by which the remembered vision yields its inmost meaning.

Here, then, as with so much that touches Forster's art, there is a paradox. As a writer he does not seek new experience. But from time to time the vision in its permanence enters into a new domain and is enriched by that which it transforms. In 1902 a valley near Ravello yields the first part of "The Story of a Panic" as though it had been waiting there for the author. In 1903 "The Road from Colonus" "hung ready . . . in a hollow tree near Olympia." In 1904 he caught fire up on the Figsbury Rings, his conception of Stephen Wonham came alive, and something vital had been contributed to *The Longest Journey*.[19] Finally in much more indirect and complicated ways he discovered in India a new body of imagery to clothe his vision. Youth and the memories of youth gave him the needed insight into what appeared on the surface a completely alien world.

The continuity of Forster's outlook and the "development" of his art are brilliantly epitomized by Elizabeth Bowen:

> With some artists the attempt at self-discovery is, itself, the art. But Mr. Forster, though his first novels were published when he was in the twenties, seems to have been adult when he began to write. Then he took up without hesitation, in fact with evident certainty, the position with regard to life that he has occupied since. . . . At all events, he went with that first book direct to his personal maturity—and in an artist that is more than a private matter. The thirty-three years since *Where Angels Fear to Tread* have given him further data, but have not changed his conclusions. . . . His "development" has been a matter of equipping himself more fully, and with wider and wider reference, to express what he has from the first felt.[20]

Forster wrote because he enjoyed writing,[21] and he enjoyed writing because he had a vision to express. He was especially pleased by those works which seemed most fully to say the things that were worth saying. That is why he could think of the short stories as better than his long books, and why in 1960 he could speak with perfect assurance and satisfaction of *The Longest Journey* as "the least popular of my five novels but the one I am most glad to have written."[22] He quit writing—and this answers the questions put earlier—because his vision had yielded all that could profitably be got from sorting and re-sorting, and because he had explored all the new orders of experience into which his vision could fully enter. He had invested and then spent what he had been given, and thereafter resisted the temptation to pass off small change as something larger.

Though the romance pattern which expresses his vision is stronger and clearer in the short stories, they do not differ essentially from the novels. They are best seen as the first statement of Forster's permanent vision and as an admirable means of radically adjusting our perspective so that we may appreciate the true character of all his fiction.

The Short Stories

The *Great Eastern,* or some of her successors, will perhaps defy the roll of the Atlantic, and cross the seas without allowing their passengers to feel that they have left the firm land. The voyage from the cradle to the grave may come to be performed with similar facility. Progress and science may, perhaps, enable untold millions to live and die without a care, without a pang, without an anxiety. They will have a pleasant passage, and plenty of brilliant conversation. . . . and, when they come to the end of their course, they will go their way, and the place thereof will know them no more. But it seems unlikely that they will have such a knowledge of the great ocean on which they sail . . . as those who battled with it for years together in the little craft which, if they had few other merits, brought those who navigated them full into the presence of time and eternity, their Maker and themselves. . . .
—Fitzjames Stephen

The direct conflict of good and evil is essential to Forster's romance pattern. When the conflict breaks down, as it does in some of the short stories, the effect is disastrous. In every case the breakdown is the result of embodying good and evil in the same character. I will deal with obvious examples of this later, after I have disposed of a story—related to this problem—that has been more written about and more generally praised than any other. The reason for its most-favored status is not far to seek. "The Eternal Moment" is more like the novels than the short stories, and more like a traditional realistic novel than anything else Forster wrote. All who dislike or are puzzled by the romance element in his work find here something to please them.[23]

Miss Raby, a famous novelist who through her writing has made an obscure mountain resort equally famous, returns many years later to see what tourism has done to her village. She cherishes memories of the place because it was here on a glorious hillside in spring that a young uneducated Italian guide confessed his passionate love for her. Though she violently rejected him, this moment has remained the most beautiful and real of her life. Now she finds the village surrounded by luxury hotels, in the plushiest of which Feo, her former lover, is the greasy, middle-aged, hypocritical concierge. The heart of the matter is not, as one might suppose, the eternal moment on the hillside, but the detailed study of Miss Raby's response to the changes in the village. It is her character and situation that must carry the story.

The tone is serious throughout. Even society, the enemy of individual vision, is treated with high-minded fairness; and Colonel Leyland's crude insensitivity, which shows him to be as vulgar as the uneducated Feo, is exposed without a single touch of irony (p. 306). Our real interest is focused on Miss Raby's struggle to be honest with herself and others, and on her determination to accept responsibility for the soulless commercial spirit inadvertently fostered by her book. In this struggle she succeeds, despite her failure to make either Feo or Colonel Leyland understand. "In that moment of final failure, there had been vouchsafed to her a vision of herself, and she saw that she had lived worthily. She was conscious of a triumph over experience and earthly facts, a triumph magnificent, cold, hardly human, whose existence no one but herself would ever surmise" (p. 307). The last statement is all too true. This superb triumph is pointed to in the narrative but not convincingly established.

Though Miss Raby's character does not encompass both good and evil, it assumes much of the responsibility for the evil of society. The story moves inward, its center is psychological. As a realistic novella it is marred by unrelieved seriousness, a moralizing tone, and stiffly handled blocks of thematic material. On the other hand, its numerous merits, which need not concern us here, make it a solid piece of respectable workmanship. For our purposes the point to be noted is that, in largely deserting his romance pattern, Forster sacrifices the dramatic, witty, urbane, and intermittently profound quality that distinguishes all his best stories. We may note too that character and scene give little sense of symbolic depth.

We turn now to three stories in which the romance pattern,

rather than being absent, simply breaks down. The result is unmitigated failure. They are "Co-ordination," "Mr. Andrews," and "The Curate's Friend."

"Co-ordination" begins in a school for girls and begins well with Miss Haddon, the old music instructor who is not musical, hectoring and cajoling Mildred and Ellen in their struggle with Beethoven's *Eroica*. The plot concerns the abolition of the "co-ordination" system of education in which all studies are related to a central theme (Napoleon in this case), and the establishment of a more meaningful co-ordination. Unfortunately not one of the characters comes alive; the best that can be said even of Miss Haddon is that she is a poor-man's version of Lolly Willowes. The plot is complicated by some heavenly episodes in which Beethoven and Napoleon are deceived by their clerks. These scenes are cleverly written but essentially frivolous.

Beethoven and Napoleon each give a command. The result of Beethoven's command is that everyone at the school experiences a sense of harmony; of Napoleon's, that everyone experiences a sense of victory. At least we are told they experience these things. The difficulty is that the same characters who before moved blindly through the deadening school routine now, without knowing what has happened to them, become the vehicle of an ostensibly transcendent vision. The development of this part of the story is marked by extraordinary poverty of imagination.[24] Forster seems to have recognized his failure for in the end he conjures up Raphael and Mephistopheles to make the point that should have been made by the human drama.

"Mr. Andrews" is a very different story—brief, bare, and tightly constructed. It makes three points. One, love is finer than doctrine or principles: Mr. Andrews and the Moslem bandit each ask at the Gate of Heaven that the other be admitted. Two, Heaven fulfills our expectations but not our infinite desires and hopes which we cannot imagine. And three, fulfillment is to be found in yielding to the world-soul which is made better by the individual's experience and by the love and wisdom he has generated. Mr. Andrews and his Moslem companion, despite a multitude of superficial differences, are portrayed as very much alike and as essentially good. This enforces the point that they share a common humanity. The combining of a weighty theme and lightweight characters in a brief narrative which is without conflict produces a dull sketch. One cannot see in it even the beginnings of an effective story.[25]

But the worst is yet to come. "The Curate's Friend" is the first-person narrative of a foolish curate who encounters a faun. He attempts to tell us how friendship with this happy creature has changed his life. The attempt is wholly unconvincing and the curate continues to appear the fool. (He indulges in one especially appalling joke at the expense of the reader.) The narrative is completely lacking in imaginative detail that might convince us of the reality of the faun and the truth of the curate's experience. The final words of the story, which I have not the heart to quote, confess as much and illustrate all too clearly the smug and precious manner of telling.

All three of these stories show how completely Forster's imagination deserted him when vision and anti-vision were expressed through the same characters or when the anti-vision was excluded. And placed alongside the successful stories, all three show how thoroughly his creative inspiration depended upon the conflict (or, at the very least, the brilliant contrast) of his two worlds of innocence and experience, and upon the incisive moral vision engendered by that conflict. Only the faint outlines of the essential pattern of Forster's fiction can be traced in these stories. There is in them no clash of opposites, no depth of symbolism, no irrevocable judgment and, in consequence, no revelation of essential reality.

"The Other Side of the Hedge" and "The Machine Stops," however deficient they may be in developing a clash of opposites, do at least succeed in creating distinct and contrasting worlds to symbolize innocence and experience. Here the world that is simply and deeply human is pitted against that which is socially oriented, progressive, and dehumanized. In the first story, the world of brown crackling hedges and dusty road is set over against the world of the other side of the hedge, the Eden-like garden with its simple pastoral way of life in which every activity is its own justification. The allegory of the road with its progress that leads no one knows where but that unfailingly induces weariness and the desertion of one's brother is effective as a generalized symbol. But when specific details are interjected, the image of the road is destroyed: "Why, even in my short life I have seen a great deal of advance—the Transvaal War, the Fiscal Question, Christian Science, Radium" (p. 43).

The allegory of the garden is, in itself, a thorough success. The scenery and simple activities are convincingly substantial and at the same time imaginatively evocative. The garden is a dream-like archetype, as its two gates suggest. The gate of ivory, of false dreams, opens onto the road; the gate of horn, of true dreams, opens into the garden. The hero, aged twenty-five when he comes from the road, hints at the twenty-five centuries of tortuous and dusty progress, of egotism and conscious effort as civilized man in the West makes his way from ancient Athens to modern London.[26] And all the time the garden is there, the timeless deeper reality of the subconscious-supraconscious mind.

The whole story, with the exception of the opening page, takes place within the garden. The hero with great difficulty crawls through the brown dusty hedge, plunges suddenly into a moat filled with cool water, and emerges to find himself in a new world. He is reborn. And as the incident shows, rebirth (like pregnancy) does not admit of degree. The hedge is an absolute barrier. In psychological terms, you are either on one side or the other; and the process of breaking through the barrier, however arduous at first, ends with mysterious suddenness. It should follow that dramatic interest will center on two points in this story: the moment of rebirth, and the absolute contrast between the hero's old world and his new world. But Forster has other ideas. Despite the admirable finality of the rebirth image, he assumes that the hero has only begun to be reborn. The story, then, deals with the inner struggle of the hero to comprehend the values of the garden. Forster hopes in this way, using a first person narrative, to bring his two worlds into dramatic conflict.

He fails. The kindly certitude of the old man who acts as guide and the blind stupidity of the narrator who blunders through the delights of the garden with a cliché of the road for ever on his lips make clear to us that life on the road is a thing to be pitied. What is more, so is the hero—which effectively destroys our interest in his inner life. Moreover at the end of the story, when we realize that the hero's vision of reality has been transformed and that he has fully entered into the life of the garden, we are left with a curious impression. Of course it is an old device to tell one's story as though the end were not known or as though one were not a changed person. But it is a dangerous device to use in this kind of story. It has the effect of denying implicitly the *power* of the transforming vision. As well, one would suppose that for the individual the great thing would be the moment of transformation and its continuing reality. Yet in the present story the transformation is outlined in two brief concluding paragraphs rendered vague by the use of the phrases "as in a dream" and "seemed to" (p. 48).

The truth is that once Forster gets off on the wrong foot, once he has denied the reality of the rebirth image and committed himself to the portrayal of psychological conflict, he cannot avoid failure. For the student of romance fiction this is an extremely interesting story. Forster has created images which adequately symbolize some important realities of the inner life but he has not succeeded in devising a narrative which will allow them to release their full meaning.

"The Machine Stops" is in many ways a contrast to "The Other Side of the Hedge." It puts most emphasis on images of experience and dehumanized civilization rather than on images of innocence and naturalness. Its narrative method is always adequate, but the initial body of symbols gives rise to difficulties.

The main preoccupation of the story is the dreary process of advancing civilization. In fact "progress" has been carried to such a pitch that it has stopped—one of the points Forster wishes to make in this space-age romance. Men live in their world-wide honeycomb within the earth, each in his cell, and the Machine does everything for them. All normal communication is by television phone, for direct human contact, from being simply inconvenient, has become actually repellent. When the Machine begins to break down there is no longer anyone who understands its complexity. Inevitably it stops and its vast nether world is consigned to darkness, airlessness, and terrible silence.

Through Vashti we are given a picture of typical day-to-day existence. She is the mother of Kuno, the youthful hero of the story who revolts against the barren and meaningless life of his machine-ridden world. In the end he dies with the rest of his civilization, but he is able to reach his mother and embrace her, thus reasserting human values. He is able also to assure her that men survive on the surface of the earth.

The image of life ruled by the Machine is set over against the image of life among the secret dwellers of the earth who may feel the incalculable living power of nature and behold the glory of the stars. The Machine is the central symbol of the lower world, the stars the central symbol of the upper world. The stars since ancient times have symbolized the eternal or, in Forster's words, harmony and salvation.[27] Since the earth-dwellers remain in the background, the story requires a major symbol for "man, the flower of all flesh, the noblest of all creatures visible, man who had once made god in his image, and had mirrored his strength on the constellations" (p. 196). The stars provide this symbol. The constellation of Orion emerges as the image of man's strength and his heroic nature (pp. 147-48, 179). Poised between the lower and upper worlds, between the Machine and Orion, is Kuno. But unlike the other heroes we have looked at, he experiences no inner conflict. He is from the beginning entirely on the side of the earth and the stars. His struggle is concentrated on escaping the Machine and on developing his basic humanity.

Kuno must contend with a whole civilization. This means, first, that he must break out of its soul-destroying routine and must discover, through a painful and touching process, that man is the measure of all things. It means, second, that he must contend with the Machine itself. The Machine enters directly into the action through one of its appendages. Kuno, who has climbed to the surface of the earth through an old ventilating shaft, is making sorties out of the dell in which he finds himself when the horrible arms of the Mending Apparatus emerge from the shaft. A "long white worm," curling round his ankle and up his leg, forces him to cry out for help. "That part" he says to his mother, "is too awful. It belongs to the part you will never know" (p. 179). The mindless tentacles, exploring and probing, grasp everything within their reach. Kuno and the grass and ferns of Wessex are dragged down together, and with them (as we learn later) one of the secret inhabitants of the earth, a girl who in coming to his assistance has been pierced in the throat by a tentacle of the Apparatus.

The symbolism is clear. Sterile society inevitably seeks to emasculate the hero and deflower the heroine. Through this terrifying episode Kuno's unequal struggle with the mindless cruelty of the Machine is given dramatic expression.[28]

We may agree that Forster has hit upon some admirable inventions. But his central image remains a problem. It is too dominant in the narrative, too vast and inescapable. This can be illustrated by comparing it with the traditional and protean symbol of the ship—of state, of civilization, of life. As a central image the ship is more readily visualized and contained in the mind. Moreover, it is always surrounded by the sea; the limits to its power and pretensions are inherent in the context of the image. As a representation of civilization it has the advantage of being obviously a symbol, whereas the civilization of the Machine, being the whole rather than a part, is first itself and only secondarily a symbol.

The vastness and inclusiveness of Forster's image is unsuited to his special capabilities as an artist. The Machine world is like his other evil societies in that it is not held to be morally responsible. But it is so monstrous (in two senses) and so inhuman that it defeats any attempt at lightness of touch. Its mechanical and dehumanized powers of evil do not arouse in Forster that intensity of imagination which can give life to the boring, the pretentious, and the conventional. Instead they arouse a solemn seriousness which in its turn opens the way to sententiousness, sentimentality, and dullness. Despite its insights and substantial virtues, "The Machine Stops" suffers from all three of these defects.

"The Point of It" is the only story of Forster's that manages to be completely serious in tone and still avoid these pitfalls. It was not liked by his Bloomsbury friends, who failed to see the point of it. They might have seen the point had they compared it with an earlier treatment of the same theme in *The Longest Journey*. Near Cambridge, Rickie Elliot had discovered "a secluded dell, paved with grass and planted with fir-trees. It could not have been worth a visit twenty years ago, for then it was only a scar of chalk, and it is not worth a visit at the present day, for the trees have grown too thick and choked it. But when Rickie was up, it chanced to be the brief season of its romance, a season as brief for a chalk-pit as a man—its divine interval between the bareness of boyhood and the stuffiness of age" (p. 25). Evergreen trees and the purity of the chalk give the dell a permanence of beauty scarcely touched by the passing of the seasons. It will, like youth, lose all its charm some day. But for Rickie it signifies the unchanging glory of his Cambridge years, the high point of his youth and of his life. However often he may neglect it, it remains for him a point of return and a place of renewal.

The same theme is explored in the short story. The first section tells of a supreme moment of youthful endeavor. Micky is rowed across the estuary by his friend Harold who, despite a weak heart, responds to Micky's exultant commands and strains every muscle in an ecstasy of physical exertion culminating in death. The second section describes how Michael gradually forgets this youthful experience as he declines slowly and gracefully toward old age, and how he is rejected by his children and dies in a fit of cynicism. The third section is an allegory telling the same story in reverse. The bobbin of experience wound in this life is unwound in the next. The first event now becomes the last. Harold and Micky again row across the estuary, moving toward the glory of the farmhouse with its windows glowing in the setting sun and "full to the brim with fire" (p. 224). The purpose of the retelling, the point of it, is not to persuade us that the bobbin of experience is actually unwound in another life but rather to reveal to us the horror that lies just beneath the surface of the conventional person's decline into the forgetfulness of respectable old age. What such a person forgets is youth and its pure sense of being.

Once this is established, we are led to the deeper truth that the desire to remember the reality of youth is sufficient for salvation, for desire will lead to memory, and memory, bursting like a star of pain, will torture its host until he is cleansed and his vision cleared. Youth is represented in the allegory as a Christ-like figure who under a thousand names—including that of Harold from the beginning of the story—has harrowed the hell of experience and forgetfulness. He does not, of course, promise the regaining of actual youth: "There is no abiding home for strength and beauty among men. The flower fades, the seas dry up in the sun, the sun and all the stars fade as a flower.

But the desire for such things, that is eternal, that can abide . . ." (p. 222).

The truth of this proposition is asserted at the beginning of the story by the quotation from Tennyson's "Ulysses." Man may grow old but the spirit of youth and heroic endeavor need not die. Youth and age are more than chronological inevitabilities; they are at all times contending forces in man's soul. Jung's brilliant account of the analogy between the life of man and the journey of the sun may deepen our understanding of this central point in the narrative.

The sun, rising triumphant, tears himself from the enveloping womb of the sea, and leaving behind him the noonday zenith and all its glorious works, sinks down again into the material depths, into all-enfolding and all-regenerating night. This image is undoubtedly a primordial one, and there was profound justification for its becoming a symbolical expression of human fate: in the morning of life the son tears himself loose from the mother, from the domestic hearth, to rise through battle to his destined heights. Always he imagines his worst enemy in front of him, yet he carries the enemy within himself—a deadly longing for the abyss, a longing to drown in his own source. . . .

The mind shies away, but life wants to flow down into the depths. Fate itself seems to preserve us from this, because each of us has a tendency to become an immovable pillar of the past. Nevertheless, the daemon throws us down, makes us traitors to our ideals and cherished convictions—traitors to the selves we thought we were. That is an unmitigated catastrophe, because it is an *unwilling* sacrifice. Things go very differently when the sacrifice is a voluntary one. Then it is no longer an overthrow, a "transvaluation of values," the destruction of all that we held sacred, but transformation and conservation. Everything young grows old, all beauty fades, all heat cools, all brightness dims, and every truth becomes stale and trite. For all these things have taken on shape, and all shapes are worn thin by the working of time; they age, sicken, crumble to dust—unless they change. But change they can, for the invisible spark that generated them is potent enough for infinite generation. No one should deny the danger of the descent, but it *can* be risked. No one *need* risk it, but it is certain that some one will. And let those who go down the sunset way do so with open eyes, for it is a sacrifice which daunts

65

even the gods. Yet every descent is followed by an ascent; the vanishing shapes are shaped anew, and a truth is valid in the end only if it suffers change and bears new witness in new images. . . .[29]

Forster's original and paradoxical presentation of this theme is reflected in the way he handles the name of his leading character. In Part I the name is Micky; in Part II it is Michael and later Sir Michael; grown accustomed to this, we are jolted by the opening of Part III: "Micky was still in bed" (p. 213). Thus Micky-Michael is characterized as protagonist-antagonist. The two roles are kept quite separate in the first two parts. In the last Michael finally becomes Micky. The separation of roles is strengthened by the fact that during each phase of the story the narrator shares the particular outlook of his character. Thus in the long second part devoted to the survey of Sir Michael's life the narrator gives us no decisive assurance that we are watching the forces of evil at work. To do so would be to destroy the sharp contrast between Part II and Part III, the contrast between the way our "sloppy civilization" sees (p. 211) and the way the true visionary sees. In this situation there can be no controlling moral vision; the vision emerges only as the allegory unfolds.

It is a dangerous technique for Forster, and there can be no doubt he runs the risk in Part II of boring us. But the real test is Part III which focuses on the inner struggle of Michael-Micky. Here Forster succeeds because he has an adequate complex of symbols to externalize and dramatize the inner life. He has, to begin with, the two names and their associations. Micky means youth and imagination, and the immediate reality of life and death. Michael means being snowed under by the steady accretion of experience, being reduced from love to sympathy to compromise, being reduced at last to futility and cynicism. In Part III Michael's world is portrayed symbolically. It is "the universe as old age," dark with a "dirtiness . . . more ancient than the hues of day and night"; it is an illimitable plain of sand over which pillars of sand move indeterminately. Men as they grow old become pillars of the past and, if like Michael they grow soft, they are pillars of sand which at a touch "fall with a slight hiss" (p. 214)—to such is the serpent of eternity reduced. Into this world as into that of the Hollow Men breaks a memory of the stars, of Orion and the

Twins, recalling adventure and youth, and recalling the love of two brothers, one human, the other divine. Like Michael, Castor dies; like Harold, who in a spiritual sense is eternal, Pollux "went down to Hell that he might be with him" (p. 217). Harold-Pollux, in his eternal and universal form as Youth, comes clothed in light and song. "Then Micky died a second death. This time he dissolved through terrible pain, scorched by the glare, pierced by the voice." He has desired to remember the magic years between childhood and age, and desire has saved him. He stumbles into a boat and finds himself being rowed away from the shore.

> As they neared mid-channel the boat went more slowly, for the tide was ebbing, and Micky knew that once carried out he would be lost eternally; there was no second hope of salvation. He could not speak, but his heart beat time to the oars—one, two. Hell made her last effort, and all that is evil in creation, all the distortions of love and truth by which we are vexed, came surging down the estuary, and the boat hung motionless. Micky heard the pant of breath through the roaring, the crack of angelic muscles; then he heard a voice say, "The point of it . . ." and a weight fell off his body and he crossed mid-stream. (pp. 223–24)

Nowhere else (not even in *The Longest Journey*) does Forster attempt so direct a portrayal of the hell that lies just beneath the surface of man's conventional life and of the vision that lies in the depths of the sky. His characteristic approach, the juxtaposing of vision and an essentially ironic and detached view of society in the comedy-of-manners tradition, is here abandoned. In the survey of Michael's life, society is seen from the point of view of an apologist; in the subsequent interpretation of his life, it is seen from the point of view of an allegorical moralist. The principle that the individual is not responsible for his failure is maintained, but with a difference: "He had mistaken self-criticism for self-discipline, he had muffled in himself and others the keen, heroic edge. Yet the luxury of repentance was denied him. The fault was his, but the fate humanity's, for everyone grows hard or soft as he grows old" (p. 219). Non-responsibility is based on commitment to the social norm rather than on individual obtuseness. This is because Michael is the symbol of the whole of our soft civilization. (His wife has a subsidiary role because the hardness she succumbs to in her pursuit of truth represents the typical vice of an earlier civilization.) Likewise, Harold is the symbol of all youth and of the vision that belongs to the time before love and truth were divided.

It is abundantly clear what kind of fiction we have here. Twentieth-century readers who can scarcely forgive Bunyan for his allegorical schematics will certainly not forgive Forster. They may attempt to escape the problem by noting that the juxtaposing of three distinct blocks of material contributes to the irony and drama of the story, that the narrative is thoroughly vivid at the right moments, and that the symbols are evoked with powerful intensity. But it must finally be apparent to them that the overall effect is starkly allegorical. Allegory is the most thematic form of romance. Yet it has its own kind of life—a point that will be appreciated only by those who have rejected the narrowness of present literary fashion. Like all effective allegory, "The Point of It" succeeds because there is implicit in it a convincing image of man's moral and spiritual nature. It is Forster's only successful attempt to break away (and it is only a partial breakaway) from the basic pattern that characterizes all the rest of his best stories.

That pattern can be seen in "The Celestial Omnibus," "Albergo Empedocle" (not one of the best but included with this group for other reasons), "The Story of a Panic," "The Road from Colonus," and "Other Kingdom." All of them create lively and satirical portraits of a society which must be judged in the light of a hero's eternal moment of vision. I will deal first with "The Celestial Omnibus" because as the least didactic of Forster's stories, its approximation to wish-fulfillment fantasy offers the greatest contrast to the moral allegory of the previous story.

It may at first glance seem surprising that one of Forster's most fantastic stories should be one of the most admired, discussed, and anthologized. The reason for its popularity is clear. The romance imagery is expressive of the poetic imagination—and every reader, like the culturally pretentious Mr. Bons of the story, makes a point of believing in the "essential truth" of poetry. The reader feels assured; there is no possibility of mistaking this romance for a realistic story gone wrong. He can respond confidently to the kind of experience with which romance deals—"experience liberated," as Henry James puts it, "experience disengaged, disembroiled, disencumbered, exempt from the conditions that we usually know to attach to it."[30]

The structure of the narrative is dictated by the need to hold two worlds in dramatic juxtaposition. "The boy who resided at Agathox Lodge, 28, Buckingham Park Road, Surbiton, had often been puzzled by the old sign-post that stood almost opposite. . . . it pointed up a blank alley, and . . . had painted on it, in faded characters, the words, 'To Heaven'" (p. 49). So the story begins with the address affixed to the one world and the sign pointing to the other.[31] At sunrise the boy enters the alley where he discovers a waiting coach. The driver is Sir Thomas Browne. After a quiet, foggy journey they come to a great gulf with a magnificent rainbow arching across it. The coach moves over the rainbow high above the everlasting river to the castle-like rocks of the other shore.

We are back at Agathox Lodge. The boy is in disgrace—he persists in lying to his parents about a journey over a rainbow. Then, in a superb little scene, Mr. Bons talks to the boy, who is so carried away by his remembrance of celestial life that he refers to Mr. Bons as though he were not present. This leads to his telling what "they" said about Mr. Bons: "I told them about you, and how clever you were, and how many books you had, and they said, 'Mr. Bons will certainly disbelieve you'" (p. 65). In all innocence the boy succeeds in playing on the vanity and pride of Mr. Bons who thereupon rashly determines to cure him by going with him to the alley at sunset.

The coach this time is driven by Dante. Mr. Bons is too appalled by the unexpected trip and too oppressed by the awful greatness of his guide to appreciate the journey. So he lectures the boy sharply about the need for sober deportment and judicious selection of acquaintances—do not waste time with trivial persons like Mrs. Gamp and Tom Jones. When he looks out during their passage over the everlasting river on a glorious lunar rainbow, he rolls to the floor in convulsions.

The last fragment of the rainbow melted, the wheels sang upon the living rock, the door of the omnibus burst open. Out leapt the boy—he could not resist—and sprang to meet the warrior, who, stooping suddenly, caught him on his shield. . . . Achilles raised him aloft. He crouched on the wonderful shield, on heroes and burning cities, on vineyards graven in gold, on every dear passion, every joy, on the entire image of the Mountain that he had discovered, encircled, like it, with an everlasting stream. (pp. 72–73)

On this mighty shield is graven the entire physical universe. Standing at its center on Mount Olympus he beholds in one great image the whole of the celestial world he has discovered. With innocent kindness he shouts to Mr. Bons, "Here is only the great Achilles, whom you knew." But Mr. Bons screams, "I see no one. I see nothing. I want to go back." Dante refuses to take him. "Mr. Bons—he could not resist—crawled out of the beautiful omnibus. . . . With a shriek of 'I see London,' he fell—fell against the hard, moonlit rock, fell into it as if it were water, fell through it, vanished, and was seen by the boy no more" (p. 73). As the tale ends the boy is crowned with fresh leaves.

It is only possible to indicate the true quality of this story by quoting from it at some length. It is easy of course to show the way Forster has arranged his narrative so that the unreal world of prose and principles and the real world of the poetic or creative imagination will reflect on each other and provide not so much a conflict as a contrast. But the point of the story and its effectiveness depend finally on the wit and irony of the worldly scenes and on the imagistic beauty and lyric feeling of the celestial scenes. The latter are enriched by a wealth of allegorical detail which Forster manipulates with a sure and light touch.[32] The result is a glorious invocation of innocence and poetic imagination and joy.

The brief epilogue to the story, coming on the heels of so mercurial a vision, leaves a distinctly odd impression:

From the *Kingston Gazette, Surbiton Times,*
and *Raynes Park Observer.*

The body of Mr. Septimus Bons has been found in a shockingly mutilated condition in the vicinity of the Bermondsey gas-works. The deceased's pockets contained a sovereign-purse, a silver cigar-case, a bijou pronouncing dictionary, and a couple of omnibus tickets. . . . Foul play is suspected, and a thorough investigation is pending by the authorities.

THE END

Forster is at once bold and playful. His purpose is not to raise awkward geographical and philosophical problems. The fact that entry into the world of the poetic imagination entails physical removal from the world of Agathox Lodge lends conviction to the first half of the story and significance to the last half, for it symbolizes the great gulf that separates the two. On the other hand, the fact that the boy, on the shield of Achilles, rests upon and is sustained by an image of the entire physical universe makes clear that the creative imagination involves not a flight from our world but an insight or vision that encompasses its oneness and its meaning.

Rather than making awkwardnesses about the two worlds of his story, Forster is demonstrating—with a modest twinkle in the eye— the power of his achievement. In the story proper he is saying: You believed the world of Agathox Lodge was real. How was I to persuade you otherwise unless, by taking advantage of your illusions, I could bring you safely into another world? Once there your vision was cleared. From the celestial world of the poetic imagination you now behold the prosy unreality and meaningless preoccupations of Agathox Lodge. You have had your revelation. You were like Mr. Bons, now you are like the boy. In the epilogue he is saying: Now that you have had your vision, you notice that the events of the real world, suitably expressed in the factual language of the press, are more bizarre and improbable than anything in my story. You notice, indeed, how unreal, how simply comic they are. That is because you see with fresh eyes; you are like the boy. And so Forster, with a playful touch of irony, arrogance, and mischief, directs us back to the central character.

It is no small thing to be like the boy. The child hero or divine child in his winged chariot symbolizes for man the promise of heroic achievement and fulfillment in the future. So does the heavenly journey which is a special type of mythic journey of the hero. The boy prefigures Achilles, and Achilles shares in "all that makes the gods immortal—their radiant visible beauty, their wonderful adventures, their capacity for happiness and laughter."[33] The boy, sharing in these immortal attributes, attains to oneness with Achilles and the gods.

"The Celestial Omnibus" presents society as a foil which

serves to heighten our appreciation of the visionary world. "Albergo Empedocle" presents the vision as a foil which serves to deepen our scorn of the social world. At least, that seems the best account of the matter. The effect is confused because the narrator's intimate friendship with the hero becomes a theme in its own right and blurs what might otherwise have been a well-defined pattern. This friendship impresses the reader by its immaturity—no doubt Forster's reason for leaving the story buried in *Temple Bar* (1903). But for all its narrative defects, it is more successful than some of the collected stories. In particular, the conventional characters are presented with conviction, humor, and as much sympathy as the situation will allow. This is especially true in the case of the "heroine," a perfect model for Agnes Pembroke of *The Longest Journey,* whose weak and selfish behavior in a moment of crisis is shocking because up to that point the reader, in judging her character, has been inclined to give her the benefit of the doubt.

Since the story is not readily available, the reader may be interested in a sample of its lively social insight. The Peaslakes are traveling in Sicily, accompanied by Harold, the fiancé of their daughter Mildred.

"It's a beautiful idea, isn't it, that the soul should have several lives."

"But, Mildred darling," said the gentle voice of Lady Peaslake, "we know that it is not so."

"Oh, I didn't mean that, mamma. I only said it was a beautiful idea."

"But not a true one, darling."

"No."

Their voices had sunk into that respectful monotone which is always considered suitable when the soul is under discussion. They all looked awkward and ill at ease. Sir Edwin played tunes on his waistcoat buttons, and Harold blew into the bowl of his pipe. Mildred, a little confused at her temerity, passed on to the terrible sack of Acragas by the Romans. Whereat their faces relaxed, and they regained their accustomed spirits.

"But what are dates?" said Mildred. "What are facts, or even names of persons? They carry one a very little way. In a place like this one must simply feel."

"Rather," said Harold, trying to fix his attention.

"You must throw yourself into a past age if you want to appreciate it thoroughly. To-day you must imagine you are a Greek."

"Really, Mildred," said Sir Edwin, "you're almost too fanciful."[34]

The characters are directly and sharply observed, the irony avoids display, and the scene comes immediately to life.

The structural weakness of the story lies in its failure to keep the balance between vision and anti-vision. Harold, an outwardly ordinary and good-natured young man, has his vision during an afternoon sleep in the ruins of a Greek temple. He knows on waking that he has lived before and in Sicily and that his life then was better. The scene is beautifully evoked. In the brilliant light, Harold lies on the flower-covered earth that has silted up the space between two fallen columns of the temple. A flower beside his face bends and flutters in the gentle gale of his breath. The image suggests both bier and marriage bed, and the whole scene suggests the eternal beauty of nature. After this admirable prelude, the vision itself is an anticlimax. We are deprived of any strong sense of revelation because Harold cannot remember the details of his earlier happier life. Thus his breakdown and insanity after Mildred ceases to believe in his experience lacks dramatic impact. Presumably Forster thought Harold so interesting in himself that he needed only a little visionary bolstering. That was Forster's mistake, a mistake no doubt related to the narrator's attitude to his "hero."

The failure in narrative structure reflects a failure in psychological penetration. The explicit subject of the narrative is Harold's entry into a previous existence; the implicit subject is his entry into the unconscious. "Remembering has made me so strong. I see myself to the bottom now."[35] Harold, through entry into man's universal past which is also *his* past, has emerged with an awareness of a higher and more inclusive self. This new self, like an emerging butterfly, can barely support its newborn splendor. Its fragility is crushed by a single blow and it sinks back into the mysterious darkness of the past, the unconscious from which it came. The result is insanity. The conscious mind, rather than reasserting its old and narrow dominance (as it does in the case of Mr. Lucas in "The Road from Colonus"), is shattered and loses itself in the unconscious; whereas, had the vision endured, it would have meant that some part of the unconscious had entered into and permanently expanded the confines of consciousness. The contradiction between Harold's feeling strong because he has seen into the depths of himself and his feeling weak and ready to collapse because it is suggested that Mildred no longer believes in his new self is psychologically convincing. Any massive reorienting of consciousness is both powerful and precarious; and, as Harold demonstrates, its collapse can be disastrous.

I hope this is a fair account of the experience underlying the narrative. One is forced to some such projection which ignores the end of the story because Forster, in representing Harold's insanity, falls into confusion and cheats. Harold, his conscious mind destroyed, is said to lead a happier life than we can know: "for the greater has replaced the less, and he is living the life he knew to be greater than the life he lived with us. . . . If things had happened otherwise, he might be living that greater life among us, instead of among friends of two thousand years ago, whose names we have never heard."[36] Sentimentality and laxness go hand in hand with the violation of psychological truth.

Neither the initial vision nor its later persistence in the disordered mind gives us a true image of man's inner life. Forster fumbles this side of the story but makes a success of the social side. He also makes a success of the prelude to Harold's vision. The image of the bed of earth between the two pillars is a just and admirable symbol. Its suggestion of death points to rebirth; its suggestion of marriage points to oneness greater than the two worlds out of which oneness is born. And the oneness is prefigured in the radiant harmony of the scene. Here is the story's true moment of vision. Harold, in the unconsciousness of sleep, experiences identity with nature and an ideal past. The implications of this will be clearer after we have looked at three stories in which a similar experience is the center of vision.

"The Story of a Panic" (date of composition, May 1902) is

the first story Forster ever wrote.[37] It describes a group of tourists in Italy. Though the characters range from a fussily innocuous old aunt to a cowardly conceited artist, our attention is focused on the boy Eustace. The scene in which he experiences identity with nature is carefully prepared. As the tourists stand on the hillside overlooking the beautiful valley, the narrator feels they are in the palm of a vast green hand. A strange silence falls, an ominous stillness. A cat's paw of wind flicks over the valley, turning the light green leaves to dark. It glides toward them over the ridge. And they flee wildly down the hill in terror and panic, gripped by an overmastering bestial fear—all except Eustace whom they later find lying in the same spot happily clutching the grass. Hoof marks like those of a goat are observed near by.

The story goes on to reveal how the pampered and listless boy is transformed by his union with the mighty and joyous power of nature as symbolized by Pan. He rushes down from the hills into the arms of Gennaro, the ignorant Italian fisherman lad who is a servant at the inn. But on his way down he stops long enough to greet the three old women from the woods and to offer thanks for the life he has been given. They are the Fates. In kissing the first of them he acknowledges Clotho, the youngest, who presides over birth (p. 21). In contrast, the adults push the encounter with Pan from their minds, and treat the boy and his new-found friend with great cruelty.

We see the result of their vicious stupidity (especially that of the narrator) in the death of Gennaro who assumes the role of surrogate for the escaping boy. Eustace, fleeing from the inn and its garden into the open country, gains his freedom and is saved; at the same time the death of Gennaro underlines the evil power of a self-righteous and spiritually dead society. It would be hard to imagine a more effective introduction to Forster's two worlds of innocence and experience, nature and society, vision and anti-vision.

"The Road from Colonus" is the story not of a youth but of an old man who regains the vision of youth. Mr. Lucas, the modern Oedipus, accompanied by his fussily helpful daughter and some of her friends is visiting Greece. Riding ahead of the others, he comes upon a little Inn surrounded by a small grove of plane trees. A pure stream bubbles musically from the roots of a great hollow tree. He steps into this natural shrine and enters into union with man and nature. He discovers "not only Greece, but England and all the world and life" (p. 130). Everything has form and meaning and purpose. Counterpointing this vision are the false raptures of the other tourists who are determined not to allow Mr. Lucas to stay at the Inn.

This is the main part of the story. It is effectively told. The vision of simplicity and harmony is quietly reinforced by a series of symbols: the river and tree of life, the natural shrine, the Inn as human dwelling prepared to receive the wayfarer, and the inhabitants (including the old grandmother who spins and the children who play) as the family of man. Set against this are the tourists with their superficial babble, their obtuseness, and their brutality. Ethel, the modern Antigone, incites Mr. Graham, her well-made young man, to use brute force in removing Mr. Lucas from the scene of revelation.

This is not the end of the story. That very night the great plane tree crashes in a violent storm and kills all the inhabitants of the Inn. Here is the blessed Oedipus-like fate Mr. Lucas has been deprived of. He returns to England where he wears out his days of doddering old age fussing about the neighbors and unable to sleep on account of the noise of running water in the drains. He is, as Ethel says, his "old self again" (p. 139).

In Forster's stories, one way of symbolizing the complete division between innocence and experience is the two-kingdom geographical setting. We have this in "The Other Side of the Hedge," "The Machine Stops," and "The Celestial Omnibus." The stories we are now looking at create the same kind of effect by more indirect means. In "The Story of a Panic" the tourists are intruders in Pan's kingdom and must flee from the place of incarnation. Later the boy must flee from the inn and garden—the world of the tourists—into the open country. In "The Road from Colonus" Mr. Lucas is alone in the grove during the moments of his vision. The rest of the party are intruders. The importance of place is beautifully symbolized when, an hour after leaving the Inn, they come round the spur of a mountain and behold the grove of trees far below them. It makes its final appeal to

Mr. Lucas but Ethel intervenes and he moves on toward the sterile inanity of his life in England.

In "Other Kingdom" the sense of a place apart is equally strong. But before coming to that, something should be said about the narrator of this story. Mr. Inskip is the employee of the prosperous, pompous, and impeccable Harcourt Worters. He is tutor to the master's ward, a very young man named Ford, and to the master's fiancée, a very unsophisticated and spirited Irish girl named Evelyn Beaumont. He is the most lively and entertaining of Forster's narrators. The first source of his allegiance to Mr. Worters is his salary; the second is a certain similarity of outlook. But the similarity is far from complete and he is able to appreciate, though never to support, Ford's scathing reactions to Mr. Worters. He is more complex than Forster's other narrators and is admirably equipped to convey the conflicting forces that ruffle the complacent surface of the Worters demesne. But he is incapable of understanding Miss Beaumont. Forster will not allow her glorious innocence and primal power to be more than guessed at by the mind of this worldly and corrupt narrator.

The characters are revealed to us through a very simple situation. Other Kingdom, a beach copse standing opposite Mr. Worters' house on the other side of a stream, is bought by him as a present for Miss Beaumont. She is in love with her property until, on a picnic to Other Kingdom, she learns that he plans to put a high fence all around it and build a path and bridge into it. Apparently broken in spirit, she at last agrees to these plans. But during a second visit to her Kingdom she escapes the deadening control of the Worters way of life by disappearing dyrad-like in her beech grove. Except for the transformation, this sketch hardly touches the heart of the story which is to be found in the first visit to the wood.

Miss Beaumont, in a green dress, leads the procession. She dances in imitation of the trees and especially the beech. As they enter the woods, she induces them to sing, as if it were a litany, a line she and Ford had been translating from the classics: "Ah you silly ass gods live in woods." Once within her wood, she welcomes them and they bow to her. For the picnic she makes the seating arrangements and

77

takes special care to have Ford stand in such a position that he will blot out her view of the Worters mansion, which the narrator cynically describes as looking "like a cottage with the dropsy" (p. 89). She goes further: "Just pull back your soft hat, Mr. Ford. Like a halo. Now you hide even the smoke from the chimneys. And it makes you look beautiful" (p. 88). And so, like a presiding deity, over them all stands "the silent, chivalrous figure of Ford" (p. 90).

Mr. Worters is not pleased. He chaffs Ford and tickles his ankles and legs. When Miss Beaumont again refers to blocking out the house, he runs his hand "up around the boy's ankle" (p. 91) and tumbles him to the ground. What follows is supposed to pass for play but Ford's cry is one of anger and pain. Later after Mr. Worters has indulged in a perfect Sir Willoughby Patterne rhapsody on the theme of the isolated and secluded bliss he and Miss Beaumont can look forward to, he stretches out his hand to cut their initials into a tree and reveals, to her horror, the "red stuff" on his finger and thumb (p. 97).

Mr. Worters is accustomed to imposing his will on others in a coldly sadistic manner. Here we have a physical symbol of his sadism. And we have more. He knows that Ford is his enemy and in precisely what way he is an enemy. The hand running up round the ankle with thumb and finger poised is a castration gesture. But unlike the parallel episode in "The Machine Stops," this one leads to a symbolic affirmation: Ford has made a blood sacrifice to the fulfillment of Miss Beaumont' ritual and, at the same time, has sealed their relationship in blood.[38]

This brilliant scene deepens our understanding of the characters. Harcourt Worters, as we learn from the finest of hints, has purchased Other Kingdom by taking advantage of a widow (p. 83). "Radiating energy and wealth, like a terrestrial sun" (p. 100), he has only to touch a thing and it turns to gold. He is Midas. Ford has told Miss Beaumont about Midas: "He just comes, he touches you, and you pay him several thousand per cent. at once. You're gold—a young golden lady—if he touches you" (p. 77). And Mr. Worters has told his mother that "in time Evelyn will repay me a thousandfold" (p. 87).

78

When Evelyn insists on remaining alive and green and enlists Ford in the carrying out of her life-giving ritual, Mr. Worters reveals the full extent of his coldly perverted selfishness.

At the same time Ford reveals his heroic nature through a kind of stillness and radiance. In his role as presiding deity and devoted lover, he belongs with Forster's archetypal primitives, Gennaro, Gino (*Where Angels Fear to Tread*), and Stephen (*The Longest Journey*). He has their kind of wisdom. But unlike them he is educated, intelligent, a biting critic, and a wit. And for good measure, he has a notable quality of virility, a characteristic rare in Forster's men. He is the most complex and finely presented male character in the short stories and a match for any in the novels.

Evelyn Beaumont is equally fine. Few novelists can convey happiness and few can portray simple, spontaneous high-spirits. Forster can do both. He can catch, too, the suddenness of collapse when liveliness is thwarted. Because he can do these things, we believe in Evelyn Beaumont and accept her extraordinary transformation. Her visit to Other Kingdom prepares for this transformation by giving symbolic value to the flowing green dress, the tree dance, the ritual procession to the wood, and the feast presided over by Ford. The preparation is continued later in the image of the large branch torn from the wood and rolled by the wind over the bridge and up the path to the very front of the house, the image of Evelyn Beaumont torn from her Kingdom. Finally, her transformation is prefigured in the magnificent description of her flight to Other Kingdom: "She danced away from our society and our life, back, back, through the centuries till houses and fences fell and the earth lay wild to the sun" (p. 108).

She becomes one with her Kingdom. As they search for her, the narrator describes their feeling that she "was close by, that the delicate limbs were just behind this bole, the hair and the drapery quivering among those leaves. She was beside us, above us; here was her footstep on the purple-brown earth—her bosom, her neck—she was everywhere and nowhere" (p. 110). She is the Earth-Mother.

The tree of life and the wood of life are traditional mother symbols. That Other Kingdom belongs in this tradition is confirmed by the mythology of the story. Boys and girls have always come up to the wood to cut their initials together in the bark. "It's called the Fourth Time of Asking. . . . They cut their names and go away, and when the first child is born they come again and deepen the cuts. So for each child. That's how you know: the initials that go right through to the wood are the fathers and mothers of large families, and the scratches in the bark that soon close up are boys and girls who were never married at all" (pp. 95-96). These are the words of Evelyn Beaumont and are followed by her plea to Mr. Worters not to fence her in by fencing her Kingdom in: "I must be on the outside, I must be where any one can reach me. Year by year—while the initials deepen —the only thing worth feeling—and at last they close up—but one has felt them."

Harcourt Worters learns that the earth, our mother, and all that is beautiful and joyous in it, cannot be bought and cannot be confined. Evelyn Beaumont has escaped him "absolutely, for ever and ever, as long as there are branches to shade men from the sun" (p. 112). But she embraces Ford in her shade for ever. No one can break him, for he is confirmed both as divine son and mortal lover of Earth, the bride-mother.

In probing the symbolic implications of "Other Kingdom," I have no doubt fallen into the error of making the story seem unduly portentous. Let me conclude by stressing the sureness and lightness of touch with which Forster handles his profoundly suggestive material. "Just pull back your soft hat," Miss Beaumont says. "Like a halo," and suddenly Ford stands before us as a radiant young god.

The central vision of this and all the best stories is the ecstatic experience of oneness with nature and an ideal past. About the past Forster is vague but evocative. It is a primitive pastoral world that looks with direct eyes on the power of nature and knows neither fences nor barriers; it is a youthful civilization in which even the old and the blind may regain youth and vision. Above all, it is the world of our ancestors which reaches into the present to give us strength and consolation. There is "no such thing as the solitude of nature, for the sorrows and joys of humanity [have] pressed even into the bosom of a tree." And silence, which so often heralds the moment of spiritual revelation, "is the voice of the earth and of the generations who have gone."[39] Whatever the image, this sense of the past gives depth to man's experience of identity with nature. Moreover it implies that what has taken place is the integration into the conscious mind of ancestrally based unconscious elements.

Such an interpretation is confirmed by the preponderance of symbols representing an expanded, enhanced, or transcendent self. The hero conveys this sense of a reborn, renewed, and greater self; and the impression of a new self is supported by symbols which convey the same meaning and which frequently act as catalysts in the process of renewal. These symbols may be characters implied or present in the narrative: Achilles, Pan, the dying Oedipus, the family of man presiding over the Inn, Castor and Pollux, and Orion the hunter and hero. They may be objects of the natural world: the constellation of Orion, the shield of Achilles with its imaged universe, the everlasting river and the gulf-transcending rainbow, the valley like a vast green hand, the beech copse of Other Kingdom, and the grove of plane trees with its three equally impressive objects, the Inn, the bubbling spring, and the overflowing vessel which is both tree and shrine. All these are traditional symbols of the self or transparent modifications of traditional symbols. Sometimes the symbol is an event and represents directly the rebirth of the self as a greater and more inclusive being. Examples are the rebirth through water into the garden on the other side of the hedge, Harold's fierce rowing which induces a mystic state of pure being, the boy's leap onto the Mount Olympus of Achilles' shield, and the religious ritual at Other Kingdom.

Forster's heroes enter into an experience which can only be described as visionary. As a result of this experience they feel a sense of strength and renewal, of expansion and fulfillment. This feeling invariably arises from their achieving identity with nature though it may be nature mediated by the poetic imagination. And nature is always rooted in the human past. Thus, for example, Harold's ancestors call to him as he rows across the estuary (p. 200). Since the experience of identity is, by definition, unconscious, it is reasonable to suppose that man's ancestral past is not simply inherent in outer nature but is inherent in his own inner nature, in the unconscious reaches of his own mind.

Once the bucket has been lowered and its contents brought up into the light, the unconscious may be mediated by the conscious mind and the renewed and greater self may enter into daily life. Such a transition is not easy. The subliminal nature of the vision calls from the depths, evoking the peacefulness of death-like oblivion; the supraliminal nature of the vision calls from the heights, evoking the exultation of splendid isolation.

In the short stories Forster is not much concerned with the way vision enters into and transforms daily life. But he gives full expression to the attraction of death and isolation as they exercise their power over the newborn self. A strange destiny awaits all those characters who are overtaken by vision. Harold in "The Point of It" dies immediately. Mr. Lucas is intended to die immediately. Gennaro dies that Eustace may live; and he can live only by escaping from society. The hero of "The Machine Stops" suffers both isolation and death. The hero of "Albergo Empedocle" is driven to the ultimate isolation of insanity. Both the divine child of "The Celestial Omnibus" and the bride-mother of "Other Kingdom" enter a place set apart; they have broken through the closed circle of the ego-centered and unimaginative worlds from which they came. Only in the thoroughly inferior stories are death and isolation of no significance—proof, if more is needed, that in these stories Forster has falsified or failed to project the deeper implications of his vision.

The achieving of identity with nature, like the breaking down of the barrier between the ego and the unconscious, can best be described as a primitive experience. The elemental and absolute nature of the experience isolates the individual from the world. In prose fiction, the first great expressions of the phenomenon of primitive identity are *Wuthering Heights* and *Moby-Dick*. In comparison with the worlds created by these fictions, Forster's world of nature may appear to be romantically conceived: the same spirit informs both man and nature, and awareness of their unity gives to the individual such a sense of expansion and fulfillment that he experiences an escape from isolation. At a superficial level, Forster is inclined to regard nature in this way. But at a deeper level, he shows by the development of his stories that union with nature isolates the individual from humanity though at the same time it reveals to the individual the primitive power and joy that lies at the root of all being. The short stories, then, are a series of probings by Forster into the immediate elemental reality of his vision. The emphasis is on the power and joy of the experience of identity; death and isolation are accepted with a kind of exultation as the price demanded by the vision; indeed they appear as the guarantee of its supreme reality.

Though Forster's interest focuses on the immediate impact of vision, he begins in three of the stories to explore the question of whether the vision can survive and become operative in the world at large. "The Point of It" approaches the problem. It shows that the vision is easy to forget but that the desire to remember can bring personal salvation. "The Eternal Moment" tackles the problem outright, thus showing its uniqueness in yet another way. Miss Raby's vision has inspired her first and most ambitious novel, it has given her the courage to hold unpopular opinions and the integrity to act straight from the center of her being, and it has made her conscious of a triumph over experience and earthly fact, a triumph magnificent, cold, hardly human.

At least that is what we are told. What we feel amounts to much less—namely, that her memory of the eternal moment helps to sustain her in the face of a series of bitter and ironic disappointments. As a memory, her vision has conviction; as a continuing reality which transforms her day-to-day life, it has neither joy nor luminousness. In other words, it has lost most of its essential quality. It has become a kind of moral residue, good for clearing the eye and stiffening the spine but no good for anything else. The truth is—and Forster practically says so at one point—Miss Raby's Italian guide and her beautiful mountain are the only things she has ever loved deeply. Though her eternal moment is one of love, that love has not entered into the world. It has touched no one, it has tranformed no one; it is a piece of movable property the possession of which gives her security and strength. This is not the impression Forster wished to create; rather it is the impression arising from his failure to portray the vision as both a continuing and a *living* reality. His failure here may be contrasted with his success in "The Story of the Siren," which approaches the same problem symbolically rather than psychologically.

"The Story of the Siren," the last of Forster's tales to be published, is one of the supreme achievements of his shorter fiction. It has been left to the end so that the fullest range of insights might be brought to its discussion. Let me add that in concentrating on its symbolic highlights I run the risk of making the story sound sensational. In fact, its power and scope are so quietly and unobtrusively conveyed that the casual reader might at first overlook them.

"The Story of the Siren" opens with a group of English tourists in Sicily. Among them is the narrator who is writing a dissertation on the Deist Controversy.[40] Beyond this silly society is that of the town corrupted by commercialism; and beyond that again is the truly evil society of the Church and its black-clad priests. The Siren never leaves the sea because the priests have blessed the land and the air. Yet, for reasons the priests cannot understand, she reveals herself only to good people. When Giuseppe, a strong Italian youth, dives into the sea without crossing himself and sees the Siren, his life is forever changed. He is appalled rather than exhilarated for his vision is one of desolation. He becomes unhappy, "unhappy because he knew everything. Every living thing made him unhappy because he knew it would die" (p. 252). When he discovers a girl who has seen the Siren, he brings her home and marries her. But love cannot alter the knowledge that makes them unhappy. Then the priests turn the people against them and it is whispered that their child will be Antichrist. Before the child is born the girl goes down to the sea one stormy night and is pushed over the cliff by a priest. Giuseppe leaves his village and roams the world, searching until he dies for another human being who has seen the Siren.

What does she represent? Homer's Sirens sing, "For lo, we know all things . . . yea, we know all that shall hereafter be upon the fruitful earth." Jane Harrison, whose book on the myths of the *Odyssey* Forster is likely to have read, notes that Homer left them "shrouded in mystery, the mystery of the hidden things of the sea . . .—

knowing all things, yet themselves for ever unknown. Nor is the manner of the death of their victims more clearly told. If, smitten with fell desire for knowledge, they hearken to the forbidden song, they must die—as, in the Semitic saga, they perish who taste of the forbidden fruit of the tree of knowledge . . .—die not at once, but by a slow wasting; . . . the hapless seafarer is cut off henceforth from all simple, human, wholesome joys of wife and babe, and consumed by a barren desire."[41] If we allow that in Forster's story knowledge of all things is simply given rather than fatally desired, this seems a fair account of Giuseppe's encounter with the Siren.

Forster wrote recently, comparing his Siren to Lampedusa's: "Mine was cosmic, and was to stay hidden until ritually summoned, when she would rise to the surface, sing, destroy silence, primness, and cruelty, and save the world. His Siren is not cosmic; she is personal. . . ."[42] If we look more closely at Lampedusa's story, however, we see through the person to a being as cosmic as Forster's Siren. The truth of her existence lies deep "in the blind mute palace of formless waters, eternal, without a gleam, without a whisper." She is the "Wise Mother" and "the current of life, with its detail eliminated." "I am immortal" she says "because in me every death meets, from that of the fish just now to that of Zeus, and conjoined in me they turn again into a life that is no longer individual and determined but of Pan and so free."[43] She is the elemental, unconscious current which underlies all life; and all individual life sinks back into her depths, blind, mute, formless, eternal, without a gleam, without a whisper. Lampedusa's Siren is a vision of age. She returns to the depths and calls man to the peace and darkness of oblivion.

Forster's Siren is a vision of youth. She too is the elemental and unconscious current of life. In her, too, every death meets. But she is also the permanent and eternal source of life. And though man, in ignorance and superstition, has confined her to the depths, she will some day—so the vision of youth asserts—be summoned into the light. When Giuseppe sees the Siren he sees life in its permanence and death in its everlastingness and he is desolate, for he knows that the vision of life's permanence is absent from the world and that death reigns over all.

"Nothing of it but will change into something rich and strange," warbles the chaplain with no slightest notion of how apposite his words are to become (pp. 245–46). Out of the vision of the world subject to death and infinite sadness comes a realization of the need for rebirth or renewal. So to a child born out of such sadness there might, as the Italian proverb says, come gladness (p. 254). This is confirmed by the prophecy of the witch: "the child would always be speaking and laughing and perverting, and last of all he would go into the sea and fetch up the Siren into the air and all the world would see her and hear her sing. As soon as she sang, the Seven Vials would be opened and the Pope would die and Mongibello flame, and the veil of Santa Agata would be burned. Then the boy and the Siren would marry, and together they would rule the world for ever and ever" (p. 255). Giuseppe's brother interprets the prophecy: "never in my life will there be both a man and a woman from whom that child can be born, who will fetch up the Siren from the sea, and destroy silence, and save the world!" Then he adds: "Silence and loneliness cannot last for ever. It may be a hundred or a thousand years, but the sea lasts longer, and she shall come out of it and sing" (pp. 257–58).

Here we have a kind of visionary map of the nature and range of the experience Forster is to explore and develop in his novels. The story does not solve the problem of how the vision can be assimilated and made operative in the world at large. But it gives fuller expression to the dark side of existence by representing death as inherent in the vision—a persistent theme in the novels. And it pictures, with greater boldness than elsewhere, the world that might be hoped for if the vision could prevail universally.

Salvation will mean the end of silence and loneliness. From his first work of fiction to his last, Forster makes splendid use of silence and loneliness. They may be associated with a revelation of spiritual power ("The Story of a Panic") or with the negation of spiritual power. In *A Passage to India* the silence beyond the remotest echo is a premonition of the nonexistence of spirit; and the cave is a symbol of narcissistic isolation, man's spirit turned inward upon itself in perfect aloneness. It is silence and loneliness of this order that the Siren will destroy. She will come up from the indestructible life-giving sea when a man, born out of the knowledge that all things must die (the preliminary truth which destroys the evil dream of the Church), recognizes the reality of death as a challenge and fashions another and greater reality: a vision of song and laughter, of love and companionship, a vision of the realities which are the highest fulfillment of man's spirit and which are coeternal with his spirit. And when the song of the Siren is heard, the Babylon of evil superstition will crash in ruin; and when the Siren marries the young man born out of the knowledge of death, it will be a sign that man's spirit reigns for ever and ever.

Forster frequently uses expressions like "eternal" and "for ever and ever." They have misled some of his readers and confused others. In fact they are a simple expression of the profoundly archetypal nature of his imaginative vision. Though most men are nonentities, one man may express the strength or beauty or wisdom of the human spirit. He is the hero whom Forster's imagination seizes upon. He is the one who in each of the short stories defines the essential character of the human spirit. It may be the poetic imagination or the active and joyous state of pure youthful being or the mighty affirmation of love and joy whose power is over death; but whatever it is, the hero or his surrogate gives expression to it. In that sense he is eternal.

In "The Story of the Siren" the total vision has a scope and profundity greater than that in any of the other stories. As a result the archetypal hero and heroine who embody the grandeur of this vision must be presented with immense skill and care if we are to believe in them. In this situation, Forster for the first time in the short stories resorts to the technique of extreme distancing. An Englishman narrates a story told by a young Italian about his brother who has seen the Siren but whose marriage fails to produce a son. The possibility of a permanent and life-enhancing vision is prefigured. But the divine child who is destined to become the hero remains unborn; the Siren, who is all unconscious life, individual and general, and the great universal bride-mother, remains in the sea; and the black priests like vultures remain guarding the cliffs.[44]

By thus distancing the purest and grandest of his archetypal romance characters, Forster makes credible the most apocalyptic of all his visions. It is the boldest and farthest stretch of his imagination and

87

the most absolute expression of his moral vision. With its two sharply divided worlds, with its boldly simple and elusively powerful symbols, and with its complex awareness of a new goodness not yet born out of the knowledge of death and an old evil not yet eradicated by the spirit of life, "The Story of the Siren" may fairly be given the central place in Forster's created world as the archetype of all his fictions.

September 24 [1938]. . . . What a tonic for me it was, having lunch with E. M. today! He says he's afraid of going mad—of suddenly turning and running away from people in the street. But, actually, he's the last person who'd ever go mad; he's far saner than anyone else I know. And immensely, superhumanly strong. He's strong because he doesn't try to be a stiff-lipped stoic, like the rest of us; and so he'll never crack. He's absolutely flexible. He lives by love, not by will. . . .

While we were eating, the manager of the restaurant came over to tell us he'd just heard on the wireless that Hitler has allowed six days for the evacuation of the Sudeten areas. . . .

To celebrate our reprieve, I ordered champagne, just for the pleasure of being extravagant, and we both got rather drunk. E. M. became very gay and made silly jokes. His silliness is beautiful, because it expresses love, and is the reverse side of his passionate minding about things. . . . We need E. M.'s silliness more than ever, now. It gives courage.

—Christopher Isherwood, *Down There on a Visit*

This entry is from a diary kept during the crises of 1938. Isherwood, like other writers who made their mark in the thirties, is a kind of permanent adolescent. But at his best he has a penetrating innocence that passes directly through the superficial to the heart of the matter. He is at his best in assessing E. M. Forster. We can see how good that best is when we observe that though he is talking about the strength of the man in a specific moment of crisis every statement is equally relevant in defining the strength of the writer. To place these remarks beside those of critics who complain of a tea-cup world is to see that the triviality is not in Forster but in his critics. The dreams of will and passion, variously deified by Nietzsche, Wagner, and D. H. Lawrence, have obscured the true strength of Forster's world.

3

Narrator as Archetype

I have defined an archetype as a symbol which, in the area of its reference, embodies a content that seems to be total in a form that seems to be universal. What, then, is the source of the symbol's power to embody a total content in a universal form? I answer that the source of power is ecstatic experience. Every one of Forster's archetypal symbols results directly or indirectly from such an experience.

This is what Forster in the short stories calls the eternal moment. Such a moment may transform a character, as George Emerson on the violet-covered terrace in *A Room with a View* is transformed to a hero in Lucy's eyes. Or it may transform an object, as in "The Celestial Omnibus" the shield of Achilles is transformed from a mere figuration of the whole world to that world as living reality. But in either case that which is transformed is the same as that which induces the eternal moment. (This is not true of all ecstatic experiences, but is true of all instances in Forster's fiction.) In "The Road from Colonus" the sacred vast and hollow tree, the spring, the grove, and the Khan are both the source and the substance of Mr. Lucas's vision. But as this story illustrates there is one great difference between the source and the substance. In the moment of identity and transformation, things which before were only so many objects (or it may be persons) expand to embrace the whole universe. "To Mr. Lucas, who, in a brief space of time, had discovered not only Greece, but England and all the world and life, there seemed nothing ludicrous in the desire to hang within the tree another votive offering—a little model of an entire man" (p. 130). This same sense of wholeness is represented literally by the shield of Achilles and—to take a very different example—symbolically by the inclusiveness of Stephen Wonham's character at the end of *The Longest Journey.*

Ecstatic experiences (as described by religious mystics, professional writers, and ordinary citizens) have been analyzed by Marghanita Laski. She finds that ecstatic states are joyful and extraordinary to the point of seeming preternatural, are of brief duration, though the afterglow may be prolonged, and are a rare and unpredictable occurrence. She finds, too, that ecstatic states are marked by an abatement of normal awareness accompanied by a sense of interpenetration or identity with the object of vision and that they give rise to a sense of totality.

Miss Laski distinguishes between intensity ecstasy and withdrawal ecstasy. The first is overwhelmingly the commonest. Though the word intensity might be sufficient to indicate its nature, I will give an example which is distinguished by briefness, preciseness, and clarity. It is from Richard Jeffries' autobiography:

> I looked at the hills, at the dewy grass, and then up through the elm branches to the sky. In a moment all that was behind me, the house, the people, the sounds, seemed to disappear, and to leave me alone. Involuntarily I drew a long breath, then I breathed slowly. My thought, or inner consciousness, went up through the illumined sky, and I was lost in a moment of exaltation. This only lasted a very short time, perhaps only part of a second, and while it lasted there was no formulated wish. I was absorbed; I drank the beauty of the morning; I was exalted.[1]

In contrast to this outgoingness and sense of transport, which is also apparent in the experience of George Emerson and Lucy Honeychurch on the violet-covered hillside in *A Room with a View,* withdrawal ecstasy is a type of introversion and is described in terms of "slow and gentle merging, melting, liquefying, dissolving, usually into something else."[2] Soundless calm and the hush of peace are also characteristic in accounts of the experience. This kind of ecstasy is frequently followed by intensity ecstasy. The process can be seen in the account of Mr. Lucas. He first loses himself in the shrine of the tree: "he lay motionless, conscious only of the stream below his feet, and that all things were a stream, in which he was moving"; then he looks out to find everything transformed: "when he opened his eyes, something unimagined, indefinable, had passed over all things, and made them intelligible and good" (p. 130). The prominence of silence in Forster's moments of vision shows that many of them at least begin in withdrawal. Examples picked at random are the stillness as the cat's-paw of wind moves over the valley in "The Story of a Panic," the silence attending Mrs. Wilcox as she moves noiselessly over the lawn at Howards End, and Rickie Elliot's dream on the Wiltshire downs in which, as he and Agnes approach the throne of God, an immense silence touches them and earth and all danger dissolve.[3]

Ecstatic experience may be set in motion by almost any thing or person. However, it is far more likely to be set in motion by an object than by a person. An impressive number of ecstasies are inspired by what Miss Laski calls a "*unitive symbol*—an object, event, or idea that can be seen as far older than the life of a man or . . . than the life of mankind. Obvious and basic symbols often found triggering this type of ecstasy are sea, earth, mountains, etc., but frequently, instead of or in addition to these, there is reference to a more particular symbol, usually a primitive form that can be seen as having existed from distant time until the moment when the ecstatic encounters it."[4] The flower-clad mountain terraces of "The Eternal Moment" and *A Room with a View* are basic symbols. The plane tree on the road from Colonus and the wych-elm at Howards End are more particular symbols. But from all of Forster's work, the unitive symbol most likely to spring to mind is the Marabar Hills.

And the Marabar Hills bring us to the experience of desolation. Miss Laski notes that accounts of desolation resemble accounts of ecstasy in that the key terms are the negation or reverse of those used to describe ecstasy.[5] The vision of Giuseppi in "The Story of the Siren" is one of desolation and clearly illustrates this point. We may note especially the emphasis on totality. But the most extraordinary instance of desolation is the experience of Mrs. Moore in the Marabar cave. Something queer happens to her normal awareness, a sense of identity with the object of vision reveals itself as the absolute identity of all things, and this identity of all things engenders an appalling sense of meaningless totality.[6]

Whether the experience is one of desolation or ecstasy, its most remarkable characteristic is this sense of totality which finds expression in such words as all, whole, complete, or universe, eternity, reality, or ineffable, indescribable, inconceivable. "It is characteristic of ecstasy that . . . its feelings are nearly always total, infinite, and measureless—due, I believe, to a loss of the sense of difference or . . . of the faculty of making distinctions. . . . What is believed to have been felt or perceived in ecstasy tends to be expressed as feelings of 'that than which nothing greater can be conceived' in the class concerned."[7]

We may now, with new insight, refer back to our definition of the archetype as a symbol which, in the area of its reference, embodies a content that seems to be total in a form that seems to be universal. We may say that an archetype is an individual person or object which, through the ecstatic moment of identity, has been transformed into "that than which nothing greater can be conceived" in the class concerned and so is experienced as the source of feelings of totality. This description of an archetype offers a psychological explanation of how the type object comes to be selected: it is experienced as an object of vision; and how it comes to have authority, which is to say how it comes to command our assent as a type: it is experienced as all-inclusive and hence greatest.

Seen in this light, an archetype is a mythic symbol. Angus Fletcher has pointed out the tendency of allegorical narrative, in which category he includes romance, to move toward central moments of great visionary intensity. Such moments transform the work: "once allegory becomes truly apocalyptic it ceases to be mere allegory and comes instead to share in the higher order or mysterious language, which we may perhaps call mythical language." He adds, by way of note, "that myth and allegory are two different stages of a single archetypal story-telling process. . . . Allegory seems usually to follow upon myth, in that the story it pulls apart into separate levels must have once been a unity."[8] Forster's stories proceed on what Fletcher calls the allegorical level. The whole image of man is pulled apart and represented in its various aspects by various characters. But the symbols and symbolic characters, which are archetypal, institute and indeed restore an awareness of ultimate unity characteristic of myth.

Achilles and his shield, caught up in the vision of the boy, institute a mythic order. The tree and its spring, the grove and Khan, Greece and the world, caught up in the vision of Mr. Lucas, institute another mythic order. But if the instrumental cause of this order is the ecstatic experience of the character, the final cause must be the ecstatic experience of the creator, the author-narrator. We may therefore ask in what sense the author-narrator is present in his work. And we may ask whether it is appropriate or meaningful to speak of the narrator as archetypal, of the narrator himself as the source through which we experience a subsuming mythic order.

The idea of the literary artist, poet or novelist, as archetypal has had since the time of the Romantics and particularly since the end of the nineteenth century a consistent and compelling attraction. The idea is explicit, for example in Westcott's insistence that the myths of Plato are "the individual expression of a universal instinct. Plato speaks not as Plato but as man." In what follows my object is to represent as fairly as I can both the idea of the literary artist as archetypal and the imagery in which the idea expresses itself. Having done that, I go on to suggest the way the idea needs to be qualified if it is to be generally applicable to works of fiction. Finally, after analyzing the role of the narrator in *A Room with a View* and *Where Angels Fear to Tread,* I explore the uniqueness of the Italian romances and the way in which they alone among Forster's works, may justify our speaking, without qualification, of the narrator as archetype.

The original model or type is God, traditionally conceived as the center and as emanating outward in a perfect circle of inclusiveness. From the idea of the creator as archetype it is an easy step to the idea of the artist as archetype. Since traditionally the artist's inspiration comes from the god, the resemblance of the human to the divine creator is more than an analogy. But whether the inspiration is thought of as coming from without or from within, the image of the artist as center and source of an inclusive universe persists. Thus Coleridge, giving the image a thoroughly subjective turn, says: "The poet, described in *ideal* perfection, brings the whole soul of man into activity. . . . He diffuses a tone and spirit of unity, that blends, and (as it were) fuses, each into each," the discordant qualities of the soul.[9] And Forster says: "Creation lies at the heart of civilisation like fire in the heart of the earth. Around it are gathered its cooler allies, criticism, the calm use of the intellect, informing the mass and moulding it into shape."[10] And here is D. H. Lawrence: "In every great novel, who is the hero all the time? Not any of the characters, but some unnamed and nameless flame behind them all. Just as God is the pivotal interest in the books of the *Old Testament*. . . . In the great novel, the felt but unknown flame stands behind all the characters, and in their words and gestures there is a flicker of the presence."[11]

With the disappearance of God and the loss of absolute moral values, the circle of creation no longer has the image of either god or man at its center. The implied author, the narrator of a story, is no longer the clearly defined presence at the heart of the fiction. For Lawrence, he has become an unnamed and nameless flame. The idea has been frequently and variously expressed throughout this century. For Marlow "the meaning of an episode was not inside like a kernel but outside, enveloping the tale which brought it out only as a glow brings out a haze, in the likeness of one of those misty halos that sometimes are made visible by the spectral illumination of moonshine."[12] In this extraordinarily intuitive sentence Conrad slides from one term to another and then to an image and then to another image and the meaning imperceptibly shimmers and slips away from us, shimmers and slips again even further away, in perfect imitation of the idea it would express. But however elusive the statement, its implications are clear. When the author is no longer the obvious center of his creation the meaning can no longer be inside like a kernel but radiates outward like an aura enveloping the tale. And through this aura as through Lawrence's flame we apprehend the creator. At the same time the creator sees himself in a different light. "I expand the emptiness within me," says Claudel.[13] And Stephen Dedalus says of the dramatic mode: "The mystery of aesthetic like that of material creation is accomplished. The artist, like the God of creation, remains within or behind or beyond or above his handiwork, invisible, refined out of existence, indifferent, paring his fingernails."[14] Ortega y Gasset offers an equally awesome but less austere view of the situation. "The artist . . . has risen above himself, above his vital spontaneity; he has soared above his own heart and above his surroundings, circling about like the eagle in majestic flight."[15]

What is striking about these statements is the way the image of the expanding circle of creation persists. Forster adds his tribute to it in the well-known plea at the end of *Aspects of the Novel*: "Expansion. That is the idea the novelist must cling to. Not completion. Not rounding off but opening out." Unlike Forster, many twentieth-century novelists have ceased to stand openly at the center. But the circle implies a center; and there, flamelike or invisible or with the emptiness of negative capability, the narrator-creator remains a presence, a voice "still dominant in a dialogue that is at the heart of all experience with fiction."[16]

In fiction the universe exists only through the narrator, either directly through the more or less omniscient author or indirectly through his mask, one or a series of authors taking part in the narrative. The author-narrator determines our point of view. He may strive for supreme objectivity, he may use dialogue to the exclusion of everything else, he may even desert the traditional past tense which gives to events the appearance of "a reality lived and remembered,"[17] but he cannot alter the basic convention of narrative. Whereas drama displays an action, narrative tells a story embracing action. Fiction not only offers but imposes a narrative point of view over and above the action, and a novelist cannot finally evade this imposition of his medium. By the fact of his being observer and storyteller (or the manipulator of the storyteller) he is apart from and, accordingly, transcends the action.

The distinction made here between the action of a novel, which apparently speaks for itself, and the narration, especially the descriptive and interpretative material, which gives a perspective over and above the action, is by no means satisfactory. The same is true of other distinctions like showing and telling or scene and summary. They are unsatisfactory because they put asunder what the narrator has joined together. Henry James states the case brilliantly:

> People often talk of these things as if they had a kind of internecine distinctness, instead of melting into each other at every breath, and being intimately associated parts of one general effort of expression. I cannot imagine composition existing in a series of blocks, nor conceive, in any novel worth discussing at all, of a passage of description that is not in its intention narrative, a passage of dialogue that is not in its intention descriptive, a touch of truth of any sort that does not partake of the nature of incident, or an incident that derives its interest from any other source than the general and only source of the success of a work of art—that of being illustrative.

Even dialogue, that most dramatic of elements, has "learned the art of being merely illustrational."[18]

It is folly to set in opposition telling and showing or description and action for these are indivisible functions. But because they are indivisible it is possible to see the one as totally subsuming the other. That is why honest men have so radically disagreed: why Ortega y Gasset can say "the novel describes" and Philip Rahv can say "the language becomes a kind of transparent envelope or medium through which we watch the action." When Ortega tells us that the petty affairs of Emma Bovary and her foolish husband are only interesting on account of the way their are described, we see what he means. And when Rahv tells us that Dostoevsky despite his being an indifferent stylist is a great novelist because "once we are caught up by the moving current of mock-reality in his narratives we cease noticing the words as such," we see also what he means.[19]

We may even find this disagreement embedded in the language of a single critic. Suzanne Langer tells us the story "is a *total action*. . . . Reflections, descriptions, and gem-like lines, and even characters are just parts of *the tale,* or *what is told*."[20] However much she may come down on the side of action and showing, her words are caught up in the dilemma expressed by Yeats in the image of the dancer and the dance. How can we know the teller from the tale? James answered this question as Yeats answered his.

A successful fiction is one and indivisible, a seamless whole. And within and behind and through the work, giving it unity, is the author-narrator. He may be a blatantly and full-bloodedly present personality like the Fielding of *Tom Jones* or he may be an unnamed and nameless flame, but whatever he is we rest in him. He opens to us the essential character of the fiction. This may be "the power of combination—the single vision," "the immense persuasiveness of a mind which has completely mastered its perspective" (Virginia Woolf). It may be the quality of the writer's mind in which the moral and artistic sense meet to furnish "the deepest quality of a work of art" (Henry James). It may be the irreducible primitive element that is the ground of every story, "the voice of the tribal narrator" (E. M. Forster).[21] However we define this essential character of the fiction, it expresses the narrator, revealing him as the type who is the source of the totality and the embodiment of the all-inclusiveness of the world he tells into creation. We might call him the ultimate man of order.[22]

He is not, however, the ultimate man of mythic order, or at least he is not usually so. From a conceptual or logical point of view he might be seen as archetypal, for as the source of all he must include all. But normally he is not in himself apprehended as a source of ecstatic experience, he does not in his own person give us that sense of totality and unity characteristic of myth. This distinction between the narrator as a center of order and the narrator as himself a visionary center will be further explored after we have looked at Forster's Italian romances. In analyzing them we proceed on the assumption, later to be qualified, that the narrator is simply the ultimate man of order.

The Italian Romances

To any vision must be brought an eye adapted to what is to be seen.

—Plotinus

The narrator is always, in Forster's novels, the more or less omniscient author. And he is always immensely important because it is his role to imply or represent to the reader the whole image of man. Forster is writing romance in which the conflicting forces of our inner life are given external representation. Life and death, good and evil, spring and fall contend with each other. The characters embodying these forces are of necessity partial. The whole image of man comes through to us only at the end of the novel when all elements are in place and all conflicts have been resolved. Here is the goal toward which the narrator has been moving all along. But from the beginning his perfect command of every detail and every moment in the fiction has been our guarantee that he was in possession of and would bring us to the integrated vision, the whole image.

Forster has said that the author's personality is conveyed through such noble agencies as "the characters or the plot or his comments on life."[23] We may take *A Room with a View* as our first text for a study of how Forster's personality is conveyed to the reader and how that personality controls the reader's response to the fiction.

There are three principles of narration in *A Room with a View* and in all the novels up to *A Passage to India*. One, dialogue and bits of incisive description and information are the main constituent. Two, normally each chapter offers access to the thoughts and inner life of one character. Three, of the various characters whose inner life offers a perspective on events, one emerges as dominant. (Lucy Honeychurch in *A Room with a View,* Philip Herriton in *Where*

Angels Fear to Tread, Rickie Elliot in *The Longest Journey,* and Margaret Schlegel in *Howards End.*)

Each of these principles of narration is qualified by the intervention of the narrator. One, description and information often turn into commentary and judgment. Two, the perspective offered by the inner life of a character very often changes to that of Forster, or the two perspectives become inextricably blended. Three, though one of the several characters whose inner life offers a perspective on events emerges as dominant, his point of view does not dominate the narrative as a whole.

The intervention of the narrator at its most extreme can be illustrated from the well-known scene at the end of Chapter 6 of *A Room with a View* in which Lucy Honeychurch and the hero, George Emerson, unexpectedly meet and, under the spell of the Italian spring, not so unexpectedly kiss. The chapter in parody of the picaresque is entitled "The Reverend Arthur Beebe, the Reverend Cuthbert Eager, Mr. Emerson, Mr. George Emerson, Miss Eleanor Lavish, Miss Charlotte Bartlett, and Miss Lucy Honeychurch, Drive out in Carriages to see a View: Italians Drive Them." In keeping with its picaresque nature the chapter permits the point of view of several characters but allows no one point of view to dominate. The fact that it is an exception to Forster's usual practice is explained by the nature of the scene toward which the whole chapter builds. After the ascent into the hills above Florence, Lucy is separated from her spinsterish cousin, Miss Bartlett, and seeks the "good man," by which term she means the Reverend Arthur Beebe.

The view was forming at last; she could discern the river, the golden plain, other hills. . . .

At the same moment the ground gave way, and with a cry she fell out of the wood. Light and beauty enveloped her. She had fallen on to a little open terrace, which was covered with violets from end to end. . . .

From her feet the ground sloped sharply into the view, and violets ran down in rivulets and streams and cataracts, irrigating the hill-side with blue, eddying round the tree stems, collecting into pools in the hollows, covering the grass with spots of azure foam. But never again were they in such profusion; this terrace was the well-head, the primal source whence beauty gushed out to water the earth.

Standing at its brink, like a swimmer who prepares, was the good man. But he was not the good man that she had expected, and he was alone.

George had turned at the sound of her arrival. For a moment he contemplated her, as one who had fallen out of heaven. He saw radiant joy in her face, he saw the flowers beat against her dress in blue waves. . . . He stepped quickly forward and kissed her.

Before she could speak, almost before she could feel, a voice called, "Lucy! Lucy! Lucy!" The silence of life had been broken by Miss Bartlett, who stood brown against the view. (pp. 85–86)

Time after time we seem about to enter Lucy's mind, about to participate fully in her point of view. And for a moment near the end we seem to see with George Emerson's eyes. But in fact we only stand in the same position he does, just as an instant before we stood in Lucy's position when "George had turned at the sound of her arrival." In this way Forster brings us close to the characters while yet maintaining his and our detachment. The detachment is apparent in other ways. The beautiful description of the violets is not an account of Lucy's impression of them; it is a statement about their ultimate reality: "But never again were they in such profusion; this terrace was the well-head, the primal source whence beauty gushed out to water the earth." Caught up in a moment of ecstasy, everything is transformed, everything is touched by greatness and completeness and becomes archetypal. The violets appear as the type of springtime glory; the characters as the type of lovers. The lovers, buoyed up by the sea of violets, appear as the image of youth and beauty and vitality. They have transcended the personal and individual.

To convey this universal quality of the lovers Forster avoids any intimate handling of their experience. Without losing immediacy or vividness he stands off and catches them in so commanding a perspective that their archetypal nature is apparent. And so we come back to Forster the narrator, for this supreme typicality is an expression of the commanding perspective of his personality.

I turn now to a second scene from *A Room with a View,* a scene much longer than the first. It is not well-known. It has no special qualities. It is strictly bread-and-butter Forster, and exemplifies perfectly all the principles of narration outlined earlier.

The scene belongs to the last half of the novel and takes place at Windy Corner where Lucy, back from her Italian trip and her stay in Florence at the Pension Bertolini, is living with her good-natured mother and brother. Her memory of that ineradicable moment on the Italian hillside when George Emerson appeared to her suddenly like a hero out of romance is now obscured by the presence of Cecil Vyse, her Sir Willoughby Patterne style fiancé. But her past as represented by Italy is pursuing her. The Reverend Arthur Beebe has become the local rector and the Emersons, father and son, have moved into the neighborhood. The Emersons are to Lucy like the grain of sand to the oyster, a persistent irritant. She tells her mother and Cecil a story about old Mr. Emerson and is disturbed to find herself telling a silly lie and saying that the name is Harris. She is upset by Mr. Beebe's story about old Miss Alan at the Pension Bertolini and how her room was filled with violets by the Emersons because they knew she loved violets. She is annoyed by a letter from Charlotte saying how unfortunate it is that the Emersons have moved into the neighborhood. And she is embarrassed at coming upon George Emerson swimming with Mr. Beebe and her brother Freddy in the Sacred Lake. In this, her first meeting with George since the kiss on the hillside, she is not prepared for a frank and happy greeting from a half-naked young man of possibly god-like appearance. To make things worse, Lucy at this moment finds her mother especially sympathetic to Charlotte because poor Charlotte is just now having the plumbers to clean her cistern and replace her boiler. (One trusts these details are not symbolic.) At the same time Freddy has invited the Emersons for tennis the following Sunday.

Lucy is haunted by George Emerson and by all the ramifications of her brief acquaintance with him. But she will not admit—indeed she cannot on account of her engagement to Cecil—that he is anything more to her than an annoyance. This then is her situation. Its difficulty is heightened by the tension between Cecil on the one side and her mother and Freddy on the other.

The scene, constituting the last four pages of Chapter 13, is too long to quote here, but I hope the reader can turn to it before going on. It begins: "Dinner was at half-past seven." It ends with the veiled insolence of Cecil's plea: "We don't want no dessert."

All the more typical narrative principles of Forster's fiction are illustrated by the scene. The importance of dialogue is obvious, as is its conjunction with description and information which tend to become the comment and judgment of the narrator. We have significant access to the mind and motives of one character, Lucy, but her perspective often shifts to or blends with that of the narrator: When Lucy hopes that her remark about seeing Emerson in Florence will pass for a reply, we have both an account of her unexpressed thought and a comment on it; and when we read the paragraph beginning "But Lucy hardened her heart. It was no good being kind to Miss Bartlett," we are seeing the matter from Lucy's point of view but her view is being summarized and presented in the words of the narrator, and it is the narrator's quality of mind that is apparent, not Lucy's. Finally we can see in miniature how, among the characters, Lucy's point of view is the dominant one and yet it does not dominate the scene, for the scene like the novel is controlled by the perspective of the narrator.

It is not my primary object to establish that Forster is a great novelist. But I must say that this everyday example of his work seems to me first-rate. Moreover, its excellence seems to me to depend on our sense of the command and poise, the perceptiveness and wit of the narrator whose presence is unobtrusive but at all times decisive. It is he who judges that Freddy "gabbled" a grace. It is he who deems it fortunate the men were hungry. It is he who sets up the little trap for Lucy when Freddy asks if Emerson is the clever sort or a decent chap. Before Lucy can say "Ask Cecil" we have already thought of Cecil as an example of the clever sort. It is he who rushes into a relatively long and breathless account of Mrs. Honeychurch's views on lady novelists in imitation of Mrs. Honeychurch and then adds—is it information or judgment?—that Lucy "artfully" fed the flames. It is he who says that "Cecil laid his hand over his eyes" and that "Cecil crumbled his bread," representing these actions not as Lucy would see them but as Cecil would hope them to be seen by a detached observer if such were present. Full justice is done to Cecil's half-despairing, half-satirical intent. At the same time by juxtaposition with the good-natured simplicity of the Honeychurches his superciliousness is justly exposed.

Again, when Lucy opposes inviting Charlotte and resorts to an argument of the most appalling triviality, it is the narrator who says "Alas!" in a tone we may guess to be a compound of humor, despair, and sarcasm. Finally it is he who blends his view with that of Lucy in describing the ghosts which plague her, so that we seem to be given at one and the same time an inner and outer perspective on her experience.

This scene is mainly dramatic. If we allowed ourselves the distinction it would be a case of showing rather than telling. What is shown is a discussion among a group of lively and convincing individuals. Yet at every turn the presence of the narrator is obvious. It is he who allows us to have a unified and commanding perspective on the whole scene.

The perfect economy of the scene may also be attributed to the narrator. Though there is a quite elaborate body of material here, including many references to past events, not a single detail is irrelevant or without value in the context. Even Mrs. Honeychurch's outburst against lady novelists is neatly illustrative of her ingenuous character and highlights by contrast the artfulness of Lucy. Besides, Miss Lavish as novelist deserves emphasis at this point for her novel is soon to play a decisive role in the story. What is most to be admired, however, is the way the trivialities—eggs and boilers, guest rooms and maids—are used not simply as realistic talking points for the revealing of character but as an important part of the Honeychurch way of life. The apparent subject of the scene is what happened to Lucy at dinner. The less apparent subject is the grounds for the tension between Cecil and the Honeychurches and the futility of Lucy's hope that she can have a foot in both worlds. Thus while she is contending with one phase of her confusion, another phase is pressing in upon her. Here again we become aware of the transcendent perspective of the narrator.

It is not especially difficult to get at the ways the author-narrator's personality is conveyed through his comment and interpretation and through our awareness of his guiding presence. But it is very difficult to get at the ways his personality is conveyed through his characters. The obvious way is by his attitude to them as implied or stated in his descriptions and comments. The less obvious way, though much the more important, is by his relationship to his characters. This relationship is not easy to define. Indeed, the attempt can be dangerous for it may lead one into the labyrinth of biographical speculation. There is, alas, no precise line separating those matters which pertain to the artist's character as a man and those which pertain to his character as a narrator. All one can do is proceed with what one hopes is discretion.

Thus I will go so far as to imagine Forster at the turn of the century saying to himself: How, in an age increasingly introspective, how after George Eliot and all her intimate involvement with the character, can I treat man's psychological nature as objectively as his moral nature was treated by Pope or Jane Austen? How, without seeming inhuman, can I achieve a detachment that will let me judge and evaluate without the emotional harassment of extreme involvement? Had Forster been born a generation later his answer to the question might have been that of Robbe-Grillet: you cannot achieve objectivity, therefore eliminate the psychology; or that of Samuel Beckett: reduce man's psychological nature to so elementary a level that it is almost beyond pathos. In fact his answer is that of romance: you can treat the inner life objectively by objectifying it, by giving it an outward representation. If life and death, good and evil contend for the soul of man, let these forces have separate representation and let them contend openly. Under such circumstances the narrator can be uninhibited in his attitude to the characters representing these forces. He can approach them with detachment and irony, with wit and playfulness, with the sense that at every moment he has the right to laugh, to ridicule, to judge. This is precisely the approach we have observed in Forster's treatment of the dinner scene. But to appreciate more fully his relationship to his characters, we must scrutinize them carefully.

It is easy to see the romance division of characters in *A Room with a View*. Since Lucy's family are on the side of light, the evils of society must be found elsewhere. In Part I they are found at the

Pension Bertolini and in the person of the Reverend Cuthbert Eager. In Part II the Reverend Arthur Beebe takes Mr. Eager's place as a source of darkness, though the meaningless sterility of society is mainly represented by Cecil Vyse. On the side of good are Mrs. Honeychurch and Freddy, though they are hardly aware of being on a side, and Mr. Emerson, a philosophical type who quotes Samuel Butler and is very much aware of being on a side. Then there is George Emerson whose good character is complicated by the fact that too severe a knock may once for all deprive him of the will to live.

Lucy Honeychurch's character is also complicated. As the scene of springtime and violets makes clear, she is by nature on the side of goodness and light. But society teaches her to flee from Florence and George Emerson and to rush off to Rome and Cecil Vyse. Society teaches her to be dishonest with herself, and the result is the artful, ghost-haunted young lady we see at dinner.

Lucy combines two roles in *A Room with a View*. As a *romance* heroine her character is fixed; she stands for the forces of life and light. As a *romantic* heroine, that is as the ingénue in a romantic plot, we would expect her character to be in the process of formation and to become formed or fixed only when she achieves happiness and marriage.[24] But Forster has modified her romantic role in order to avoid seriously disrupting the romance pattern of the novel. We do not get the impression that Lucy's character is being formed. Her nature is already established and the only question is whether it will triumph or go under. When she deceives herself the darkness comes on. She is not changing so much as moving toward nothingness. And when Mr. Emerson rescues her, more through his voice, his seriousness and his age than through any words, she finds as he speaks that the darkness is withdrawn "veil after veil," and she can see to the bottom of her soul (p. 248). "It was as if he had made her see the whole of everything at once" (p. 250).

Essentially Lucy remains a romance heroine. This same pattern is obvious in the characterization of George Emerson whose role as *romantic* hero is decisively subordinated to his role as *romance* hero. What concerns us about these young people is not their psychology but their fate. Forster is not interested in the inwardness of their experience. For instance the first five chapters of Part II, which take us from Lucy's engagement up to the dinner scene and which include the first meeting of George and Lucy since Italy, offer little insight into the heroine's mind and feelings. Forster implies that confusion and darkness reign—what more is there to be said? Then in the dinner scene which comes after Lucy's meeting with George, that is to say, after she has been disturbed by contact with reality, her inner life begins again to take on significance. But in discussing it, Forster repeatedly uses images of ghosts and darkness to dramatize the starkness of the issue. "The ghosts were returning." They invade and usurp all the places Lucy has valued: Italy, the Sacred Lake, Windy Corner. The juxtaposing of that which suggests death with that which suggests life is striking and gives a kind of public quality to Lucy's thoughts.

The reader may justly observe at this point that had Lucy gone under she would not on that account have entirely ceased to exist and that if we are to see adequately the issue that confronts her we should have some idea of what might become of her. We are given a very good idea of the dark side of her fate in the character of Miss Bartlett. In keeping with Forster's economy of means in this novel she has several other roles in addition to that of Lucy's double. She is a Jamesian *ficelle,* a representative of the triviality and evil restrictiveness of society, and unconsciously she is a promoter of the romance between George and Lucy. But of course her great interest is as a model of what Lucy will be thirty years from now if she denies the life force— and her love for George Emerson.

And what, the impatient reader may ask, does all this tell us about the personality of the narrator? It tells us, in the first place, that he is interested not in psychological processes but in the great forces that make or break a character. It tells us, too, that he is a strenuously committed moralist who sees the conflict between fulfillment and negation as a conflict between life and death, good and evil. And it tells us that he is uncompromising in his attitude to both sides in this struggle, being ready at all times to satirize and mock the representatives of darkness and evil and to honor at all times the representatives of goodness and light. He never hesitates to evaluate and judge his characters.

We are now in a position to sum up Forster's relationship to his characters. He is not, like George Eliot, the careful analyst who scrupulously weighs every detail before reaching a judgment. He is not, like Henry James, the equally careful analyst who scrupulously maneuvers every detail into place in an attempt to do justice to his heroine. Indeed, he is a narrator who has no responsibility to his characters. This is the remarkable fact about his relationship to them. But however remarkable it may be, it should not surprise us. We have already established in the earlier discussion of romance that Forster's negative characters are not morally accountable for the evil that attends them and that his positive characters have not quite earned the given moments of their deepest insight and highest goodness. Forster's non-responsibility to his characters is the corollary of their own non-responsibility.

Only the whole image of man—not the aspects of his nature as symbolized by romance characters—can be thought of as morally responsible. Hence the narrator is responsible not to his characters but to a whole image of man which he bears within himself and which, being implicit throughout his narrative, must in some sense be made explicit before the story ends. The narrator is responsible to the values and the total vision for which he stands. He is responsible to himself in the sense that he must at all times judge according to his vision, and he is responsible to the reader for he must at all times help the reader to judge also according to the vision. It follows from this that he must be responsible *about* his characters but not *to* them. He must make sure that they subserve his values and forward the development of his total image of man; there his obligation ends.[25]

To fulfill this obligation will require skill and ingenuity in the manner of presentation. Romance characters are by nature fixed and unchanging.[26] But the narrator is free to withhold knowledge about their true natures and to reveal this knowledge progressively or suddenly at such times as will be most effective. Thus in Part I Mr. Beebe appears in a favorable light, but in Part II we more and more see that he stands against life. *He* has not changed. But the hidden springs of his nature have been exposed by events and the comments on events. An example of a different kind is to be seen in the potential likeness of Lucy and her cousin. This is not at first apparent to the reader. Indeed, even later it comes as a kind of revelation. From these illustrations we see that the presentation of fixed characters leaves the narrator a great deal of freedom; and further that the exercise of this freedom, because it is so obviously a part of the strategy of telling the story, shows us the interests and moral intentions of the narrator.

It is not possible to keep in separate compartments the treatment of plot and character. But insofar as it is possible we will now go on to look at how the ordering of events reveals the same decisive moralist apparent in the presentation of character.

It is true, of course, that at first glance *A Room with a View* looks like having a thoroughly romantic plot. The heroine is unexpectedly kissed by the young man for whom she is obviously intended. She thinks herself insulted and runs away. In time she thinks herself in love with another man, a man very unlike the first and one for whom she is just as obviously not intended. Having got over this error in judgment by seeing the two men together, she is still deluded enough to think she must uphold her reputation and must refuse to admit her love. Through the kindly intervention of an old wise man she is able to recognize the truth of her own feelings. And so she marries the young man and lives happily ever after. It is obvious that the central interest of such a plot, if it is indeed romantic, must be the development of the mind and character of the heroine.

When we look more closely at Forster's plot, however, we see that its central interest is the development of a series of contrasts. In Part I, Lucy moves toward light and the fulfillment of her nature, but at the last moment she is overcome by darkness—and flees. In Part II she moves towards darkness and the denial of her nature, but at the last moment she sees the light. This parallel with contrast is also represented in the detailed plotting. Lucy, having been kissed by George, confides in Charlotte who dismissses George and arranges Lucy's departure for Rome. Charlotte confides in Miss Lavish, who in turn confides in the readers of her novel, including George and

Lucy. As a result George kisses Lucy again, and Lucy confides in Miss Bartlett again. But this time her former chaperone is helpless and Lucy must herself dismiss George. Now Charlotte confides in Mr. Beebe and the two of them help Lucy in her plan to go to Greece which is in fact a plan to run away from George for the second time. The difference here is that her plan fails.

Forster also provides contrasts and parallels at a more detailed level. Thus for example the expedition of the tourists to the Italian hills (Chapter 6) is echoed in the expedition of Lucy, Mrs. Honeychurch and Cecil to the garden-party (Chapter 9: "Lucy as a Work of Art"). Again we have a social outing, including a carriage ride. Again the party breaks up, but this time the lovers are openly and deliberately together. They walk through woods. Lucy appears to Cecil as a work of art rather than as flesh and blood. George, you will recall, saw "the flowers beat against her dress in blue waves" (p. 86); Cecil, whose taste inclines to the artificial and exotic, sees her as "some brilliant flower that has no leaves of its own, but blooms abruptly out of a world of green" (p. 131). They are in a small clearning, the view is restricted, and the Sacred Lake (reminiscent of the sea of violets) is now a puddle. Cecil, deliberate and passionless, asks Lucy for a kiss. Here no Miss Bartlett roams the woods to threaten interruptions, yet Cecil suffers from the fear of being observed. In case anyone should miss the parallel between the two scenes, Lucy's first words after the kiss are about the Emersons.

Forster's tendency to construct his plot by juxtaposing related but contrasting episodes and blocks of material is powerfully reinforced by his handling of setting. Here and elsewhere Forster designs his settings with such economy and relevance that they may be interpreted as extensions of character and plot.

"Windy Corner lay, not on the summit of the ridge, but a few hundred feet down the southern slope, at the springing of one of the great buttresses that supported the hill. On either side of it was a shallow ravine, filled with ferns and pine-trees. . . . Whenever Mr. Beebe crossed the ridge and caught sight of these noble dispositions of the earth, and, poised in the middle of them, Windy Corner—he laughed. The situation was so glorious . . ." (p. 215). Earlier the scene is described from Lucy's point of view. "Seated on a promontory herself, she could see the pine-clad promontories descending one beyond another into the Weald. The farther one descended the garden, the more glorious was this lateral view" (p. 139). There can be no doubt Windy Corner is intended to parallel the violet-covered terrace overlooking Florence. And this is as it should be, for Windy Corner is on the side of light.

Then there is darkness. Forster's handling of light and dark is the most significant feature of the settings in this novel. In Part I, after experiencing the glorious sun-drenched slopes of the Italian mountains, Lucy descends into storm and darkness. In Part II, after encountering George at the Sacred Lake in a setting of sunshine, clear water, and happiness, she finds during the dinner scene that the Sacred Lake and Windy Corner, formerly the world of life and light, are being usurped by ghosts and darkness. Again, when George comes for tennis the Sunday following, the day is glorious. And again Lucy is kissed. She dismisses George, but going outdoors becomes aware of the approach of autumn and darkness (pp. 206–7). That same night she dismisses Cecil and determines never to marry. "The night received her, as it had received Miss Bartlett thirty years before" (p. 214).

The next chapter (18), much of it from Mr. Beebe's point of view, reinforces the pattern. It is a blustering, windy day, autumn has come and the flowers are being broken down. Mr. Beebe and Miss Bartlett, returning from tea, "hurried home through a world of black and grey," while Mrs. Honeychurch "still wrestled with the lives of her flowers. 'It gets too dark,' she said hopelessly" (p. 229). When Mr. Beebe leaves, he sees Windy Corner poised below him—"as a beacon in the roaring tides of darkness" (p. 232). It has been agreed that Lucy may go to Greece. Thus she will be leaving this one point of light in a dark world. The following chapter is one of rain and dismalness. Up the dark hill stands the dark church. In Mr. Beebe's study, Lucy and Mr. Emerson are surrounded and pressed in upon by books—"black, brown, and that acrid, theological blue" (p. 244). And Mr. Beebe himself appears as a "long black column" (p. 249).

But at this moment, the blackest in Lucy's life, Mr. Emerson points the contrast: "Now it is all dark. . . . I know. But remember the mountains over Florence and the view" (p. 250). The recurring movement from light to dark is halted and reversed. Yet the mountains and the view appear only as a memory; the returning light is more subdued.

And so George and Lucy, again in Florence and in the spring, are aware of the dying evening and the roar of the river Arno (p. 255). At the novel's end passion is requited, love attained. "But they were conscious of a love more mysterious than this. . . . they heard the river, bearing down the snows of winter into the Mediterranean." Their love is related to the cycle of nature and to the related cycle of life and death. When there is life, when there is light and spring and fulfillment, then darkness and winter and death can be accepted and integrated into the total vision. Here the simplified romance characters attain wholeness.

Character, plot, setting, and commentary unite to dramatize and enforce a decisive moral outlook. That outlook is embodied from the beginning in the personality of the author-narrator. He is the center which emanates outward in a perfect circle of inclusiveness.

A briefer treatment of *Where Angels Fear to Tread* will be sufficient to show how it differs from *A Room with a View* and how it's narrator differs. Unlike George and Lucy, the principal characters in this novel no longer bear even a superficial resemblance to those of romantic convention. Gino, the Italian antagonist-protagonist, shares in the paradoxical qualities of his country, in its energy and reality, its brutality and mystery. He may be a possible hero of romance, but as a romantic hero he is quite out of the question. The same is true of Lilia Herriton, the English woman whom he marries. She is no ingénue, but a thirty-five-year-old widow, vulgar, superficial, and fun-loving. It is true that her brother-in-law Philip Herriton is the right age for a romantic lead, but he is content to be a spectator of the world's comedy. And it is true that Caroline Abbott is the right age to play opposite a romantic lead, but she is of a matronly disposition. Besides, by the time Philip has stopped being a spectator and fallen in love with her, she has developed a helpless passion for Gino. The world of romance is more bizarre than that of romantic comedy but even by the freer standards of romance, these characters are an odd lot.

The plot too is an extraordinary and melodramatic affair. Many writers of fiction have—in Richard Chase's words—excelled in the skillful use of melodrama: "They have known . . . how to take advantage of the abstractness of melodrama and its capacity to evoke ultimates and absolutes, in order to dramatize theological, moral, and less frequently political ideology."[27] This capacity to evoke ultimates explains melodrama's great appeal to the romance writer and its prominent role in the romance tradition.

Romance narratives, especially of the quest type, sometimes take the form of an apparently endless sequence of adventures. More frequently, as the result of thematic commitment, they are highly structured. Forster is not much interested in the capacity of romance to encompass adventures, but he is intensely interested in its capacity to dramatize moral confrontations. Hence his plots, exploiting the direct appeal of melodrama, tend to be highly ordered, though by Jamesian standards the ordering falls short of tidiness. It is true, of course, that in *Aspects of the Novel* he shows himself to be thoroughly modern in his "oh dear yes" attitude to plot. That is because his symbols and his vision of life came to him through people and places and the inwardness of his own experience and could best be expressed in fiction through character and setting. Thus his low opinion of plot does not stem from the realist objection that it is arbitrary and unmimetic but from the simple fact that it was not central to his vision of life. On the other hand, when he needed plot to bring out the implications of his vision, he used it with a casual boldness which can still agitate and astound the realistic brotherhood of critics. The daring and rigorous use of plot pattern is especially notable in *Where Angels Fear to Tread* which falls neatly into two parallel parts, the first part (Chapters 1 to 4) being much the shorter.

The opening chapter, after showing us Lilia's departure for Italy, offers a detached survey of the Herriton family and their typical suburban life in Sawston. We do not see events from the point of view of the characters nor do we get a look at their inner lives except incidentally in the way of necessary information. Thus the chapter is more than usually rich in brief comments and judgments by Forster.

Chapter 2 brings Philip Herriton to Monteriano to prevent the marriage of Lilia and Gino. He leaves when he finds he has come too late. Chapters 3 and 4 describe the breakdown of the marriage, the birth of a son, and the death of Lilia.

Chapter 5 is like Chapter 1. Lilia's death is like Lilia's departure. Everyone in Sawton can now settle down into an orderly and undisturbed existence. Then Caroline Abbott makes an issue of the baby; and Philip, this time accompanied by his stiff-necked sister Harriet, is despatched to Monteriano on another rescue operation. The remaining chapters, fully half the novel, show the catastrophic failure of that operation.

Contained within this orderly framework is a series of dramatic and melodramatic episodes: in part one, Lilia's hasty marriage to Gino, her attempt to flee from Monteriano, and her sudden death in childbirth; in part two, the exciting visit to the Monteriano opera,[28] the kidnapping of the baby, the intervention of the grotesque idiot who assists Harriet, the collision of the carriages in the darkness and the wet—with the consequent death of the baby—and the weird scene also in the dark in which Gino, frenzied on account of the loss of his son, tortures Philip by alternately twisting his broken arm and compressing his windpipe. Philip faints and the scene takes another extraordinary turn. As he comes to, he hears a voice saying to Gino that his son is dead. "The room was full of light, and Miss Abbott had Gino by the shoulders, holding him down in a chair. She was exhausted with the struggle, and her arms were trembling" (p. 190). Yet this like all the other melodramatic moments is thoroughly convincing.

The odd assortment of characters and exceptional incidents are credible because the story is furnished with a narrator whose tone is consistently serious and, when satire is in order, biting. This mature and almost somber nature of the storyteller is especially obvious in the presentation of setting and in some of the descriptions and commentary.

The settings are symbolic, the object of the symbolism being to sharpen the contrasts between Sawston and Monteriano. Here to begin with is a Sawston scene from the opening chapter of the novel. Mrs. Herriton, assisted by her daughter Harriet, is planting the kitchen garden; she is practical, we may suppose. She says, "We will save the peas to the last; they are the greatest fun," thereby evincing her "gift of making work a treat." When they come to the peas, Harriet holds the string "to guide the row straight" as is appropriate for a person strict, narrow, and lacking pliancy, while her mother "scratched a furrow with a pointed stick," an act suggestive of the injurious decisiveness of her interfering nature. She sows the peas evenly and well—then the letter arrives from Lilia with the shocking announcement of her engagement to an Italian—and Harriet forgets to cover the peas. Before nightfall the sparrows have taken every one. "But countless fragments of the letter remained, disfiguring the tidy ground." The best laid plans come to nought and what would be wished away persists, disrupting and disfiguring ordered existence.

Mrs. Herriton has three successive plans for her daughter-in-law: to cultivate Lilia and make a lady of her, to save her from the Italian marriage, and finally to rescue the child of that marriage from its Italian father. In each, Harriet is her assistant. Each plan fails. In the last, Harriet is directly responsible for the death of the child. So the kitchen garden has weighty implications. As a functioning symbol, however, it is light-weight. It appears once only, it comes early in the novel, and it lacks archetypal reference. In other words it is perfectly suited to the spiritual dimensions of Mrs. Herriton and life in Sawston.

At the heart of Monteriano is the Piazza with its three great attractions—the Palazzo Pubblico, the Collegiate Church of Santa Deodata, and the Caffè Garibaldi: "the intellect, the soul, and the body. . . . For a moment Philip stood in its centre . . . thinking how wonderful it must feel to belong to a city, however mean" (p. 163). Here then is a symbol of the self, of the complete man, which in turn is a symbol of and is symbolized by the city, the image of a complete society. The tower commanding the Siena gate reaches up to heaven and down to hell. Philip, looking at it with Miss Abbott, and seeing the summit of the tower radiant in the sun while the base is in shadow and pasted over with advertisements, asks "Is it to be a symbol of the town?" (pp. 126-27)

The symbolism of the complete city, contrasting with the triviality of Sawston, is the narrator's device for enlarging our understanding of the characters and of the issues confronting them. But more than that, the symbolism greatly assists him in achieving an overmastering perspective. It is true that at the end of the novel Philip believes himself to have seen all round the sequence of events and to have got hold of its meaning. "And to see round it he was standing at an immense distance" (p. 204). It is true too that he has a fuller grasp of the symbolism than any other character and that he has been helped by it in arriving at his whole and distanced view of things. In this sense he may be thought of as dramatizing the experience of the reader. But the reader in his turn is helped by the symbolism and by the narrator to attain a perspective more complete and more immense than Philip's.

The symbolic settings are only one of the narrator's means of putting himself and us in a commanding position with reference to the action. Of even more importance are a series of comments and descriptions which obviously go beyond the knowledge, observation, or interest of the characters. Here, for example, is a comment inspired by Gino's intense love for his son: "For a wonderful physical tie binds the parents to the children; and—by some sad, strange irony—it does not bind us children to our parents. For if it did, if we could answer their love not with gratitude but with equal love, life would lose much of its pathos and much of its squalor, and we might be wonderfully happy. Gino passionately embracing, Miss Abbott reverently averting her eyes—both of them had parents whom they did not love so very much" (pp. 155-56). As the last sentence shows, this commentary places the experience in a perspective greater than the characters in their involvement can command.

The most impressive descriptions of this kind relate to Monteriano and its legends. One of these legends concerns Santa Deodata. She is not an important saint and during her lifetime she did not achieve much, yet a church has risen over her grave. Her strength was in her denial of the world, in her determination not to participate. In this she is both a parallel and a contrast to Philip. Like her, he refuses to participate; but he remains a spectator for personal and trivial reasons whereas Santa Deodata, however misguided she may have been, was deeply serious in her refusal to take part in life. This implied analogy gives us an added perspective on Philip's character.

But of all the descriptions relating to Monteriano and its legends, the most extraordinary is the following exercise in historical imagination (Philip and Miss Abbott are looking out from their hotel which was once a castle):

> She removed a pile of plates from the Gothic window, and they leant out of it. Close opposite, wedged between mean houses, there rose up one of the great towers. It is your tower: you stretch a barricade between it and the hotel, and the traffic is blocked in a moment. Farther up, where the street empties out by the church, your connections, the Merli and the Capocchi, do likewise. They command the Piazza, you the Siena gate. No one can move in either but he shall be instantly slain, either by bows or by cross-bows, or by Greek fire. Beware, however, of the back bedroom windows. For they are menaced by the tower of the Aldobrandeschi, and before now arrows have struck quivering over the washstand. Guard these windows well, lest there be a repetition of the events of February 1338, when the hotel was surprised from the rear, and your dearest friend—you could just make out that it was he—was thrown at you over the stairs. (p. 126)

These moments in the narrative have almost an autobiographical quality. By this I do not mean that in any way we know them to be autobiographical. Nor do I mean that if we did know them to be autobiographical our perception of their literary quality would be altered. We know Philip Herriton is somewhat like Forster but there is scarcely a hint of autobiographical quality in Forster's presentation of him. Rather I mean that at these moments the narrator seems to look through or over the heads of his characters and their situations and to speak directly to us about his own experience of the situation or place or legend. But he does not seem to speak to us intimately or privately, and for this reason I judge the effect not to be autobiographical. Indeed, even in *The Longest Journey,* an admittedly personal novel, the narrator seldom strikes an autobiographical note.[29] What we have in *Where Angels Fear to Tread,* and to a lesser degree in *A Room with a View,* is a narrator who can be thoughtful and imaginative beyond the range of his characters and a narrator who wishes to share with the reader an enriched and commanding perspective. This is not incompatible with what we also have, a narrator capable of a large measure of detachment and objectivity. The ability to unite the two roles of presiding genius and detached observer gives a very distinct character to the personality of Forster the narrator.

At the same time the narrator's personality has its own distinct character in each novel. In *Where Angels Fear to Tread* his personality has a certain somber and mature quality; in *A Room with a View* it has a witty and urbane exuberance. The difference in personality may be related to the order of composition. The Italian part of *A Room with a View* was first written in 1903. The story, though not completed for publication until 1908, was obviously carried through very much in the spirit of its beginning. For this reason it is justifiable and indeed right to treat it as Forster's first novel. The high-spirited youthfulness of the narrator, contrasting as it does with the graver insight of the narrator of *Where Angels Fear to Tread,* is a decisive indication of the correctness of such an order.

I now turn to a more general way of regarding the presence of the author's personality in his work, a way of regarding it which applies to all Forster's novels equally and indeed to all successful fiction whatsoever. Charles Morgan has put the case admirably with reference to drama:

> Form is *in itself* valuable only in those works of art into which the time-factor does not enter, and which, therefore, come to us whole. Painting, sculpture and architecture come to us whole; they are directly formal arts. An epic poem does not come to us whole, but a short lyric or a particular line therein may almost be said to do this, so slight, by comparison with an epic, is the time-factor involved. A play's performance occupies two or three hours. Until the end its form is latent in it. It follows that during the performance we are not

influenced by the form itself, the completed thing, but by our anticipations of completion. We are, so to speak, waiting for the suspended rhyme or harmony, and this formal suspense has the greater power if we know beforehand, as the Greeks did, what the formal release is to be.[30]

This same principle applies to the novel. But in the novel much of our sense of anticipated form will relate to the narrator and to our confidence in him. This is what Forster is saying in *Aspects of the Novel* when he tells us that "a character in a book is real . . . when the novelist knows everything about it. He may not choose to tell us all he knows—many of the facts, even of the kind we call obvious, may be hidden. But he will give us the feeling that though the character has not been explained, it is explicable, and we get from this a reality of a kind we can never get in daily life" (p. 61). In a similar way the form, though incomplete, is assured and real and meaningful. Such a sense cannot be attributed to anything abstract, it must be attributed to the personality of the author-narrator. In some works the personality may be detached or invisible. In Forster's works it is strikingly present in the form of a narrator who, as the more or less omniscient author at the center of the fiction, expands outward to include all in a formal unity which is from the first anticipated and at the last fulfilled.

The author-narrator is the ultimate man of order, the ultimate source of the reader's experience of the work as a totality. But this is not in itself sufficient grounds for speaking of the narrator as archetype. To this way of speaking it must be objected that such a conception of the narrator is applicable to all fiction, or at least to all fiction successful enough to create a sense of unity, and that logically a narrator so defined as archetypal belongs to a category different from that of archetypal objects or characters or moments of vision within a fiction. The force of this objection is demonstrable in the short stories. There the ecstatic moment of identity with nature gives rise to the sense of a living totality. The author-narrator exists in or behind the fiction, but in the reader's actual experiencing of the story he appears as a secondary source of totality; the moment, or the character participating in the moment, appears as the primary source. It is the moment which is archetypal. Similarly, in the later novels, archetypal characters and objects are primary in the reader's experience of a subsuming mythic order and unity.

Here the Italian romances reveal their unique character. In them, the object of vision is apprehended more fully and the moment of ecstasy is participated in more wholeheartedly by the narrator than by his characters. George and Lucy are transformed in each other's eyes, but our vision of the two of them as the type of young lovers caught up in an eternal springtime of violets goes beyond their own comprehension. It is finally the vision of the narrator. In like manner, the presentation of Monteriano is one of abiding visionary insight into the permanent reality of the archetypal city. This ecstatic insight, transcending the characters and their individual moments of experience, adheres to the author-narrator.

Such a situation is unique in Forster's fiction (always leaving *A Passage to India* aside). In every one of the short stories at least one character fully apprehends the object of vision or fully experiences the moment of ecstasy. The same is true of the characters in the later novels, though every reader will be able to detect examples of vision which belong essentially to the author-narrator. In *The Longest Journey,* to which we will be turning next, the splendid account of the Wiltshire downs as the center of England begins as Rickie's view, but ends as the narrator's. Even so, we come to understand this vision as the conscious expression of what Stephen Wonham experiences unconsciously. And Stephen, in his turn, assumes the role of hero in our eyes because that is the way he is seen by other characters in the novel.

It will be understood, in view of what has already been said about romance, that the total order in each of Forster's works transcends the individual characters and their moments of ecstatic experience. And it will be understood that this total order, though it embodies the visionary, is not itself visionary. Even in the Italian romances, where the narrator is a visionary center, the vision does not touch all, for which reason its all-inclusiveness is limited to those areas where is does touch. Only the narrator with respect to order is a center expanding outward to include all.

But within this total order, the narrator as a focus of vision, as a personality directly related to moments of ecstatic experience, creates in his own person an awareness of visionary totality and mythic unity. Accordingly he takes on a status closely resembling that of archetypal characters within the fiction. For this reason *A Room with a View* and *Where Angels Fear to Tread,* alone among Forster's works, may justify a conception of the narrator as archetype.

One must behave as if one is immortal, and as if civilization is eternal. Both statements are false—I shall not survive, no more will the great globe itself—both of them must be assumed to be true if we are to go on eating and working and travelling, and keep open a few breathing holes for the human spirit.

Abinger Harvest

These words, which belong to the Forster who addresses international congresses, nonetheless epitomize the art of the novelist. The first sentence is grand and one might say poetic in conception. The second begins forthrightly, moves again toward grandeur in the Shakespearean echo of "the great globe itself," then sinks to the mundane with eating, working, and traveling. But when these sentences are recalled—as they have been frequently—"a few breathing holes" gives place to "one is immortal." We respect the qualification but respond to the grand conception as it reverberates in the mind. It is the same with Forster's fiction. The characters who assume their immortality and achieve their moments of admirable luster reverberate in the mind. The witty qualifications of irony and the dreary qualifications of fact pattern themselves in an ominous but almost magical circle around the point of spiritual illumination. The prophet of vision appears in the simplest of clothes and the shabbiest of settings, but he nonetheless appears.

4
Hero as Archetype

$\mathcal{T}$he hero is a splendid illustration of the nature of an archetype. Like any other mythic character, and like the narrator under special circumstances, he is transformed through ecstatic apprehension into "that than which nothing greater can be conceived" in the class concerned. But here the class concerned is mankind in its completeness; and the hero is the individual who eminently possesses the attributes characteristic of mankind. He is not a defining concept, nor a drawing of the circle of definition which excludes. He is literally a man who on account of his central position and extended affinities expands outward to include most men. He is a uniting symbol.[1]

The hero, whether of myth, legend, epic, or romance, has a fixed character which distinguishes him from the so-called "romantic hero" (the romantic lead of drama and film) and from the ordinary protagonist of most realistic novels. The novelistic protagonist, like the romantic lead, has a character only partially formed. The development of the story is related to the development of his character. That is to say, the various and often conflicting possibilities open to him are narrowed down until at the end he has achieved a definite and final character. His destiny is likely also to have become final, a fact often represented by marriage.

The hero of epic and romance is a person of established character, and his unalterable nature is his greatest glory. He will allow himself a few digressions and regressions. Setting these aside, he will, in a quite unyielding way, pursue the course he has set for himself and in so doing will remain faithful to his nature. The hero (and it is true of other archetypal characters as well) is always of fixed disposition and represents being rather than becoming. His actions reveal his heroic nature and are the fulfillment of the destiny inherent in his character.[2]

The type of the hero is god-like in that potentially he represents the sum of man's nature and destiny. The problem in portraying him is how his individual character is to be prevented from obscuring his universal nature. Myth and legend avoid this difficulty by stressing the representative nature of his actions or destiny and by understressing his individual character. Epic and romance, because of their greater circumstantiality, are committed to a more individual hero. Forster, as a writer of romance fiction, gets round this difficulty by strictly limiting our view of the hero, and in particular by keeping him out of situations likely to reveal his individuality. In the short stories, he relies on the brevity of form to limit the appearances of the hero and so limit the kind of excessive detail that is destructive of typicality. And in the novels—with the single exception of Stephen Wonham in *The Longest Journey*—he confines himself to archetypal characters who typify only certain aspects of the hero's total nature and destiny. Their role in the action is limited and their significance restricted; but within their limits, within the range of their significance, they are typical and universal. Though they express only a part or fragment of the total nature of the hero, they are nonetheless heroes.

In all of Forster's fiction, the most extreme instance of an archetypal character with a limited heroic role and a restricted significance is the nameless Italian in *A Room with a View* who is unexpectedly stabbed as George Emerson and Lucy Honeychurch look on. Their eyes, meeting over the dying man, share a new knowledge, an understanding that life is violent and real and meaningful. The glance Lucy receives from the man as he dies tells her that death is in life and that man is mortal. But he who silently tells her this has no name, no personal attributes; as a hero he is open to any signification the narrative can project onto him. And because he plays so simple and so brief a role, there is no problem of individual detail undermining or detracting from the universal significance of his character. But of course his character can have only a very limited role in the action when it is so thoroughly deprived of individual attributes.

A Room with a View offers another instructive example of the way the archetypal character is stripped of individuality and restricted to a subordinate role. George Emerson and Lucy Honeychurch, suspended in a sea of violets and swept into each other's arms, cease to be individual English tourists in Italy and become the type of young lovers. The episode conjures up a world of romance: innocent maiden, in the glorious countryside of spring, ravished by impetuous and irresistible youth. Beyond that lies the image of a green and growing garden, a springtime of flowers and innocent first love. In the words of Dylan Thomas: "it was all / Shining, it was Adam and maiden." George and Lucy transcend their individual identities and rest for the moment in a deeper stratum of being than they have known. They do not and indeed could not continue simply and wholly as the type of young lovers. But the reality of what they *are* at this moment becomes the center round which they revolve, however erratically, until they settle in the fixed orbit of marriage.

But what happens when an archetypal character or a character in his archetypal capacity assumes a more prominent role in the narrative? Gino in *Where Angels Fear to Tread* will give us one answer to this question. But the answer will be in two parts, for Gino plays a major though still subordinate role as natural man and a more minor role as father.

In his role as father, he is superbly archetypal. This is largely the result of the celebrated episode in which he bathes his infant son. Here his individual actions and attitudes are in perfect keeping with his universal role. He is pridefully joyous at the sight of his son, at the sight of this perfect incarnation of his own flesh. His delight is completely selfish and completely beautiful. It seems to us god-like. Gino is not, as he would be in Tolstoy, an individual who comes face to face with a great mystery of the universe and in that confrontation represents us all. Rather, he is one whose personal identity is subsumed in a timeless image of man as father.

We may be helped to understand the nature of Forster's success here if we compare his presentation of Gino with Tolstoy's presentation of Levin-as-father in *Anna Karenina*. Forster maintains a certain detachment. We see Gino close up, but we do not see inside. He appears very clearly as a person to be apprehended and appreciated but not to be entered into. In addition he is presented in a way which we might call absolute. That is, he receives an exclusive focus of attention and he is not even incidentally compared with anyone else or allowed to be seen in any larger context—except the largest context of all, a mythic one.

Quite the reverse is the case with Levin. We are exposed to all the agonies of his mind as he imaginatively experiences his wife's suffering during the birth of his child. But along with the intimacy of this approach, Tolstoy gives us the point of view of the doctor who has delivered many hundreds of babies and wishes despairingly that husbands at times like this would act like men. And so we see Levin as one father among many, and as the last in a long line stretching as far back as the imagination can reach. We see him as representative, as typical. In contrast, we don't see Gino *as* anything. Rather he *is* the type of man-as-father. To see him as one of many would be to violate his heroic nature and so obliterate the sense of totality inherent in his image.

Forster makes precisely the same point in *Aspects of the Novel* when he compares Hetty Sorrel and Mitya Karamazov. Of Mitya and his good dream he says: "We cannot understand him until we see that he extends, and that the part of him on which Dostoevsky focuses did not lie on that wooden chest or even in dreamland but in a region where it could be joined by the rest of humanity. Mitya is— all of us" (p. 123).

Gino's more major archetypal role, which should include his role as father, is as a natural man. Forster intended him to be unself-conscious, selfish, thoughtlessly brutal, but at the same time powerful, virile, spontaneous, and joyous. Unfortunately he becomes involved in too many drawingroom-style scenes and in too many social contretemps which naturally enough lend to his character detailed individual attributes that obscure or distract from his image as natural man.

The discretion needed in presenting a character of the heroic type is discussed by Forster in connection with his unfinished novel "Arctic Summer," the opening chapter of which was written in the spring of 1914. In 1951 he had this to say about its hero:

> He is first and foremost heroic, no thought of self when the blood is up, he can pounce and act rightly, he is generous, idealistic, loyal. When his blood is not up, when conditions are unfavourable, he is apt to be dazed, trite and sour—the hero straying into the modern world which does not want him and which he does not understand. . . .
>
> How should such a character be presented? Impressionistically—that is to say he should come and go, and not be documented, in contrast to the [non-heroic characters] who can't be documented too much. . . . The only way to present this hero was to root him as little as possible in society, and let him come and go unexplained.[3]

Such an injunction could be applied to all archetypal characters, though it is especially relevant when the character has a major rather than a minor role in the narrative. But Forster's really important point is not *how* to present a hero but *why* it is necessary to present him with such care. The hero is not at home in the modern world. His heroic nature and the essential pattern of the heroic life cannot be effectively portrayed in a straightforward sequence of events set in that world. Therefore his appearances must be carefully staged and he must begin with very few commitments so as to be free to take on whatever significance the narrative may require. Precise commitments are to be avoided because they lead inevitably to other precise commitments, all of which lead in their turn to awkward and unwanted realistic detail. Thus in looking back at "Arctic Summer" Forster shudders at the thought of the family circle he has given his hero, for in this way he has irrevocably placed him in society.

This is precisely the kind of difficulty Forster encounters in his portrayal of Gino as a natural man. And again in *The Longest Journey* the same hazards of overcommitment in the placing of the character and of overexposure in the treatment are apparent in the presentation of three archetypal characters: Ansell, Mrs. Elliot, and Stephen Wonham.[4] Of the three, Stephen is the most important. Though he begins as a supporting character it is his destiny to become the hero. As a result, his frequent appearances, sometimes in quite ordinary circumstances, partially but—as the following discussion is intended to make clear—by no means wholly obscure the mythic power of his role.

Forster's first problem with the hero may be summed up in the question: How is such a character to be presented? His second and more urgent problem may be summed up in the question: How is such a character to be contained? And in particular, how is he to be contained within the framework of a society which permits the free development of the individual?

The archetype of the hero had a strong psychological attraction for Forster. His first piece of fiction, "The Story of a Panic," prefigures the hero in the boy Eustace. "The Celestial Omnibus" sums up the course of the hero in the two journeys of the boy. The first journey parallels the dragon fight in which the hero breaks from the ties of the unconscious and the parents. The boy, back at Agathox Lodge, has established his own identity and now regards his parents as belonging to another and unreal world. His second journey parallels the hero's later triumph over the dragon of the world. The boy on the shield of Achilles is no longer mastered by the world but sees it whole and transcends it. Presented as no more than a boy, he yet prefigures the triumph of the hero Achilles. Finally, in "The Story of the Siren," Forster looks to the boy not yet born as the hero who may encompass the permanent salvation of mankind. The closing vision of this story is remarkably similar to the conclusion of *Howards End*. Mrs. Wilcox, who is a universal feminine figure like the Siren, continues even in death to be a living presence and indeed a dominating influence at Howards End, and Helen Schlegel's son, though only an infant, is pointed to as the future hero.

In each of these instances the heroic character is no more than a boy, but the quality and significance of his presentation show how greatly Forster was fascinated by the archetype of the hero. Why, then, did he not complete "Arctic Summer" in which we suppose a heroic type was to be the leading character? And why is Stephen Wonham—though not the leading character of *The Longest Journey* —his only fully developed adult hero?

Viewed psychologically, the hero is the epitome of man's fuller or higher development as an individual. Viewed socially or culturally, the hero is ambiguous. Mythically seen, he is the bringer of civilization, order, and spiritual advance. Pragmatically seen, he is the bringer of mob rule and tyrannical authority.

We can now see Forster's dilemma. The hero of the individual psyche is vastly attractive; the hero of the mass psyche, being a potential tyrant, is dangerous and distasteful. This is one of the reasons Forster first opts for boy heroes or for the young in spirit like Achilles of "The Celestial Omnibus" and Harold of "The Point of It." These pose no threat as leaders and instruments of the mass psyche. In large measure the same is true of Stephen Wonham whose portrayal as young in spirit and as preferring the isolation of the country can be explained on this basis.

Besides the cultural danger of the hero archetype, Forster had another reason for hesitating to embrace it, a reason which had to do with national character. Early in 1938 he said: "The Hero is an integral part of the authoritarian stock-in-trade. We in England don't produce him much; we produce varying types of humanity, a much finer achievement."[5] This idea of varying types is developed in *Howards End*. Also in this novel and in *A Passage to India* he turns with a new decisiveness and subtlety to the archetype of the Great Mother. Along with her the boy-hero of the short stories appears again—in the first as a child, in the second as the mythic Krishna who at midnight is born yet who cannot be born for he has always been.

Once we have focused our attention on the prominence of the universal mother in the later work and the boy-hero in the earlier work, we can see the uniqueness of Stephen. He will be our one opportunity to see how Forster confronts the full range of psychological dangers and presentational difficulties implicit in the hero archetype.

We may approach the subject by returning once more to Forster's first piece of fiction. In Part I of "The Story of a Panic" the hero journeys up the mountain and all alone confronts Pan. In doing so, he discovers his true nature and so achieves identity. He pays tribute to Clotho because he has been born into selfhood. He should now as hero set out to find and slay the dragon of the world and so assert his mastery. Instead he is imprisoned in his small room without a view.

It is at this point that "The Story of a Panic" becomes of special interest, for in the Eustace-Gennaro relationship we have in fact a double hero very like that implicit in the Rickie-Stephen relationship in *The Longest Journey*. Gennaro in betraying the boy allies himself with the sterile or monstrous world that must be destroyed by the hero before new life may arise. Thus Gennaro's death prefigures the death of the old order. But in helping the boy to escape into the world which is to be the theater of his action, he performs the sacrificial act and enters into the death out of which new life comes. Seen in this way it is most meaningful to take Eustace-Gennaro as archetypal hero in the dual role of dying and reviving god-man.

In *The Longest Journey* Rickie parallels Eustace and Stephen parallels Gennaro, but the destiny of the characters is reversed. Rickie must die and Stephen live. There are other differences too. The novel casts Rickie Elliot for the part of hero. From this point of view Stephen Wonham is one of several archetypal characters who have very important but subordinate roles to play in Rickie's life. When Rickie fails completely in his heroic role, Stephen emerges as hero. If we think of Rickie-Stephen as dual aspects of one heroic role, we will understand finally that Rickie is included in Stephen as the novel moves smoothly to its appointed end. But if we think of Rickie and Stephen as having separate heroic roles, we will understand finally that Rickie is displaced by Stephen as hero and that the whole structure of the novel is shifted on its foundations.

However this matter is decided—and I may as well say in advance what my conclusion is, that Forster wavers but at last comes down on the side of the second and more drastic alternative—it is still true that in the total perspective of the novel Stephen, the authentic hero, is a subordinate character. Even his journey as a hero is condensed and symbolic, whereas Rickie's is rather fully developed. For this reason we should begin by looking at Rickie's life as it parallels and frequently parodies the career of the traditional hero. Only then will we be able to evaluate the role of the archetypal characters who find their center in Rickie's life, and in particular the role of Stephen who is Forster's one fully developed example of the hero as archetype.

The reader may find it convenient in approaching this discussion of *The Longest Journey* to have before him an objective standard against which he may measure the heroic adventures of Rickie and Stephen. To provide such a standard, I quote in its entirety Joseph Campbell's summary of the traditional hero's adventure:

The mythological hero, setting forth from his commonday hut or castle, is lured, carried away, or else voluntarily proceeds, to the threshold of adventure. There he encounters a shadow presence that guards the passage. The hero may defeat or conciliate this power and go alive into the kingdom of the dark (brother-battle, dragon-battle; offering, charm), or be slain by the opponent and descend in death (dismemberment, crucifixion). Beyond the threshold, then, the hero journeys through a world of unfamiliar yet strangely intimate forces, some of which severely threaten him (tests), some of which give magical aid (helpers). When he arrives at the nadir of the mythological round, he undergoes a supreme ordeal and gains his reward. The triumph may be represented as the hero's sexual union with the goddess-mother of the world (sacred marriage), his recognition by the father-creator (father atonement), his own divinization (apotheosis), or again—if the powers have remained unfriendly to him—his theft of the boon he came to gain (bride-theft, fire-theft); intrinsically it is an expansion of consciousness and therewith of being (illumination, transfiguration, freedom). The final work is that of the return. If the powers have blessed the hero, he now sets forth under their protection (emissary); if not, he flees and is pursued (transformation flight, obstacle flight). At the return threshold the transcendental powers must remain behind; the hero re-emerges from the kingdom of dread (return, resurrection). The boon that he brings restores the world (elixir).[6]

The Longest Journey

A Type is an example of any class, for instance, a species of a genus, which is considered as eminently possessing the characters of the class. . . . the Type must be connected by many affinities with most of the others of its group; it must be near the centre of the crowd, and not one of the stragglers. . . . The class is steadily fixed, though not precisely limited; it is given, though not circumscribed; it is determined, not by a boundary line without, but by a central point within; not by what it strictly excludes, but by what it eminently includes; by an example, not by a precept; in short, instead of a Definition we have a *Type* for our director.

—William Whewell

Rickie Elliot's parents are dead and his half-brother is unknown to him. In other words he has that foundling background common to the tradition of heroes. He is living in Cambridge which is both a city of spires and a university passionately in search of reality and truth. Balancing this masculine symbolism is the beautiful dell near Madingley. Because its soil is chalk and its trees are evergreen it is not subject to the influence of the seasons. It suggests timelessness and security, feelings strongly associated with a mother figure. This traditional significance of the grove or wood as a mother symbol is also employed by Forster in "Other Kingdom."

Cambridge and the dell near Madingley enable Rickie to succeed in the first of the hero's quests, the attainment of his own identity. This involves separation from the real parents and acceptance by or identity with the other, higher, or trans-personal parents, here represented by Cambridge and Madingley. The issue of the story is whether Rickie who has mastered himself can master the world. For the hero, like every man, must answer the call to adventure in the world; and failure will bring with it not only loss of the world but loss of the self.

134

The issue is given philosophic emphasis at the opening of the story as the undergraduates debate the nature of reality. Ansell insists that the cow is still there when no man is present to see her. Here Agnes Pembroke bursts into the room. Rickie has forgotten about her coming. She chides him, she says he should be horsewhipped; she speaks with that noisy, friendly, domineering impertinence which in its self-indulgence makes clear that the speaker has no real interest in the person spoken to. Ansell, dominating the room from the mantel, notices that no one in the room, not even Rickie, has any reality for Agnes. Hence he concludes that it is Agnes who is without reality. He rudely ignores her. As he says later, she is one of those phenomena "which, to our destruction, we invest with the semblance of reality" (p. 24). For the hero she is the shadowy figure that guards the entrance to the mysterious world of his adventure. He must overcome or in some way get round this figure. Instead, Rickie invests the shadow with reality, rejects Ansell whose true role is that of guide and helper, and accepts Agnes in this role. The result is ruin. Agnes invades the precincts of Cambridge and the holy ground of the dell near Madingley, the very places which symbolize Rickie's sense of identity.

In case the reader should think this account a little exaggerated and the hero imagery grandiose, let me present Forster's own account of the matter: "Cambridge is the home of Rickie, the elder brother, the legitimate, his only true home: . . . the fearless uninfluential Cambridge that sought for reality and cared for truth. Ansell is the undergraduate high-priest of that local shrine, Agnes Pembroke is its deadly debunker. Captured by her and by Sawston ["which poses as the great world in miniature"], Rickie goes to pieces, and cannot even be rescued when Ansell joins up with Stephen and strikes."[7]

Accompanied by Agnes, Rickie journeys into Wiltshire to the home of Mrs. Failing, his father's sister. Here he meets Stephen, the Pan-like figure so frequently encountered by the hero once he has passed over the threshold into the world of his adventure. Pan is the representative of nature's power and health and brings the wisdom of the World Navel, the universal source.[8] So Stephen presides over Wiltshire where the whole system of the land is spread before us. "Here is the heart of our island: the Chilterns, the North Downs, the South

Downs radiate hence. The fibres of England unite in Wiltshire, and did we condescend to worship her, here we should erect our national shrine" (pp. 145-46).

Thrust into action by Mrs. Failing (an admirably ironic touch) Rickie sets forth with Stephen as guide on a journey of wonder and adventure toward Salisbury and "the most beautiful spire in the world" (p. 127). But he is in no fit state for adventure. The spirit of life has been swallowed up by his love for Agnes. Fresh people fail to interest him and he no longer cares for the unknown. Despite infinite space, brilliant sunshine, the unconquerable chalk, and a land which suggested "there had been no lack of drama to solace the gods" (p. 127), Rickie turns his back on Salisbury and returns to Agnes and his Aunt who do *not* await him in "Cadover, the perilous house" (p. 127). His only adventure has been an ecstatic dream in which he and Agnes touched by an immense silence float toward the Throne of God: "the earth and all danger dissolved, but ere they quite vanished Rickie heard himself saying, 'Is it exactly what we intended?'" It is noteworthy that Rickie's moments of vision are now confined to dream states. We might also notice the setting in which this dream took place: the "path lay upward, over a great bald skull, half grass, half stubble" (p. 128).

Rickie later comments to Stephen on this episode: "Ever since then I have taken the world at second-hand. I have bothered less and less to look it in the face—until not only you, but every one else has turned unreal" (p. 283). His sense of unreality is objectively imaged in the character of Mrs. Failing. She is the dragon that must be destroyed if the hero is to win through.

Rickie's aunt seems to him a kind of evil genius. She epitomizes the diabolical character of the Elliot family and presides over its misfortunes (pp. 116–17 especially). Her diabolical nature is symbolized by the family limp which she shares with her brother, Mr. Elliot, and with Rickie. It is symbolized also by the imagery of serpent, snake, and dragon. Mr. Elliot had in his London rooms flowers rising gracefully in their vases "from frames of lead which lay coiled at the bottom, as doubtless the sea serpent has to lie, coiled at the bottom of the sea" (p. 30). When we first encounter Mrs. Failing the serpent reappears as a "snake of water," "thick white water which was sliding like a snake down the gutter of the gravel path" (p. 100). After a brief acquaintance, "Agnes began to find Mrs. Failing rather tiresome. Wherever you trod on her, she seemed to slip away from beneath your feet" (p. 122). But finally we are not dependent on mere association. Mrs. Failing, displaying her usual cold facetiousness, disparages Agnes's notion of the hero as a strong wonderful champion: "Ah, wait till you are the dragon! I have been a dragon most of my life, I think. A dragon that wants nothing but a peaceful cave. Then in comes the strong, wonderful, delightful being, and gains a princess by piercing my hide" (p. 120).

The snake image has a further implication. The suppression of the unconscious and the instinctual by the conscious mind is the curse of the Elliot family. As with Philoctetes, this is the evil which looses the serpent which stings the foot.[9] Thus, for the would-be hero, the serpent-dragon nature of Mrs. Failing is ambiguous in its evil implications. It represents the conscious mind, rationalism, materialism, that emphasis on the obvious and superficial which is in fact a retreat from the sources of life, a withdrawal into the cave of unreality. But this cave is not the quiet retreat it appears to be. The process of cutting oneself off from the sources of life is the process of losing one's identity until suddenly the Great Mother takes shape as the devouring world dragon. The cave of unreality becomes the pit of involuntary oblivion. The would-be hero loses both his world and his identity. This is the horror Forster enables us to glimpse through the serpent-dragon image.

Rickie now approaches his great test. After the unsatisfactory ritual of Sunday church service, he visits the double entrenchment of earthworks high on the downs known as Cadbury Rings. Mrs. Failing conducts him through the two entrenchments to the single tree which stands at their center. Three times the cracked church bell intrudes directly in the narrative calling "Pang". Three times Mrs. Failing refers to Stephen as "your brother." As they reach the tree she allows Rickie to understand the truth. All these years she has guarded this hoard, the treasure hard to attain. Now carelessly, in a moment of diabolical mischievousness, she has left it unguarded, she has allowed it to be seen.

Rickie's unqualified soul cannot rise to the heroic occasion. At first he had connected the Rings with the dell near Madingley. Now he realized he was gazing at the past which gaped "like an unhallowed grave. Turn where he would, it encircled him. It took visible form: it was this double entrenchment of the Rings" (p. 150). Here then is the movement inward, to the center, to rebirth or renewal. The past must be passed through and included in the act of renewal. It is like a grave because death must precede rebirth. It is unhallowed because Rickie has not reconciled himself to his new knowledge about the past. He flees the reality at the heart of the encircling past. Unable to find the exit he stumbles on the inner barrier and falls into darkness.

"He woke up. The earth he had dreaded lay close to his eyes, and seemed beautiful. He saw the structure of the clods. A tiny beetle swung on the grass blade. . . . For one short moment he understood. 'Stephen—' he began, and then he heard his own name called: 'Rickie! Rickie!'" (pp. 150–51) His cry of acceptance is interrupted and Agnes catches him to her breast. As he and Agnes pass out of the Rings, Mrs. Failing who stands at the opposite entrance is again on guard while Stephen, the symbol of reality and rebirth, the treasure hard to attain, leans against the tree at the center of the Rings.

Rickie must endure yet another test. Though it is an anti-climax so far as the action goes, it gives new emphasis and significance to that moment when Agnes intervened between the brothers. As Stephen leaves Cadover, the perilous house, he calls to Rickie three times. Again Agnes intervenes. At Madingley he yielded to her thrice repeated call; now he yields to her entreaties and denies Stephen's thrice repeated call. Stephen, unaware of any kinship, shouts as one man to another; Rickie, knowing it is the call of a brother, denies him. Yet he also knows that here is one of those rare and momentous occasions which have immense symbolic value, and that in denying Stephen he is denying life (p. 157).

Rickie does not yet know that Stephen is the son of his mother. When Mrs. Elliot is presented at the beginning of Part III she appears as the Earth-Mother, that is as the Great Mother in her benign aspect as the fertile and sustaining earth. In this respect Mrs. Elliot has as her counterpart Mrs. Failing who appears as the Great

Mother in her terrible aspect, the world dragon. When the child goes into the world, the world takes on the role of the mother and appears both as the great sustaining power and as that which envelops and swallows up the individual independence of the child. The hero's quest frequently culminates in a holy marriage with the bride-mother. This signifies that the hero has conclusively secured his own identity, has mastered the tendency to lose himself in the dragon cave of the maternal embrace, and has established his right to the sustaining power and fertility of the Great Mother in her benign aspect. In other words, he assumes the role of the father. This supreme event in the hero's career is echoed in Rickie's cry of acceptance as he awakes in the Rings and finds himself in intimate contact with earth and with Stephen, the son of the Earth-Mother. But Agnes catches him to her breast. The moment for union with the bride-mother has passed.

Part II, "Sawston," shows us the consequences of this heroic debacle. Rickie returns from Wiltshire and marries Agnes. Instead of a holy marriage, the hero contracts with the world and finds himself slowly and inexorably swallowed up in darkness and misery. His journey becomes a descent into the underworld of Sawston. "He stood in the twilight that fell from the window, she in the twilight of the gas." Even as he accepts Agnes and his role as teacher his prayer is "to be delivered from the shadow of unreality that had begun to darken the world" (p. 173). He trusted "that his wound might heal as he laboured, and his eyes recapture the Holy Grail" (p. 174).

At the heart of this low-grade hell, at the heart of Sawston and Sawston school is Dunwood House presided over by Mr. Herbert Pembroke. At the entrance to temples or other sacred buildings it is usual to find certain guardian figures, gargoyles, winged beasts, defenders with drawn swords. The entrance hall of Dunwood House has its guardians too: "a framed certificate praising the drains, the bust of Hermes, and a carved teak monkey holding out a salver" (p. 175). Herbert is Rickie's guide through the labyrinth of the school and from Herbert he learns at second hand the correct response to each situation. The sense of unreality and horror grows upon him. He realizes he does not love his wife and indeed that he had ceased to love her before they were married, his daughter is born deformed and soon dies, and his denial of Stephen recurs to him every day and hurts him in his subconscious self (p. 216).

In this situation he experiences the most terrible journey of all, the dark night of the soul. The night ends with a mysterious dream in which his mother seems to speak to him. But the result of this dark journey is not a purification of the soul. "Henceforward he deteriorates. ... He had lost the work that he loved, his friends, and his child. He remained conscientious and decent, but the spiritual part of him proceeded towards ruin" (p. 218).

Forster ends Part II with the short chapter on spiritual coinage.[10] Rickie—so the chapter suggests—has put all his faith in coinage stamped with the image of his dead mother, whom he now learns was Stephen's mother also. His image of her was false, and so he is bankrupt. Here is the end of the hero's fatal choice and false marriage. Here is complete ruin.

Part III, "Wiltshire," is brief. Rickie, with Stephen rather than Agnes as guide, now makes his last journey to Mrs. Failing. Confirmed in his illusion that Stephen is the incarnation of their mother, he is shattered when his brother behaves according to the laws of his own nature (not the laws of Rickie's hero worship) and indulges "his sacred passion for alcohol" (p. 295). The result is Stephen lying drunk on the railway tracks. And though Rickie rescues him, he does so in a spirit of weariness and at the cost of his own life.

The railway is artificial and destructive, the road of death intersecting disastrously with the road of life which runs down to the village and the farm where the stream of life flows for ever. Mrs. Failing *fails* to bridge the crossing whose death-dealing nature is thus associated with the Elliots. In this sense the Elliots, who deny the spirit of life, may be said to destroy themselves—a fulfillment of Tony Failing's prophecy: "Cast bitter bread upon the waters, and after many days it really will come back to you" (p. 156). The crossing stands for arbitrary and meaningless death. The fact that it has been bridged at the end of the novel brings it into harmony with the final world of comedy in which death is a meaningful event in the life of each generation.

The train runs over Rickie's knees and he dies up at Cadover whispering to Mrs. Failing, "You have been right" (p. 312). Mrs. Failing had warned him to beware the earth, to beware "throwing away the artificiality which . . . is the only good thing in life" (p. 304). And so Rickie dies young, a fate not uncommon for the hero, but dies in despair and defeat, having lost all contact with reality. Mrs. Failing, the world dragon, provides a suitably impersonal obituary: "one who has failed in all he undertook; one of the thousands whose dust returns to the dust, accomplishing nothing in the interval" (pp. 312–13).[11]

It would be fair to say that in Part III Stephen emerges as the hero, but from a strictly narrative point of view Rickie remains the central character. Thus Ansell, Mrs. Elliot and Stephen are all subordinate characters, and their role is to guide the hero. They represent the reality—that is to say the spirit of life—to be found in books, in the fertile earth, and in man. The meaningfulness of what they represent is in each case fortified by a symbol. Stephen signifies the reality of man; his symbol is Orion. Mrs. Elliot signifies the reality of earth and earth's fertility; her symbol is Demeter. And Ansell signifies the reality of books; his symbol is the repeated square-within-circle diagram. As the novel progresses these three modes of reality are brought to a single focus in Stephen. It is toward this focal point that the discussion will move.

In novels as in other things, it may be worthwhile to begin with the wisdom of the philosopher. Ansell says: "If you ask me what the Spirit of Life is, or to what it is attached, I can't tell you. I only tell you, watch for it. Myself I've found it in books. Some people find it out of doors or in each other. Never mind. It's the same spirit, and I trust myself to know it anywhere, and to use it rightly" (p. 205). He is in the reading room of the British Museum, where he "looked up at the dome as other men look at the sky. In it the great arc lamps spluttered and flared, for the month was again November" (p. 203). The association of dome with sky and arc lamps with stars, and especially Orion the constellation of November, assures us of the reality of his world. And more, it connects him with Stephen through the implied reference to Orion.

Circle and square, each within each, constitute Ansell's symbol. "Are they real?" asks Rickie early in the story. "The inside one is

—the one in the middle of everything, that there's never room enough to draw." The appearances of this symbol are in conjunction with two kinds of phenomena: "*one,* those which have a real existence, such as the cow; *two,* those which are the subjective product of a diseased imagination" (p. 24). The circle appears to stand for that which has real existence, the square for the subjective and unreal. The persistence of the square has the same philosophic basis as the persistence of absence in *A Passage to India.* Absence implies presence or existence. Similarly, unreality implies reality. Ansell, who seeks the circle, shows wisdom in recognizing the persistence of the square and the necessity at all times of fashioning a new circle.

His assertion that only the one (presumably the circle) in the middle of everything is real is later clarified in Forster's summing up: "It was worth while to grow old and dusty seeking for truth though truth is unattainable, restating questions that have been stated at the beginning of the world. Failure would await him, but not disillusionment" (pp. 199–200). The circle in the middle of everything that there's never room enough to draw is truth which is unattainable. The progression of square within circle within square is the answering of recurrent falsehood by the restating of truth-seeking questions that have been stated at the beginning of the world.

For Ansell the philosopher the circle of reality expresses itself as truth. For Rickie it takes a more concrete form. Before his child was born he was like "one who spies a new symbol for the universe, a fresh circle within the square. Within the square shall be a circle, within the circle another square, until the visual eye is baffled. Here is meaning of a kind" (p. 207). The suggestion is that reality, at each moment fenced in by unreality, must continually be reborn or restated, whether in thought, image, or child. Each circle is "a new symbol for the universe," a symbol for the real present.

Ansell's circle is further echoed in Rickie's journey to Wiltshire and to the downs which are the center of England and to the Rings which are the center of the downs and to the tree which is the center of the Rings.[12] It is no accident and more than amusing that to the young and funny Cadbury Rings are known as "Cocoa Squares"

(p. 113). Here at the tree Rickie confronts both truth and reality—they are the same thing—and flees.

The symbol of the circle and of the square within the circle has a long history and a traditional basis in European thought. In the *Timaeus* we are told that the body of the world was created out of the four elements but its form or figure which was to comprehend within itself all other forms was that of a globe "having its extremes in every direction equidistant from the centre, the most perfect and the most like itself of all figures."[13] Here the form is divine, the four elements earthly. Thus Plato's image approximates the widely distributed image of the circle as celestial, as God, as wholeness and perfection, and the square as earth combining the four elements, and as goddess or soul.

The coming together of the circle and square is a symbol of union and harmony: the dome of the sky unites with the four quarters of the earth, and "the square chamber is *obliged* to forsake its plan and strain forward to meet the round dome in which it must terminate."[14] Microcosm imitates macrocosm. "Circles and squares drawn from a common centre appear in ancient Italy as well as in the Buddhist East as the ground-plan *par excellence* on which everything is built. Upon it all the little worlds—cities and shrines—are constructed. . . ."[15] The shrine, temple, or isolated sacred place is symbolized by the circle. The altar at its center marks the spot where the hero performed the deed which the shrine is intended to commemorate, or alternately it is a depersonalized symbol of the divine man protected by the magic circle of the shrine.

In Ansell's symbol the center is depersonalized, but like the stone which is the central concern of alchemy the circle in the middle of Ansell's drawing is an ultimate uniting figure. In the dell near Madingley, however, the center is not depersonalized. The center is Rickie. And Rickie is the not very heroic child-hero, who tells his own story. And in Wiltshire it is Stephen, hero or divine man, who stands by the central tree. This of course is the most profound connection between Ansell and Stephen. Stephen is that which is real and is at the center.

This central point at the heart of both past and present is a symbol of rebirth. "A great many traditions trace the creation of the

143

World to a central point (navel) from which it is supposed to have spread out in the four cardinal directions. To attain to the centre of the World means, therefore, to arrive at the 'point of departure' of the Cosmos at the 'beginning of Time'; in short, to have abolished Time."[16] Thus one may be said to participate in the instant of the world's creation which is the instant of one's own rebirth. The ecstatic or transcendent quality of the experience arises from the sense that time has been abolished. This is the experience which brushes against Rickie at the center of the Rings. It is the experience he glimpses as he waits for the birth of his child.

We might now restate what was said a little earlier about the implications of Rickie's vision of a fresh circle within the square. The suggestion is that reality or the timelessness of creation, at each moment fenced in by the temporal, must continually be reborn or restated in thought, image, or child. Each circle is "a new symbol for the universe," a symbol for the present as the moment of rebirth.

Circles in the form of the Cadbury Rings are also symbols of the past. At the moment when Rickie sees that he has made false idols of Stephen and his mother and has worshipped a torn photograph instead of the reality of Demeter the goddess, he envisages the Rings as "those mystic circles" (p. 284). Later the burning ball of paper set floating on the stream by Stephen and associated with the mother is recalled as "that mystic rose."[17] It is appropriate that Mrs. Elliot who died when Rickie was fifteen should be connected with the Rings representing the past, and that she should be included along with Stephen in the circularity and cocoa-squareness of Ansell's symbol of truth and reality. It is to her we turn now as the second of Rickie's potential guides.

"She is the first of the mystic mothers that haunt Mr. Forster's work—earth mothers, portentous, half-mythical figures who embody his concept of continuity, of an essential race-life."[18] Mrs. Elliot is Demeter, a goddess much written about at the end of the nineteenth century. Erwin Rohde observes that "Demeter, in whose name there was early a tendency to recognize a second 'Mother Earth,' in many places took the place of Gaia in religious cult, and thereby entered into closer connexion with the realm of the souls below the earth."[19] Her

144

connection with death is frequently stressed. Thus Walter Pater, referring to the Demeter of Cnidus, says: "Here she is represented in her later state of reconciliation, enthroned as the glorified mother of all things. . . . the goddess of the fertility of the earth and of all creatures, but still of fertility as arisen out of death; and therefore she is not without a certain pensiveness, having seen the seed fall into the ground and die, many times."[20]

Forster, writing about Cnidus, says that he will not pity the Demeter exiled from her Mediterranean home and now situated in her little recess in the British Museum: "if, as I believe, she is alive, she must know that she has come among people who love her, for all they are so weak-chested and anæmic and feeble-kneed, and who pay her such prosaic homage as they can."[21] Thus in 1904 Forster appears to have found the British nation Rickie-like but not unacceptable on that account. By 1907 he appears to suspect that the weak-chested and feeble-kneed may be too poor in spirit to truly appreciate Demeter.

But worship her they must. "Demeter alone among gods has true immortality. The others continue, perchance, their existence, but are forgotten, because the time came when they could not be loved. But to her, all over the world, rise prayers of idolatry from suffering men as well as suffering women, for she has transcended sex." (In *Howards End* the wych-elm which stands as guardian of the house is also described as transcending sex; it is associated with Mrs. Wilcox, another Demeter-like mother figure.) The goddess transcends sex because her sexual meaning is included in a context so large and full of implication that it will always appeal in one way or another to men's minds. As Mircea Eliade puts it, "the Earth-Mother constitutes a form that is 'open' to, or susceptible of, indefinite enrichment, and that is why it takes in all the myths dealing with Life and Death, with Creation and generation, with sexuality and voluntary sacrifice."[22]

Mrs. Elliot is primarily associated with trees, streams, and stars. It is natural that the Earth-Mother should have connections with vegetation. When Rickie learns that he has a brother, Mrs. Elliot who is *of* the past is present in the pastness of the Rings. She is specifically represented by the tree at their center which, like the little wood near Madingley, is a traditional mother symbol. (Stephen

145

leans against the tree, it sustains him; but it is small, it does not overshadow him.) The relation of a fertility goddess and flowing water needs no comment. Forster's specific treatment of the symbol I leave till later.

The relation of Demeter and the stars is less obvious, though it is by no means obscure. In *Aspects of the Novel* Forster has quoted Meredith's description of the stars as "the brains of heaven, the army of unalterable law" (p. 104). And speaking of Dante in 1907, he said that the conflicting forces of man's nature "are reconciled in the orbits of the stars."[23] When we set beside these statements the fact that the Great Mother represents the nature of being and the law of being, we see that Demeter and the stars are different ways of looking at and of symbolizing the same reality. If we think of the maternal figure as Nature or the Universal Mother, then the stars will be subsumed in her image. Thus in *The Mystical Hymns of Orpheus,* a new edition of which was published in 1896, the hymn "To Nature" salutes the goddess in these words:

> Untam'd, all taming, ever splendid light,
> All ruling, honour'd, and supremely bright.
> Immortal, first-born, ever still the same,
> Nocturnal, starry, shining, powerful dame.

A note to the hymn quotes Proclus: "But she governs the whole world by her powers, containing the heavens in the summit of herself, but ruling over generation [or the sublunary realms] through the heavens; and every where weaving together partial natures with wholes."[24]

These hymns ever assimilate Pan to the star image, describing him as "starry light." They also enlarge on the water image. It is said that from Rhea "ev'ry river flows." As a previous note explains, Rhea, the mother of the gods, "is one of the zoogonic or vivific principles of the universe. . . . Plato [says Proclus] assimilates her prolific abundance to the flowing of waters; signifying nothing more by the word *flowing* than that fontal power by which she contains in transcendent union the divisible rivers of life."[25]

The Demeter of *The Longest Journey,* though she participates in all these associations, is not presented finally as a subsuming figure.

Rather, as we shall see when we come to Stephen, she appears in a supporting role in relation to the hero.

The picture of the Demeter of Cnidus must not be confused with the goddess or with Mrs. Elliot. The picture has been dismissed from the drawingroom at Cadover and hangs in Stephen's attic. It is a possession of the Elliot family and in its specific details symbolizes Rickie's defective embodiment of the spirit of life, the Elliot distortion of his inheritance from his mother. The broken nose of the lady suggests, not very happily to be sure, the sterility of the Elliots, while the shattered knees reflect the family limp and, more particularly, Rickie's knees crushed by the train. The presence of the Demeter of Cnidus in Stephen's room earlier portends and later affirms the truth, so obvious in retrospect, that Mrs. Elliot is the mother of Stephen.

Earth was the mother of Orion, so legend tells us. Orion is Stephen's symbol. Its first appearance will show how Forster has put it to dramatic use. Rickie, in an agony of despair after the death of his child, falls into a troubled sleep. In the darkened room he hears distinctly his weeping mother. "He whispered, 'Never mind . . .' and a voice echoed, 'Never mind—come away—let them die out—let them die out.' He lit a candle, and the room was empty. Then, hurrying to the window, he saw above mean houses the frosty glories of Orion" (p. 218). For the moment we are baffled by the dream: we cannot be certain that "them" signifies Rickie and the Elliots; we mistakenly believe Stephen is the son of Rickie's father; and though the stars have been suggestively introduced earlier, Orion appears here for the first time. Sixty pages later, Rickie, after learning that Stephen is his mother's son, recalls his mother's words and thinks his dream must surely have been a vision. "To-night also he hurried to the window—to remember, with a smile, that Orion is not among the stars of June. 'Let me die out. She will continue,' he murmured, and in making plans for Stephen's happiness, fell asleep" (p. 278).

In this second scene we actively participate in Rickie's sense of vision and revelation. Orion becomes fixed in our minds; each new appearance of the symbol reminds us of Stephen and, beyond him, of strong and adventurous man, a son of earth whose destiny is

147

imaged in the harmony and glory of the stars. This is the hero whose parentage, childhood, journey, and destiny we shall now consider.

The hero as foundling is one way of expressing his independence of the parents, and one way of explaining his having two mothers or two complete sets of parents. Frequently the foster parents are representative of his lower or carnal nature and the real parents of his higher or divine nature. In particular, his real mother is likely to be the Mother Goddess. So it is in Stephen's case. His mother is Demeter. His father breaks into her life, fathers a son, and disappears by drowning. As so often in legend father and son have one identity. We are told that for generations before Salisbury cathedral was built the villages of the surrounding country "were clinging to the soil, and renewing it with sheep and dogs and men, who found the crisis of their lives upon Stonehenge. The blood of these men ran in Stephen; the vigour they had won for him was as yet untarnished . . . the last of them had rescued a woman of a different kind from streets and houses such as these"—of suburban London (p. 275). Here is the long and noble line of ancestors of which Robert is the last. Having united with the Earth-Mother he is swallowed up in the great maternal sea to re-emerge in the form of the son, who now becomes the last of the noble line. It is very obvious that Stephen's parents are heroic or divine.

His foster parent is Mrs. Failing. (Tony Failing's role is of another kind, and will be dealt with later.) Forster tells us that it was an uncle who gave him "hints for the character of Mrs. Failing and whose house up in Northumberland provided the architecture and the atmosphere for Cadover."[26] Such a background to her character is quite appropriate and not at all surprising for she is essentially an androgynous figure; even her perversity is shared by Rickie's father. Her androgynous role in the novel is important because she is the living representative of Mr. Elliot. "Rickie admired his aunt, but did not care for her. She reminded him too much of his father. She had the same affliction, the same heartlessness, the same habit of taking life with a laugh—as if life is a pill!" (p. 115). Through Mrs. Failing, Stephen shares with Rickie the same carnal father; whereas in Mrs. Elliot they share the same divine mother.[27]

We learn little of Stephen's childhood. But he makes one memorable appearance as a child hero. Slipping wet from his nurse's hands, he emerges onto the roof at Cadover. He is an image of nonsense and beauty. Tony Failing afterward wrote: "I see the respectable mansion. I see the smug fortress of culture. The doors are shut. The windows are shut. But on the roof the children go dancing for ever" (p. 138). Like the squaring of the circle, the child hero or divine child signifies the union of opposites. This union of joy and dancing and youth with the smug fortress of culture is in the future, for the child hero is only potential mediator. But he promises to be *one who makes whole.*[28]

It frequently happens, as was the case with Hercules, that the hero in his youth must labor at the command of another. Stephen is at this stage in his career when Rickie and Agnes go into Wiltshire. He is subject to Mrs. Failing and has not yet entered fully on his heroic course. Before he does so, we may pause to consider his qualities as a hero. These include his resemblance to the elements, his animal simplicity, his elemental or primordial humanity, and his heroic prowess.

Forster more than once suggests that Stephen is like an ancient Greek (pp. 239, 240–41). He would agree with Pater that the "body of man . . . was for the Greeks, still the genuine work of Prometheus" and that "its connexion with earth and air . . . [was] direct and immediate."[29] Stephen's ride with Rickie over the sun-and-wind-swept downs to Salisbury clearly establishes such a connection between the hero and the elements. This is confirmed when Stephen is described the morning after his drunken onslaught on Dunwood House as having "recaptured motion and passion and the imprint of the sunlight and the wind." And his eyes recall "the sky unclouded" (pp. 279–80), for his parents had given him "a cloudless spirit—the spirit of the seventeen days in which he was created" (p. 269).

Stephen in his simplicity is first interpreted by Rickie as "an inexperienced animal" (p. 125), but Forster says simply that "he knew nothing about himself at all," adding that in his living relationship with the horse he rode he was "a centaur" (pp. 127, 134). Ansell's judgment is the most conclusive: "He gave the idea of an animal with just enough soul to contemplate its own bliss" (p. 239).

Stephen's elemental humanity stems from an absence of self-denial. This aspect of his heroic character is clearly foreshadowed by Forster in an essay of 1903 which describes a Greek toilet case engraved with a legend from the story of the Argonauts. The heroes have landed to refresh themselves at a spring and one "has hastened back to the Argo, and is pouring water down the throat of a sick friend. But he has drunk himself first." This man, says Forster, "is as many centuries from self-denial as he is from self-consciousness."[30] Mrs. Failing interprets Stephen's freedom from self-consciousness and self-denial as obtuseness and brutality. In one sense she is right, as we learn from Forster's use of the word brutality later in the story. Stephen, in his relations with Rickie, "was man first, brother afterwards. Herein lay his brutality and also his virtue" (p. 296). That is, he saw Rickie for precisely what he was which might mean treating him brutally but assuredly meant treating him honestly and forthrightly. Life was "no decorous scheme, but a personal combat or a personal truce" (p. 272). This same capacity for direct confrontation gives liveliness and eccentric truth to Stephen's meeting with Ansell at Dunwood House.

In addition to his primordial humanity, his animal simplicity, and his resemblance to the elements, Stephen is described or referred to in heroic terms. Riding over the downs to Salisbury—we have already noted how the setting is appropriate to a hero—with the soldier who has become his drinking companion, he finds himself defending Mrs. Failing's honor because his own honor is involved. "For the moment he would die for her, as a knight would die for a glove. He is not to be distinguished from a hero" (p. 133). Later as he stood before Rickie with the imprint of the sunlight and the wind upon him he is described as "not consciously heroic" (p. 279). And just before the catastrophe Rickie catches Ansell's enthusiasm: "Stephen was a hero. He was a law to himself, and rightly" (p. 309). Rickie's opinion might seem exaggerated and unreliable, coming as it does immediately before his disillusionment, were it not confirmed by Ansell's judgment.

Ansell is clear-headed enough to know that he is not himself a hero (p. 200). Yet he has every confidence in Stephen: "Let him do what he likes. . . . He knows more than we do. He knows everything" (p. 290). His confidence arises from the profound impression Stephen made on him when they first met at Dunwood House: "A silence, akin to poetry, invaded Ansell. Was it only a pose to like this man, or was he really wonderful? . . . Certain figures of the Greeks, to whom we continually return, suggested him a little. One expected nothing of him—no purity of phrase or swift-edged thought. Yet the conviction grew that he had been back somewhere—back to some table of the gods, spread in a field where there is no noise, and that he belonged forever to the guests with whom he had eaten" (pp. 240–41).

Stephen's heroic nature is more important than his heroic adventures. His adventures begin late in the story and tend to be telescoped and symbolic. In Part I the fundamentals of his heroic nature are established and his essential stance with respect to the world is defined. Late in Part II when less than a third of the novel remains, he begins his adventures. Dismissed from Cadover, he puts its corrupting influence entirely behind him. In a "great symbolic act" he casts his clothes into the pond and wades "through the dark cold water" to new clothes on the other side of the stream (p. 243). This is a symbol of purification rather than baptism and rebirth.

Stephen journeys to Sawston, the threshold of the strange world he must now enter. In the garden of Dunwood House he meets Ansell. They participate in an almost dream-like and markedly ritualistic brother-combat. (They are brothers because each is real and recognizes the other as real.) Next he enters Dunwood House which is the entrance into suburbia which is the entrance into the modern hell of the great city. Here he encounters Agnes, again the shadowy figure of the threshold, a kind of suburban dragon whose corrupting fire is money rather than flame. But money cannot tempt Stephen, its fire cannot touch him. He goes alive into the dark kingdom, passing through one suburb after another:

Far into the night he wandered, until he came to a solemn river majestic as a stream in hell. Therein were gathered the waters of Central England—those that flow off Hindhead, off the Chilterns, off Wiltshire north of the Plain. Therein they were made intolerable ere they reached the sea. But the waters he had known escaped. Their course lay southward into the Avon by forests and beautiful fields, even swift, even pure, until they mirrored the tower of Christchurch and greeted the ramparts of the Isle of Wight. Of these he thought for a moment as he crossed the black river and entered the heart of the modern world. (p. 273)[31]

After surviving in London for a short time he suddenly encounters one of those helpers so common in the career of the hero, in this case a man who mistakenly gives him an excessive tip. With this money he gets drunk, returns to Dunwood House, and smashes up the guardians of the front hall. From here he leads Rickie out of bondage.

Stephen's journey has taken him from Wiltshire to Sawston to London. His return, after the ordeal of crossing the black and majestic Thames and enduring the modern hell of the great city, is from London to Sawston and so to Wiltshire. At Salisbury he and Rickie find a trap and drive to Cadover. It is November, the time of Orion, and night comes on. "The horse went slowly forward into the wilderness, that turned from brown to black" (p. 300). Stephen tells Rickie of his thoughts and doubts: "While he spoke even the road vanished, and invisible water came gurgling through the wheel-spokes. The horse had chosen the ford." As they continue to talk, "Rickie watched the black earth unite to the black sky. But the sky overhead grew clearer, and in it twinkled the Plough and the central stars" (p. 301). The shining stars point to Stephen's future while earth and sky united in a single blackness foretell Rickie's doom.

Meanwhile Stephen has left the cart. Down in the stream he lights a crumpled ball of paper handed him by Rickie, who is intent on Stephen's transfigured and illumined faced. He sees in that face the incarnation of their mother.

> The paper caught fire from the match, and spread into a rose of flame. "Now gently with me," said Stephen, and they laid it flower-like on the stream. Gravel and tremulous weeds leapt into sight, and then the flower sailed into deep water, and up leapt the two arches of a bridge. "It'll strike!" they cried; "no, it won't; it's chosen the left," and one arch became a fairy tunnel, dropping diamonds. Then it vanished for Rickie; but Stephen, who knelt in the water, declared that it was still afloat, far through the arch, burning as if it would burn for ever. (p. 302)

In this moment Mrs. Elliot and Ansell's circle come together and are united in Stephen whose immersion in the stream suggests not simply purification but baptism and rebirth. The hero attains to a higher nature, and becomes a god or supreme man. Here the mystic rose reveals its immense richness and complexity. It symbolizes Stephen's attainment of heroic stature; it is the unfolding, flowering, flaming out of his higher self. It symbolizes also the transfiguration of the body. Fire and water are the traditional means of transformation—in Christianity as well as in alchemy—by which matter is transmuted and becomes the incorruptible body. Stephen is now ready for the supreme event, the consummation of his destiny. In his face, illuminated by the mystic rose, is reflected his union with Earth, the bride-mother. And in the sacred marriage the fire is the fire of creativity. Thus Ansell's symbol is subsumed in the ball of paper, the mystic rose of the mother who in turn is subsumed in the hero-son Stephen. For the reader as for Rickie, Stephen has come to represent all reality, whether found in books or in the earth or in man.

While Stephen bathes in the stream, Rickie drives on to Cadover, believing earth has confirmed him. His belief is shattered by Stephen's drunkenness: "Tell him he's broken his word, and I will not go with him to the Rings" (p. 310). Thus he rejects the past, a part of earth's confirmation. In the belief that Stephen will ruin himself, that his mother will die out, and that there will be no future, he rejects all: "That mystic rose and the face it illumined meant nothing. The stream—he was above it now—meant nothing, though it burst from the pure turf and ran for ever to the sea. The bather, the shoulders of Orion—they all meant nothing, and were going nowhere" (p. 312).

Here then is the river of life springing from the earth and flowing forever to the great sea of change and unknown possibility. The unlighted arch on the right is Rickie's, the one on the left is Stephen's. (Compare the bend sinister.) For Rickie the light is short-lived; but for Stephen, immersed in the stream, it seems to burn for ever, giving promise that he and his descendants, the sons of earth, will continue to journey down the river of life.

Erwin Rohde has noted that in Greece the "worship of Heroes

began as an ancestor-cult and an ancestor-cult it remained in essence."[32] Forster has followed the Greek tradition in his creation of Stephen. Even before Rickie learns that Stephen is his mother's son, he is aware that Stephen rather than himself "would contribute to the stream; he, through his remote posterity, might be mingled with the unknown sea" (p. 217).

This imagery of river and sea is recurrent. It makes a notable appearance in Rickie's thinking at the moment when he realizes that the dream about his mother ("Let them die out") was a kind of vision. "On the banks of the grey torrent of life, love is the only flower. A little way up the stream and a little way down had Rickie glanced, and he knew that she whom he loved had risen from the dead, and might rise again" (p. 278). This image prepares for the mystic rose at the ford, for "the only flower" can appear again only through the continuation of the race. And so Stephen, at the close of the novel, stands between his ancestors who century after century found the reasonable crises of their lives at Stonehenge and Salisbury, and his descendants in whom century after century his thoughts and passions would triumph in England. "The dead who had evoked him, the unborn whom he would evoke—he governed the paths between them" (p. 320).

Keith Johnstone has most eloquently related this theme of continuation to the theme of death: "Death is almost a rhythm in *The Longest Journey,* a rhythm which emphasizes Stephen's survival. The sudden deaths, like a progression of great chords, culminate in the death of Rickie. Surrounded by all this death, it is marvellous, it seems the work of fate, that Stephen should survive. His theme, as it were, expands, and continues after the novel has ended."[33]

The hero includes all who go before and all who come after, for he is the beginning and the end, the human totality. It is, I believe, this all-embracing and god-like quality of Stephen's character which most explains Forster's special fondness for *The Longest Journey.* It has often been supposed that the novel is his favorite because it is autobiographical. But this is true only in a very special sense. Forster does not prefer the novel because Sawston school is like the school he attended or because Rickie Elliot is like his creator (though both are true); he prefers it because here more prodigiously than in any other of his works he has liberated a whole constellation of deeply felt and profoundly significant symbols. If these sometimes bring the work close to intellectual and structural confusion, it is the price to be paid for the liberating of symbols the explosive pressure of which is everywhere apparent. The theme of the death-wish and the loss of reality is juxtaposed to that of the spirit of life. It is the latter which is so intensely represented in the symbolism and especially in the figure of Stephen as hero. One senses that this intensity is possible because it is balanced (one might almost say compensated for) by the theme of spiritual death. One extreme begets the other.

The liberation of symbols from what Forster calls the subconscious has another notable consequence. It exposes more fully than anywhere else the paradox, or if you like, the conflict of interest, that lies at the heart of Forster's thinking and his artistic practice. The conflict is between individuality and universal nature. We may begin to understand it by studying Rickie's uncle.

Tony Failing seeks reality in books, out of doors, and in others. In terms of myth and legend he is the old wise man and a guide for the hero. His writings are gathered into a book of wisdom which throws light upon the various characters who come in contact with it. For instance, Stephen has no thoughts on the subject of rural silence which Tony Failing said was a practical need for all men (p. 237), but Ansell's insight tells us that Stephen takes silence for granted because it is so much a part of his being. The hero, because he encompasses every aspect of humanity, may be expected to include the image of the old wise man. However, I do not find that Tony Failing is presented by Forster as an archetypal character nor do I find that he is subsumed in Stephen as Ansell and Mrs. Elliot are subsumed.

Mrs. Failing says that Rickie is her husband's spiritual heir (p. 220). The remark, which foretells Rickie's failure, is not less true for coming from a nasty source. What Rickie and his uncle have most in common is the desire to appreciate all forms of reality and by so doing to foster their own individuality and that of others. This would seem a commendable goal. But is it not strange that those who most cultivate their individuality should fail? And is it not strange that a supposedly wise man in a Forster novel, after noting that the Beloved Republic (Swinburne's phrase) will not be brought about by love alone should say: "Self-sacrifice and—worse still—self-multilation are the things that sometimes help it most" (p. 265)? A little reflection tells us that these words of Tony Failing point toward Rickie's self-sacrifice and self-mutilation in rescuing Stephen from the oncoming train. By this act—we are told on the last page of the novel—he bequeaths "salvation" to Stephen.

Behind this relationship of the brothers lies the ancient mythological figure of the twins. Forster continues to show interest in this figure when he develops the parallel between Harold-Michael and Castor-Pollux in "The Point of It." The persistence of the twin motif in the traditional account of the hero's life has been explained by Otto Rank as a carry-over from the primitive belief in a double which was thought to have an existence independent of the person and to survive after the person had died:

> The idea prevalent in the traditions of civilized peoples that one of the twins is immortal emerged from the earlier belief in the double, since the twin appeared as a concrete personification of the soul resembling the body like a double, in other words, as the soul in person. This not only makes him independent and invincible but also the fearless revolutionist who dares all mortal men and even the immortal Gods. It is this utter independence which makes the twin the prototype of the hero. In this sense, the traditions of the birth of the hero whose life is saved by the death of a twin are not merely mythical biographies of these individuals, but in their totality they epitomize the birth of the heroic type as such from the magical conception of twinship.[34]

The twin (or a reasonable facsimile thereof) must die that his brother may have life and life immortal.[35] What is implied here is that the first twin is subsumed in the figure of his heroic brother who then represents the fusion of body and soul, the union of the mortal and immortal self. I cannot read the scene at the ford or the closing account of Stephen's inarticulate gratitude to the brother who has bequeathed him salvation and life without thinking at those moments that something very like the above account is reflected in Forster's portrayal of

Rickie and Stephen. Such a view is rendered the more probable by our understanding of the nature of romance fiction. Since the characters are partial we cannot be surprised at the end of the story that Stephen, who finally appears as the whole image of man, should include Rickie.

On this view, Rickie's individuality, rather than being denied and sacrificed, is significantly included in and reconciled with Stephen's impersonality. This is what we should expect from Forster's earlier novels and from "The Story of a Panic"; it is what is traditionally implied by the myth of the twins and by the nature of romance. But for all that, I cannot believe it is what the novel shows us. The fact that so many forces press in the direction of inclusion and reconciliation only make the failure to include the more striking. I do not see how we can get round Tony Failing's words nor round the complete misery and disillusionment of Rickie's death. He is offered up, mutilated, and destroyed.[36]

The mythological figure of the twins gives us a valuable insight into Forster's story. But in the end the pattern offered by the figure of the twins is displaced by the less ancient pattern of the double as the dark side of human nature. The primitive notion of the other self, because it was associated with the other world and an other life, came in time to be connected with evil and death and all that is dark. The resulting figure of the double as evil may be a minor character and as totally abhorrent as Orlick in *Great Expectations* or it may be a major character and as fascinating as Mephistopheles in Goethe's *Faust*. Psychologically, it may express no more than certain corrupt features of the ego or it may express the whole power of chaos and the unconscious in its threat to overwhelm consciousness. The antinomies represented by the hero and his double in darkness have found their most extreme polarization in God and Satan, Christ and Antichrist. Such a polarization implies the desire to eliminate the dark side of the equation. The rule here is simple: the more ideal the hero the more likely it is that his double in darkness will be sacrificed or eliminated and that any redeeming qualities which the double may have had will be sacrificed too. Something like this happens in *The Longest Journey*.

We have already seen that Stephen, through the foster parentage of Mrs. Failing, shares with Rickie the lower carnal father, Mr. Elliot. When Rickie voluntarily foregoes his hereditary interest in his mother who represents for him the higher parentage and takes upon himself the carnal nature of the brothers, he sacrifices himself so that Stephen, purged of carnality, may stand as the representative of man's higher nature. Individuality is sacrificed to the universality and impersonality of the hero.

In *The Longest Journey* Forster finds the fully developed hero a dangerous archetype. At the very least he may require the sacrifice of the struggling individualist; and there is the possibility he may turn into a brute and a tyrant. Forster avoids this latter possibility by stressing Stephen's youthful spirits and his devotion to country life. This in turn relates him to the archetype of the mother which also serves to contain the hero. Stephen's close ties with Mrs. Elliot are dramatized at the story's end. The picture of the Demeter of Cnidus and the picture of Stockholm, the city of canals where Stephen was conceived, have found a place in Stephen's home and are seen as pink in the light of the setting sun. The life-like color suggests their vitality and connects them with the mystic rose. As the sun sets and silence descends on the earth, Stephen with his daughter in his arms goes out onto the hillside to sleep. As hero he is finally placed in the context not of the world and the mass psyche but of the earth and the universal feminine.

So placed, he dominates the novel. Symbols and symbolic characters meet in him to enforce an eminence confirmed by Rickie's death. With the rising of his star the novel shifts focus and a tragedy of rejected possibilities is transformed into a comedy of man triumphant.

At the same time Forster has found that there is no easy way to contain the hero and keep him within bounds. We may suppose this to be one of his reasons for not exploring the type further. The other reason, outlined in the first part of this chapter, relates to the difficulty of presentation. How to bring a hero into the modern world, how to keep him free of social commitments, how to make him consistently heroic: these are the difficulties Forster solved only partially in his handling of Stephen. Within limits they are the difficulties posed by all archetypal characters, for such characters must be free to come and go, free to expand and take on a full complement of meaning. We may assume on the basis of Forster's two last novels that he understood the dangers which beset him in the presentation of Ansell and Mrs. Elliot and Stephen. The hazards implicit in the creation of archetypal characters are carefully avoided in the portrayal of Mrs. Wilcox and Mrs. Moore. They are the flawless achievement of an assured technique. They are also a sign of Forster's turning away from the greatest hazard, the portrayal of the hero as archetype.

The Melanesian mind is entirely possessed by the belief in a . . . power or influence, called almost universally *mana*. This is what works to effect everything which is beyond the power of the ordinary man, outside the common processes of nature; it is present in the atmosphere of life, attaches itself to persons and to things. . . . It is a power or influence, not physical . . . but it shows itself in physical force, or in any kind of power or influence which a man possesses. This *mana* is not fixed in anything, and can be conveyed in almost anything; but . . . it essentially belongs to personal beings to originate it, though it may act through the medium of water, or a stone, or a bone.

—R. H. Codrington, *The Melanesians*

This sense of the ineluctable power manifest in a multiplicity of phenomena, a power mysterious but not supernatural, incomprehensible but not improbable, is wonderfully analogous to the spirit that moves through E. M. Forster's fictions. This spirit "essentially belongs to personal beings . . . though it may act through the medium of water, or a stone." Guided by intuitive insight, Forster penetrates through the advanced abstractions of energy, power, and natural law to the concrete reality of elemental psychic experience. Square-within-circle, constellation, and man, or again, tree, house, and woman, express in their multiple ways the same powerful energy, the same pervasive spirit. But in doing so, these symbols and beings express not the abstraction that makes them one but the multiplicity-out-of-oneness that makes them themselves.

160

5
Object as Archetype

*A*n object, a form, any nonhuman thing becomes a symbol when it takes on human meaning. (I exclude from consideration the notion of symbol as a sign having a precise meaning conventionally agreed upon.) Most such symbols—rock, cave, fountain, tree, animal—come directly from nature. But they may come from nature indirectly, as does the circle in *The Longest Journey*.

A circle's symmetry and perfection of form must be apparent to most. And the way it is drawn from a center—with the end going the long way round to come back to a perfect meeting with the point of beginning—has an almost magical quality. This may be called the object's natural inclination. Such an inclination will influence the development of the object as a symbol, for it will determine the kind of human meaning it is most likely to assume or, if it seems better to put it negatively, the kind of meaning it is most likely *not* to assume. Dark clouds may suggest rain and fertility or darkness and dismalness but they are unlikely to suggest anything bright and carefree. Likewise a circle is unlikely to suggest anything ragged, distorted, or formless.

Within the range of its natural inclination, an object takes on human meaning through its context, through its association with events and characters, and through the attitudes towards it expressed by the characters and narrator. We can see this by glancing once more at the circle in *The Longest Journey*.

Through Ansell's square-within-circle drawing and Rickie's experience before his child is born, the circle comes to signify the continual rebirth of the present. This is the heart of its meaning and a way of stating the novel's theme. The glory of man and his universe as represented by Stephen and Wiltshire would be matter for tragedy were it not for this assurance of continuity. The circle expands to encompass every form of rebirth whether in thought, image, or child. It expands also to include the Cadbury Rings, those mystic circles within whose bounds Rickie encounters the past; and the mystic rose, symbol of the mother who is of the past and who, in her sons and in her role as Earth-Mother, is of the future as well. Contained and ordered within the harmony of the circle, these references tell us that the rebirth of the present exacts a continuing return to the past which is the beginning, and offers a continuing assurance of the future which is our hope this side of the grave. Change and mutability are seen as subserving the continuing act of renewal. This process is rendered permanent in the image of the circle. Is it the circle that Ansell could never find room to draw, the one at the center of all circles, the one, perhaps, that contains all circles? Forster has drawn it for us and made his myth.

He has made his myth because the image of the circle, by virtue of its power to convey a sense of totality and ultimate unity, has become an archetype or mythic symbol. This is to define an archetype more narrowly than is customary today. As illustration, let me present the views of two of the best-known practitioners of archetypal criticism, Northrop Frye and Leslie Fiedler.[1] For Frye an archetype is a symbol seen in its capacity as an instrument of social communication. It is a typical or recurring image, "a symbol which connects one poem with another and thereby helps to unify and integrate our literary experience." Looked at in this way an archetype is a "communicable unit" and poetry is "the focus of a community." Forster's fiction is generously supplied with typical and recurring images. The tree of life has a prominent place in *Howards End*. And in *The Longest Journey* we find stars, Demeter, Orion, rose, river, and of course the circle.

Fiedler's definition of archetype does not exclude Frye's meaning but it places the emphasis very much elsewhere. By archetype he means "a coherent pattern of beliefs and feelings so widely shared at a level beneath consciousness that there exists no abstract vocabulary for representing it, and so 'sacred' that unexamined, irrational restraints inhibit any explicit analysis. Such a complex finds a formula or pattern story, which serves both to embody it, and, at first at least, to conceal its full implications. Later, the secret may be revealed, the archetype 'analyzed' or 'allegorically' interpreted according to the language of the day." The reader may ask what covert body of beliefs and feelings are implicit in Forster's contrast of the educated, sophisticated, sterile Elliots with a complex of images that includes the open Wiltshire downs, the country hero Stephen, the Demeter-like Mrs. Elliot, the circle, and the mystic rose? The reader may ask, but I do not propose to answer.

My principal interest in Forster's archetypes is not the interest of either Frye or Fiedler. Though I hold it entirely correct to do so, I do not in this book call a symbol archetypal because it is traditional or because it embodies a widely distributed and secret psychological pattern of beliefs and feelings. When I present a traditional interpretation or a common late nineteenth-century interpretation of a symbol, my main purpose is to establish what is likely to have been Forster's conscious intention or unconscious inclination in employing that symbol. And when I present a psychological interpretation of a symbol or a constellation of images, my concern is to open out the significance of the symbol within the work rather than to relate it to the psychology of Forster or the nineteenth century or any number of centuries. Even in the study of the hero where I have used an approach like Fiedler's and have taken the archetypal story pattern of the hero, which has been "analyzed," and have superimposed it on Forster's heroes and his one failed hero, my principle object has been to make clear to the reader unused to prose romances that Forster *intends* these characters to be heroes and that he intends their stories to have the kind of significance found in other and earlier accounts of the hero. It is for this reason only that I have become involved in a certain amount of psychology necessary to present the sacred coherent pattern of beliefs and feelings embedded in the hero archetype.

My interest in those symbols of Forster's which I call archetypal is an interest arising from their strange and unique power, a power which has its origin in the moment of ecstatic experience and which expresses itself through the transformation of objects and persons into symbols of totality and mythic unity. But how does this transformation take place? Or rather, since ecstatic experience is contingent on identity with the object of vision, how does the perceiver become aware of what he perceives?

Forster has discussed this perplexing question in *A Passage to India* in connection with the festival of Gokul Ashtami. The festival itself presents an added difficulty in that it is a *deliberate* attempt to achieve oneness with the other-than-self here designated as God. A prolonged and elaborate ritual is devoted to this end. Such a ritual does not contradict the principle that ecstatic experiences are rare and come at irregular intervals. Forster glosses the point admirably in *Howards End* when he says that "visions do not come when we try, though they may come through trying" (p. 216). We have also seen that certain phenomena are especially likely to set an ecstatic experience in motion. A ritual is not a guarantee that anything will happen, it is simply a device for putting oneself in the way of an ecstatic experience: "the human spirit had tried by a desperate contortion to ravish the unknown, flinging down science and history in the struggle, yes, beauty herself. Did it succeed?" Precisely here is the problem. "Books written afterwards say 'yes.' But how, if there is such an event, can it be remembered afterwards? How can it be expressed in anything but itself? Not only from the unbeliever are mysteries hid, but the adept himself cannot retain them. He may think, if he chooses, that he has been with God, but as soon as he thinks it, it becomes history, and falls under the rules of time" (p. 300).

How can such an event be remembered afterward? How, when one's normal awareness is suspended and one has fallen into a state of identity with the other-than-self, can there be anything to remember? The answer must involve the paradox that awareness is only in part suspended and that identity rather than being complete is subject to degree.

Next, how can such an event be expressed in anything but itself? The first answer: insofar as knowledge of the event is ordinary it may be expressed by the means normally used to express knowledge. The second answer: insofar as the knowledge is strange and beyond the bounds of discursive thought processes it may best be expressed in images which are modeled on or emerge from the event itself. This is the procedure followed by Forster in the short stories where the eternal moment is the center of the story. Yet the moment is no sooner thought about than it becomes history and falls under the rules of time. This difficulty is met by contrasting the visionary moment and mundane reality in such a way as to project the deadening sense of history and time onto the mundane reality. So it is not simply romance convention but the very specific nature of Forster's material that makes necessary the decisive contrast—discussed in Chapter 2—between vision and anti-vision.

A procedure so well-suited to the short story is not without problems when applied to the novel. After the eternal moment has been "given," it must be kept alive through the remainder of a long narrative. When Forster came up against this problem in *A Room with a View* and *Where Angels Fear to Tread*, it appears that he unconsciously hit upon the procedure of attaching the moment of vision to the narrator himself. At the same time he began to explore the possibility of portraying the person or object of vision without portraying the eternal moment itself. By devising a series of less intense moments he could make the impact created by the person or object of vision more continuous and diffused. The presentation of Stephen as hero and Gino as natural man are examples, not wholly successful, of this method.

The process of dissolving the single moment of vision is a natural development in Forster's art. It is natural for this reason: a character is precisely like a tree or a stone in that it is rendered archetypal only when it becomes an *object* of vision; a character is not rendered archetypal by virtue of having a vision. Thus the subjective fact of ecstatic identity with something outside the self must take second place to that something outside which in its transformation becomes archetypal and gives the impression that "nothing greater can be conceived." But when the ecstatic himself becomes an object of vision he too is transformed. It may be noted that the above distinctions are largely irrelevant in the short stories since typically the ecstatic and the world with which he achieves identity are presented as a unit and together are rendered as an object of vision.

All Forster's characters who attain to archetypal stature have had or are assumed by others to have had ecstatic experience. On the other hand, by no means all who have had ecstatic experience attain to archetypal status, as witness Helen and Margaret Schlegel, Rickie Elliot, Philip Herriton, and the narrator of "Other Kingdom." (In this last instance the narrator's vision is markedly defective and must be pieced out by the reader; none the less it is *through* him that we apprehend Miss Beaumont as an object of vision.) Everything depends on the manner of beholding, on whether the character himself is perceived as an object of vision either by other characters (the usual means) or by the omniscient author (as in "The Road from Colonus"). Even when the visionary moment, transcending the characters, attaches directly to the author-narrator (*A Room with a View* and *Where Angels Fear to Tread*) a strange objectification takes place. That is why it is so important to the effect that there should be nothing personal or intimate in the presentation. The narrative must transmute both the narrator and his experience into an object of vision.[2]

Ecstatic experience is the well-spring of archetypes, whether objects or persons. But in view of the fact that the ecstatic himself is not necessarily archetypal, it is a natural development that Forster should pass over the single and unique phenomenon of the eternal moment and should instead invoke the sense of archetypal power and significance by means of a series of less intense moments distributed through the narrative. Such a procedure, well-suited to the longer form of the novel, has an added merit. It allows Forster to introduce a variety of characters who are capable of vision, but does not commit him to an equal variety of archetypal characters who would confront him with immense difficulties of presentation.

166

After taking his risks with three prominent archetypal characters in *The Longest Journey,* Forster displays a new caution in *Howards End* and restricts himself to one such character, Mrs. Wilcox. The consequence of so limiting himself is two-fold: a greater emphasis on archetypal objects, and a more skillful deployment of other characters to reinforce and sharpen the impact of the archetypal character. To take up the latter point first: by the end of the novel Helen and Margaret Schlegel share in Mrs. Wilcox's attributes and participate fully in her significance. But because they are not themselves archetypal, they support her effect from the outside, so to speak.[3] At the same time their frequent visionary experiences help both to confer archetypal power on Mrs. Wilcox and to sustain that power throughout the narrative.

As counterpoint to the economy of one mythic character, Forster invests a cluster of archetypal objects with a vitality and complexity surpassing anything in the earlier fiction. These archetypal symbols are doubly effective by virtue of their coherence, for all lend support to and find their focus in Mrs. Wilcox.

The skill requisite to the creating of archetypal symbols and to the sustaining of them through a full-length novel cannot be overestimated. When such symbols are confined to an individual moment or scene they may be easier to handle than an archetypal character, for they do not have to be put into action or even paid attention to when they are unwanted. But when the symbols are intended to have something approaching a continuous and living presence in a long narrative, the difficulty of keeping them animated and luminously significant is greater than with a character. Howards End, with its house and tree, will give us a chance to study Forster's success in creating a highly developed and complex set of archetypal symbols.

"There is a sense" writes Kenneth Burke "in which the *word* for tree 'transcends' the thing as thoroughly as does the Platonic idea of the tree's perfect 'archetype' in heaven. It is the sense in which the name for a class of objects 'transcends' any particular member of that class."[4] Since our day-to-day language is saturated with totality *concepts* it is not surprising that we should feel something approaching unholy fascination in the presence of a physical object which embodies such a concept and so becomes a totality image. The totality image of ecstatic experience is not simply an image of the all-tree, for it takes on human significance. The tree transformed expresses the all-meaning of the all-tree. In the words of Erich Neumann: "When things, a landscape or a work of art, come alive or 'grow transparent,' this signifies that they are transformed into what we have called 'unitary reality.' What we see becomes 'symbolic' in the sense that it speaks to us in a new way, that it reveals something unknown, and that in its actual presence, just as it is, it is at the same time something entirely different: the categories of 'being' and 'meaning' coincide."[5]

Two things at least deserve comment here. First, the object is said to "come alive." You will recall Lord Raglan's dictum that the sun is worshipped only when a god has been put into it. He notes also that "to savages, as to the ancients, a god is any person or thing with power to confer life."[6] When an object comes alive, speaks to us in a new way, and reveals to us something unknown, it is in Lord Raglan's sense a god with life-giving power. It is valuable to consider the archetypal symbol in this way if for no other reason than because it shows how arbitrary is the distinction between object and person. The same god-like function may be performed by both.

The second point that deserves comment is Neumann's statement that in a symbolic object the categories of being and meaning coincide. After the event, after the apprehension of "unitary reality" has passed, we must suppose that it is possible to analyze such an occurrence and extract or decipher some part of its "meaning." If a writer uses the event without having made any effort to analyze it, we as readers will find ourselves in the same position Westcott and Stewart thought they were in when confronted by Plato's myths and in the same position Symonds thought he was in when confronted by myth generally (see Chapter 1). In other words we will be confronting the representation of a reality in which the being and the significance are one and can be expressed in no other way. Still, you cannot stop an active mind from analyzing. And analysis will almost certainly open the symbol to some degree of rational ordering and so make possible some limited discursive comment.

Indeed, so inveterate is the tendency to analyze that Forster himself, though emotionally and intuitively opposed to such activity, has probed his symbols to the degree that he knows what ideas to associate with them. Let me emphasize this phrasing, for I think it the best way to handle an unavoidable difficulty. I do not say that Forster tells us what his archetypal symbols "mean." I only say that he tells us or at least implies what ideas may appropriately be associated with them. Such a distinction is important, though not I think important enough to justify the use of elaborate and cumbersome language throughout this study. But the reader is asked to remember that when I say, for example, the tree means comradeship, I mean that the tree may appropriately be associated with the idea of comradeship.

We approach the object as archetype with these expectations: that it will have some idea or meaning associated with it, will be to a limited degree analyzable, will give us a sense of its being alive and god-like, will seem wholly significant, and will create an irreducible impression of totality and mythic unity.

Howards End

Rigidity and Chaos, these two forms of the negative are directly opposed to the creative principle, which encompasses transformation, hence not only life but also death. Across the diabolical axis of rigidity and chaos cuts the transformative axis of life and death.

—Erich Neumann

The center of our attention in *Howards End* is to be the object as archetype rather than the character as archetype. But if we are properly to understand the symbolic objects of the novel, we will have first to take some notice of Mrs. Wilcox, for every one and every thing is a fragment of her mind (p. 331). She is the most inclusive of all the symbols of totality. Knowing this, we may find it especially interesting to observe the way she is first described and the way she first breaks into the action.

Helen Schlegel writes her sister Margaret that early in the morning she saw Mrs. Wilcox walking in the garden. "Then she walked off the lawn to the meadow. . . . Trail, trail, went her long dress over the sopping grass, and she came back with her hands full of the hay that was cut yesterday . . ." (p. 4). When Mrs. Wilcox next appears, it is a moment of crisis. Helen's Aunt Juley has let Charles Wilcox know that his brother Paul and Helen are secretly in love. Helen speaks first:

"Aunt Juley . . . I—I meant to stop your coming. It isn't— it's over."

The climax was too much for Mrs. Munt. She burst into tears.

"Aunt Juley dear, don't. Don't let them know I've been so silly. It wasn't anything. Do bear up for my sake."

"Paul," cried Charles Wilcox, pulling his gloves off.

"Don't let them know. They are never to know."

"Oh, my darling Helen—"

"Paul! Paul!"

A very young man came out of the house.

"Paul, is there any truth in this?"

"I didn't—I don't—"

"Yes or no, man; plain question, plain answer. Did or didn't Miss Schlegel—"

"Charles dear," said a voice from the garden. "Charles, dear Charles, one doesn't ask plain questions. There aren't such things."

They were all silent. It was Mrs. Wilcox.

She approached just as Helen's letter had described her, trailing noiselessly over the lawn, and there was actually a wisp of hay in her hands. She seemed to belong not to the young people and their motor, but to the house, and to the tree that overshadowed it. One knew that she worshipped the past, and that the instinctive wisdom the past can alone bestow had descended upon her—that wisdom to which we give the clumsy name of aristocracy. (pp. 22–23)

Mrs. Wilcox is an Earth-Mother figure but that is not what makes her entry into the story so strangely powerful and compelling. The hush that surrounds her, the aura of timelessness and mysterious strength, creates an extraordinary effect; an effect like that of a perfectly spinning top which without moving sustains all motion.

Here we have a subdued awareness of something like a moment of ecstasy. The moment arises from the encounter with the house and tree as well as from the encounter with Mrs. Wilcox. Though the effect is naturally less extraordinary when repeated, Mrs. Wilcox creates much the same impression in later scenes. Forster allows us to see her close up but always from the outside. He gives her only a few characteristics but they are notable ones. She is consistently associated with certain objects, she moves in a slow but irresistible—almost ghost-like—way, suggesting a timeless figure, and she does not think or scheme, her effect is that of being. Her full significance can only be developed by the full novel. But from the beginning we may apprehend her as a form which contains all other symbols and is itself contained only within the totality of the novel.

Howards End has another containing symbol. It takes shape

in Helen Schlegel's visual imaginings as she listens to the third and fourth movements of Beethoven's *Fifth Symphony*. This symphony becomes her special symbol. "The music had summed up to her all that had happened or could happen in her career" (p. 36). But its significance extends beyond the limits of her own career. Indeed, Beethoven's music emerges as a symbol of the whole of life and the whole of the novel.

The third movement opens with goblins walking over the universe. They remind Helen of her affair with Paul Wilcox. Panic and emptiness! It closes in joyous splendor, reminding the reader of Helen rushing in from the hayfield at the close of the novel. The music does not, however, specifically parallel the story.[7] Rather, it defines two poles of human experience. One may feel there is splendor and poetry and love in the world; one may feel there is "no such thing as splendour or heroism in the world" (p. 34), that even love and hatred have decayed (p. 121); and like Helen one may feel now the one, now the other. Moreover, Forster's Beethoven shows no desire to assert that heroic splendor exists in any absolute sense. It exists, as does its negation, in man's experience. No other reality is insisted upon. The symphony, then, defines the scope and nature of the experiences to be encountered by the characters of *Howards End*.

If one were to ask what *Howards End* is about, the answers would probably be as varied as if one were to ask what the *Fifth Symphony* is about. The novel is about the Schlegel sisters, young ladies of independent means and cultivated taste. Of them it might be said: "the imaginative life is distinguished by the greater clearness of its perception, and the greater purity and freedom of its emotion." It is about the Wilcoxes, men of business with plenty of money and not much independence or taste. Of them it might be said: "do we not feel that the average business man would be in every way a more admirable, more respectable being if his imaginative life were not so squalid and incoherent?"[8] It is even about Leonard Bast, the clerk with one foot on the slippery first rung of the middle-class ladder, who is a displaced yeoman and so another version of the decline of the yeoman class as symbolized in the dying out of Mrs. Wilcox's family, the Howards.

From the point of view of plot, the novel is about the attempt to connect the two main families through the marriage of Margaret Schlegel and Henry Wilcox and so unite the practical competence, the expertise, and the immense energy of the Wilcoxes with the thoughtfulness, the self-analysis, and the culture of the Schlegels. Like the marriage itself, the attempt to connect the outer and the inner life moves toward ruin when it is intersected by another plot which has as its center the one-night love affair of Helen Schlegel and Leonard Bast. This plot culminates in a violent crisis and brings all the characters together in a final confrontation at Howards End.

There are many ways of indicating what the novel is about, but the most effective is to say it is about Howards End. The story begins and ends there. To Mrs. Wilcox the place is sacred. When shortly before her final illness she asks Margaret to come down to Howards End with her, a lasting bond is established between the two women. Her dying wish that Margaret should have Howards End creates a crisis for the Wilcoxes. They respond in a business-like way, for they are—however much coarsened—the true descendants of Forster's own ancestors, the Thorntons.

When the Thornton family declined and Battersea Rise, which had been their home for over one hundred years, fell vacant, "London knocked and everything vanished—vanished absolutely, and has left no ghost behind, for the Thorntons do not approve of ghosts." They do not approve of ghosts because they have "no sense whatever of the unseen."[9] So it is with the Wilcoxes. A house—even such a house as Howards End—means nothing to them. It is simply a possession and they mean to keep it. Judged from a legal or practical point of view, they may be said to have acted correctly. Mrs. Wilcox had been looking for a spiritual heir to Howards End, and a consideration of this kind cannot be muddled up with the practical business of transferring property. At least, so the Wilcoxes think. But the little fact that cannot be got round remains: they have ignored the last wish of a woman whom they had reason to value. The Schlegels would not have ignored such a wish.

Now that Mrs. Wilcox is dead, a series of coincidences bring Margaret and Henry Wilcox together. Yet after their marriage Howards End still eludes Margaret as a home. Instead it becomes the place where the furniture from Wickham Place is stored and where, on her own initiative, it is convincingly arranged by Miss Avery. And so, unknown to any of the principal characters, the house is now in readiness. Helen, who is pregnant, returns from Germany. She longs to spend one night with Margaret, surrounded by their possessions from Wickham Place. Henry refuses permission, Margaret revolts, Charles asserts himself, Leonard dies, Henry breaks down. The result, Margaret is after all to inherit Howards End and from her it is to go to Helen's son. For Margaret has drawn Henry and Helen and the child together, assisted by the benign influence of Howards End with its meadow, its house, its tree, and, overarching all, the unseen presence of Ruth Wilcox.

Within this context we may define, in a preliminary way, the symbolic import of hay, house, and tree. The hay symbolizes individual life; the house, individual life in relation to family, that is to ancestors and heirs; the wych-elm, individual life in relation to the total life of man rooted in an unknown past and branching into an unknown future.

The word *life* is prominent in these formulations. But death is everywhere implicit. Hay is dead grass, and ancestors and the whole of man's past life are dead too. At the same time we notice that death, the most inescapable of evils, is conspicuously associated with the heroic splendors of Beethoven. Its meaning for man is supremely ambiguous: "Death destroys a man: the idea of Death saves him" (p. 253). This statement, out of the mouth of Michelangelo,[10] is the key that unlocks the symbolic mysteries of hay, house, and tree, and at the same time relates them to the theme of "Only connect." Putting first things first, then, we may begin with this theme.

In his 1907 paper on Dante, Forster commented on the barrier that exists between body and soul: "Most modern thinkers realize that the barrier eludes definition. . . . and the wisest of our age, Goethe for example, and Walt Whitman, have not attempted to find it, but have assayed the more human task of harmonizing the realms that it divides."[11] Or as Margaret says in writing of the seen and unseen: "Our business is not to contrast the two, but to reconcile them" (p.

109). In Forster's scheme of things to reconcile or connect is to harmonize; and to harmonize is to attain proportion. The body of the world was created out of four elements, says Plato, "and it was harmonized by proportion, and therefore has the spirit of friendship."[12] Like Plato, Forster will arrive at friendship or comradeship as the end to be attained through proportion. But first he observes with reference to the division between body and soul, between seen and unseen: "The business man who assumes that this life is everything, and the mystic who asserts that it is nothing, fail, on this side and on that, to hit the truth." And truth is not halfway in between. Rather, it is "to be found by continuous excursions into either realm, and though proportion is the final secret, to espouse it at the outset is to insure sterility" (p. 206).

We will have a better understanding of what Forster means by proportion if we relate this statement to his later analysis of love and truth. In the passage just quoted truth means the answer or the final secret—which is proportion. In the later passage it is used more precisely. Love is the acceptance of things as they are. Truth is the yearning for things as they ought to be. Only through love, which is acceptance, can a man make useful excursions into the realm of the seen; and only through truth, which is yearning for what ought to be, can he make useful excursions into the realm of the unseen. And out of many such excursions, balancing each other, emerges proportion, the final secret. The warfare of love and truth may seem eternal, the whole visible world and all of life may rest on it, but proportion brings them together, harmonizes them, introduces the spirit of friendship or comradeship. To begin with proportion is to begin with an abstract formula. It is to begin without love or truth, without making sorties into the realms of body and soul, seen and unseen, what is and what ought to be. And so it can result only in sterility (p. 243).

For each man, the first and inescapable division is that between body and soul. Continual excursions into each realm result in that development of the inner life symbolized by the ability to say "I." The ability to say "I" is to the inner life what proportion is to the outer life. It is the final secret to be attained through prolonged and honest effort. The Wilcoxes cannot say "I." They have evaded the realities of the inner life and are hollow in the middle. They are muddled and when the crisis comes all within is panic and emptiness. The inner life of proportion which results in personal relations and the outer life of proportion which results in comradeship are equally beyond their reach. But to someone like Margaret there are "moments when the inner life actually 'pays,' when years of self-scrutiny, conducted for no ulterior motive, are suddenly of practical use. Such moments are still rare in the west; that they come at all promises a fairer future" (p. 206).

It is now apparent that Forster's terms are more precise than they may at first have seemed. Body and soul, seen and unseen, love and truth, the inner life that says "I" and the outer life of proportion can be precisely defined in relation to the theme of man's divided nature and the necessity to connect.

The theme becomes more complex and requires new terms and a new definition of love when the divided individual experiences sexual love. Then the beast and the monk emerge and it is necessary to connect them. The connection robs them of life and establishes the rainbow arch of love. Mr. Wilcox illustrates the failure to achieve such a connection, for he is beastly in his relations with Mrs. Bast and monk-like in his distrust of the flesh (pp. 196–97, 194). Beast and monk, though at odds, do not represent a real polarity. Rather they are alike in that each in its own way places value upon the flesh as such. The essential conflict here is between beast-monk whose materialistic nature degrades the flesh, and love whose spiritual nature transcends and redeems the flesh.

The half-life of the divided beast-monk is clarified by another set of terms: "Margaret greeted her lord with peculiar tenderness on the morrow. Mature as he was, she might yet be able to help him to the building of the rainbow bridge that should connect the prose in us with the passion. Without it we are meaningless fragments, half monks, half beasts, unconnected arches that have never joined into a man" (p. 196). And a little later: "Only connect! That was the whole of her sermon. Only connect the prose and the passion, and both will be exalted, and human love will be seen at its height" (p. 197). It is not particularly fruitful to parallel beast with passion and monk with prose. But observe that the missing term in beast-monk is love, while the missing term in prose-passion is poetry. Here poetry, like love, signifies the spirit's power to transform and exalt. In sexual love, the law of the spirit must triumph, the flesh must be redeemed. For the law of the flesh, if it triumphs, leaves behind it lust and shame, passion and final drabness.

Forster's basic division is between flesh and spirit. But if we extend the logic of the image in which beast and monk are robbed of life and transformed through love, it should follow in the case of the broader conflict of matter and spirit, seen and unseen, that matter will be transformed through spirit into a reality of another kind. Forster does not, of course, entertain such a possibility. The material things of the world, as Margaret so often tells us, are to be accepted. The freedom and culture of the Schlegel sisters is made possible by the islands of money upon which they stand. Ruth Wilcox makes the same point in a different way when she twice asserts that a house cannot stand without bricks and mortar (p. 81).

The flesh is the only part of material existence which Forster sees as directly subject to the spirit. In the context of the flesh, love means transformation. In other contexts it means attachment to things as they are. And always, I think, it has a third meaning. It is libido, the energy or power that impels us both to accept things as they are and to yearn for things as they ought to be, that impels us to make sorties into the realms of the seen and unseen. Love in this sense is a kind of preliminary connection which in its higher and more self-conscious form expresses itself as proportion and comradeship.

The theme of the epigraph, only connect, and the various usages of the word love are most richly illustrated in the failures and triumphs of the Schlegel sisters. In the central portion of the novel we discern a sharp contrast in their development. Helen, who has the kind of qualities Forster admires—"spontaneity, natural gaiety, recklessness"[13]—through a failure to connect, remains spiritually stagnant. The drab intellectual companion of her European stay is proof of her inner condition. Yet when she returns to England, Howards End nourishes a spectacular evolvement, a sudden opening out, like a flower, into the fresh air and sunshine of the clear spirit. In contrast, Margaret makes a steady, non-spectacular progress toward the same goal.

It is in the realm of sexual love that Helen fails to connect.

She misinterprets Wilcox prose and is willfully deluded by Paul Wilcox's momentary passion. Her later reaction of hate is inverted passion, while her devotion to Leonard Bast is founded in another misinterpretation of prose. "There's an odd notion . . . running about at the back of her brain" Margaret tells us, "that poverty is somehow 'real'" (p. 191). Helen's divided nature reveals itself in her confusion and error. But the division is apparent only in a sexual context. When she returns to Margaret's love and the strong associations of the past, intelligibility and joy triumph.

Helen's failure to establish a meaningful or durable relationship with a man is not disastrous. Human beings may have defects, limited areas of failure (Margaret, for instance, cannot love children), but they are not on that account debarred from bliss. Indeed, imperfectness, by fixing limits to the range and direction of growth, becomes an important source of individuality. Thus variety characterizes the human scene, relieving the monotony of life's daily grey. The Schlegel sisters are the best illustration of that variety, and the best assurance that in moving toward proportion the individual does not thereby move toward monotony.

Margaret, differing from her sister, shows us how love and connection can lead to a series of spiritual triumphs, each more far-reaching than its predecessor. It is true that she is modest about her accomplishments. When she visits Oniton before her marriage to Henry Wilcox, she notes that it is imperfect like herself: "Its apple-trees were stunted, its castle ruinous. It, too, had suffered in the border warfare between the Anglo-Saxon and the Kelt, between things as they are and as they ought to be" (p. 244). Nevertheless, her love for Henry Wilcox establishes a bridge, albeit a shaky one, between his worldliness and her own spiritual insight. Her love for Ruth Wilcox connects her with Howards End and from loving Howards End she comes to love the countryside and all England. And through the final secret of proportion she is able to achieve a broader vision, her "unexpected love of the island . . . connecting on this side with the joys of the flesh, on that with the inconceivable" (p. 216). Later, visiting the farm near Howards End, she perceives that "the graver sides of life, the deaths, the partings, the yearnings for love, have their deepest expression in the heart of the fields." Yet at this moment nature is filled with the happiness of light and sound and color. "It was the presence of sadness at all that surprised Margaret, and ended by giving her a feeling of completeness. In these English farms, if anywhere, one might see life steadily and see it whole, group in one vision its transitoriness and its eternal youth, connect—connect without bitterness until all men are brothers" (pp. 283–84). Margaret is more than once referred to as heroic. Here then is her final and heroic goal, and love's highest destiny—the brotherhood of man. The word for it is comradeship, a word to be considered in a later place.

The countryside has a prominent role in Margaret's vision of brotherhood. As in the previous novels, the living world of vegetable nature supports the spirit of man. But how long it may do so is now in doubt. "Under cosmopolitanism . . . we shall receive no help from the earth. Trees and meadows and mountains will only be a spectacle, and the binding force that they once exercised on character must be entrusted to Love alone. May Love be equal to the task!" (p. 275) Love here may be presumed to have its full complement of meanings.

Forster does not assert that alone love will be equal to the task since the binding force of earth is still at work. But he comes close to such an assertion by establishing death, which is meaningful in purely human terms, as the most powerful influence in strengthening the wings of love. The significance of death is enforced by two memorable passages in the novel. The first is from the scene in the Hotel at Oniton and represents, fairly directly, the thoughts that Helen tries to express in her talk with Leonard Bast:

"Death destroys a man: the idea of Death saves him." Behind the coffins and the skeletons that stay the vulgar mind lies something so immense that all that is great in us responds to it. Men of the world may recoil from the charnel-house that they will one day enter, but Love knows better. Death is his foe, but his peer, and in their age-long struggle the thews of Love have been strengthened, and his vision cleared, until there is no one who can stand against him. (p. 253)

The second passage concerns Leonard as, eight months later, he walks to Howards End:

To Leonard, intent on his private sin, there came the conviction of innate goodness elsewhere. . . . Again and again must the drums tap, and the goblins stalk over the universe before joy can be purged of the superficial. It was rather paradoxical, and arose from his sorrow. Death destroys a man, but the idea of death saves him—that is the best account of it that has yet been given. Squalor and tragedy can beckon to all that is great in us, and strengthen the wings of love. They can beckon; it is not certain that they will, for they are not love's servants. But they can beckon, and the knowledge of this incredible truth comforted him. (p. 342)

The idea of death strengthens a man's power to love and to connect because it shows him (in Helen's words) "the emptiness of Money" (p. 252), the emptiness of all things material, and it shows him that death destroys the flesh and that the destiny of the flesh is neither heroic nor splendid. Thus squalor and tragedy and death, by saving a man from exclusive fixation on material things, invite him to respond to the unseen as well as to the seen, to things of the spirit as well as things of the flesh. They beckon to his capacity for love and joy and at the same time purge his love and joy of the superficial.[14]

"Death destroys a man: the idea of Death saves him." We may now go on to see how this theme is associated with the symbols of hay, house, and tree.

The hay. Perhaps the most tantalizing passage in *Howards End* is that in which Margaret protests against the "jangle of causes and effects": "Here Leonard lay dead in the garden, from natural causes; yet life was a deep, deep river, death a blue sky, life was a house, death a wisp of hay, a flower, a tower, life and death were anything and everything, except this ordered insanity . . ." (p. 348). To take this statement literally is to compound confusion. What it says is that each of these items is an image of life-and-death. The river of life implies the death of the individual; the blue sky, image of infinity, enforces a recognition of earthbound transcience; a flower is as short-lived as it is beautiful; and a tower is reminiscent of both the ruined castle at Oniton (p. 244) and "the Six Hills, tombs of warriors, breasts of the spring" (p. 326). This passage, then, suggests the context within which we will find the meaning of the hay symbol.

Flowers, grass, and hay, the smaller flourishings of vegetable nature, are symbolically associated with the individual human life. The most decisive piece of evidence of this is to be found in Margaret's discussion with Helen about individual differences in the grey world of every day. The most important part of the discussion will be quoted later. It is noteworthy also that these images of grass and hay are never presented in their own right but always in association with one or another of the characters. Both the garden with its flowers and the meadow of hay are persistently associated with Ruth Wilcox. She knows that grass and flowers fall, cradled by the sickle of death. Her devotion to the living plant is revealed to us in the garden image; her devotion to the dead plant, in the hay image. We read: "Ruth knew no more of worldly wickedness and wisdom than did the flowers in her garden, or the grass in her field" (p. 94). More frequently we read of her connection with the hay—already illustrated from the novel's opening scenes.

In contrast we note that Margaret, except in the final scene, is always associated with grass rather than hay. For the moment we shall assert that grass stands as an image for the individual seen under the aspect of life; hay as an image for the individual seen under the aspect of death. The meaning of hay is further defined at the close of the novel.

> Helen took up a bunch of grass. She looked at the sorrel, and the red and white and yellow clover, and the quaker grass, and the daisies, and the bents that composed it. She raised it to her face.
> "Is it sweetening yet?" asked Margaret.
> "No, only withered."
> "It will sweeten to-morrow." (p. 357)[15]

This image in its structure, in the relation of its parts, directly parallels the structure of the proposition "Death destroys a man: the idea of Death saves him." Facing up to the reality of death, we find our lives sweetened and made meaningful; and we find the lives of those now dead to have freshness and value for us. This has been Ruth Wilcox's experience: "she cared about her ancestors, and let them help her" (p. 23). Her attachment to hay symbolically asserts what she could never find words to express and what she herself now stands for.

The saving power of the idea of death, already elaborated by

Helen, is defined in a somewhat different way by Margaret as she contemplates Leonard's death and the manner in which cause and effect "go jangling forward to some goal doubtless, but to none that she could imagine. At such moments the soul retires within, to float upon the bosom of a deeper stream, and has communion with the dead, and sees the world's glory not diminished, but different in kind to what she has supposed. She alters her focus until trivial things are blurred. Margaret had been tending this way all the winter. Leonard's death brought her to the goal" (pp. 350–51). We can now see why Margaret, up to this moment, has been associated only with grass and why she is able shortly after to understand that the hay will sweeten.

Another image is summed up in the hay symbol. In the course of the story many references are made to life's daily grey and to the relieving of its monotony. The passage in which Helen takes up the bunch of grass and looks at the many varieties and colors that compose it comes immediately after Margaret's little sermon on the differences planted in a single family "so that there may always be colour; sorrow perhaps, but colour in the daily grey" (p. 357). The differences arise from variety in the objects of our love; hence the hay represents not just individual man, but man in his individuality.

The hay is associated with the meadow, and a strange meadow it is. A boundary separates it from the garden, and the wych-elm stands on the boundary and leans a little over the house (p. 3). Mrs. Wilcox walks "off the lawn to the meadow" whose corner to the right Helen can "just see" (p. 4). Margaret on her first visit looks into the garden. "Farther on were hints of the meadow and a black cliff of pines. Yes, the meadow was beautiful" (p. 212). And as the novel moves to its close we see the farmer, "amid whirring blades and sweet odours of grass, encompassing with narrowing circles the sacred centre of the field" (p. 354). Here surely we catch a glimpse of the unseen. The meadow confirms Helen's plea that "the Invisible lodges against the Visible" (p. 253). And it confirms the spiritual incapacity of the Wilcoxes. Just as they cannot endure any deep emotion, so they cannot tolerate the unseen. The meadow breaks them up. Shattered and congested by hay fever, they flee the outdoors and seek refuge in the house and in the city. In contrast, Mrs. Wilcox's life was of the garden and the meadow. She was sustained by the unseen, by the spirit. The meadow continues to represent that sustaining power but now it includes Mrs. Wilcox as a part of the unseen. Before her death she says to Margaret: "I cannot show you my meadow properly except at sunrise" (p. 91), thereby implying that the things of the spirit are not subject to decay. Properly seen the meadow belongs to the light and the beginning of things, it belongs to eternal youth.

"'The field's cut!' Helen cried excitedly—'the big meadow! We've seen to the very end, and it'll be such a crop of hay as never!'" The close of the novel asserts the power and the spiritual vision of Ruth Wilcox and the sharing of that vision by the Schlegel sisters. More specifically it is a dramatic counterpart to the proposition that cultivation of the inner life "pays" and that attention to the unseen and to the significance of death "saves."

The house. The meaning of Howards End is clearly established in the early account of Ruth Wilcox, who belonged to the house and the tree, and who worshiped the past and the instinctive wisdom of the past—"that wisdom to which we give the clumsy name of aristocracy" (p. 23).

Clinging to the house is the vine which Ruth Wilcox fought to preserve and which Helen instantly loves. It is Margaret's symbol. When Charles Wilcox heard of his mother's bequest of Howards End to Margaret, he looked at the house—"the nine windows, the unprolific vine. He exclaimed, 'Schlegels again!'" (p. 101) The vine has already been described as encumbering the south wall (p. 98), precisely the word to represent the Wilcox view of Margaret. And, like Margaret, it is unprolific. In reality, of course, the vine is attached to and embraces the house. Margaret is the spiritual heir of Ruth Wilcox and of Howards End. The vine is the physical sign of her heirdom. The fact that it had been there all the time is strangely suggestive. The same is true of the fact that the furniture from Wickham Place fits perfectly into Howards End. When Helen returns from Germany it is her love of the vine and of the books and furniture from their former home that enables her, and also Margaret, to appreciate Howards End in something like the way Mrs. Wilcox had appreciated it. "'Ah, that greengage tree,' cried Helen, as if the garden was also part of their childhood" (p. 315).[16]

"Explanations and appeals had failed; they had tried for a common meeting-ground, and had only made each other unhappy. And all the time their salvation was lying round them—the past sanctifying the present; the present, with wild heart-throb, declaring that there would after all be a future, with laughter and the voices of children" (p. 315). The house gives a new dimension to the proposition that the idea of death saves, emphasizing as it does the wisdom to be gained through those now dead and the hope to be attained through those who have yet to live.

The sense of the ancestral is strengthened by the six Danish tumuli. Margaret settles that beneath the Six Hills "soldiers of the best kind lay buried. She hated war and liked soldiers—it was one of her amiable inconsistencies" (p. 209). The inconsistency is hardly surprising, since her father was a soldier. The Six Hills are Margaret's symbol. They give her a sense of an ancestral background in the vicinity of Howards End. And like Mrs. Wilcox's home, they are associated with the earth (p. 211) as well as the past, and so with the living as well as the dead. Covered with spring herbage (p. 320), they are not only tombs of warriors, but "breasts of the spring" giving promise for the future (p. 326). Margaret and Henry Wilcox sit on one of these hills when Henry, broken by the turn of events, tells her that Charles will go to jail for manslaughter. "Margaret drove her fingers through the grass. The hill beneath her moved as if it was alive" (p. 353). Mrs. Wilcox had found Howards End a continuing source of strength and insight and new life. Margaret finds the Six Hills such a source also.

At this point it will be valuable to look more closely at the idea of ancestors and the family. Forster's outlook is Greek, and may be summed up in these words of Erwin Rohde:

All cult, all prospects of a full life and future well-being . . . of the soul on its separation from the body, depends upon the holding together of the family. To the family itself the souls of its former ancestors are, in a limited sense, of course, gods—*its* gods. It can hardly be doubted that here we have the root of all belief in the future life of the soul, and we shall be tempted to subscribe to the belief . . . of those who see in such family worship of the dead one of the most primitive roots of all religious belief—older than the worship of the higher gods of the state and the community as a whole; older even than the worship of Heroes, and of the ancestors of large national groups. . . . Among the Greeks . . . this belief lived on in the shadow of the great gods and their cults, even in the midst of the tremendous increase in the power and organized influence of the state. But these larger and wider organizations cramped and hindered its development.[17]

Even the concluding sentences have ominous relevance. We see Howards End and the Six Hills pitted against the endless advance of the sprawling city, symbol of the superstate.

Yet all is not relevant. If Forster's view of family is much the same as that expressed by Rohde, and if Rohde's view is much the same as that expressed by I. A. Richards—who was the first but not the last to comment at length on this aspect of Forster's work[18]—what are we to make of the fact that Margaret's "ancestors" are ancient Danish soldiers who are not her ancestors at all, and what of the further fact that Howards End is not inherited by a descendant of Mrs. Wilcox, not even inherited by a direct descendant of her spiritual heir, Margaret Schlegel, but rather is inherited by the son of Leonard Bast and Helen Schlegel? I suggest that these two facts make untenable the usual account of Forster's attitude to family. That account suggests that Forster's interest in ancestors and heirs has its basis in genetic inheritance. The truth seems rather to be that he values ancestors because they symbolize the one thing that can give stability, the collective and universal past; and he values children because they symbolize a potential hope and a potential wholeness greater than we know at present. Forster's interest in the living continuity represented by ancestors and descendants is a general rather than a particular interest, it is universal rather than individual. That is why the same novel can encompass ancestor worship, child glorification, and the admirable Margaret Schlegel. That is why it is not supremely important who fathers Helen's child, but is supremely important that there be a child.

Because Forster's values are not restricted to the genetic, his emphasis falls not on the "family tree" but on the house and on the wych-elm which is a universal tree and is the genius of the *place*.[19] This emphasis is confirmed in many ways. Miss Avery, who has been a friend of the Howards, is described as "the heart of the house." And the heart of the house beats "faintly at first," suggesting Mrs. Wilcox, "then loudly, martially," suggesting Margaret. On this, Margaret's first entry into Howards End, a "noise as of drums seemed to deafen her." The drums marked the transition in Beethoven's *Fifth Symphony;* now Miss Avery, descending the stairs, marks the transition in the house—from Ruth Wilcox to Margaret Schlegel (p. 213). The birth of Helen's child also confirms the importance of the house. There are nine windows in the front of Howards End. They are arranged in three-above-three fashion and each looks from a room. The heir to Howards End is "born in the central room of the nine" (p. 359).

The final meaning and beauty of Howards End as a symbol is to be discovered in its connection with Wickham Place. At the beginning of Chapter 31 Forster, in one of his finest passages of subdued poetry, describes the death and destruction of Wickham Place, the home of the Schlegel family for thirty years. Its death is compared to that of a person from whom "the spirit slips before the body perishes." The phrasing reminds the reader of Ruth Wilcox. During Margaret's visit to her shortly before her final illness, she conveys a haunting impression of dissolution and of withdrawal into the shadows. There was a long pause in their conversation—"a pause that was somehow akin to the flicker of the fire, the quiver of the reading-lamp upon their hands, the white blur from the window; a pause of shifting and eternal shadows" (p. 76). The reader is also reminded that Mrs. Wilcox has spent the thirty years of her married life at Howards End. The description of Wickham Place as "void of emotion, and scarcely hallowed by the memories of thirty years of happiness" (p. 271), suggests the attitude of the Wilcox family to Howards End and to Ruth Wilcox herself.

If the demolition of Wickham Place parallels the physical dissolution of Ruth Wilcox, then Wickham Place living may be said to have the same value for Margaret as Ruth Wilcox living, while Howards End has the same value for Margaret as Ruth Wilcox dead. This may be put in another way: Wickham Place is to Howards End as grass is to hay. Wickham Place was a house of life and happiness, but as the rented home of an alien adventurer it was, like the flesh, a temporary habitation. The past is concentrated in the movables, the sword, the books, the furniture, which are finally established at Howards End. It is as though this house in the country had been the home of the Schlegel sisters for all their lives, as though Wickham Place, through death and the vision that Ruth Wilcox enforces, had been transformed (sweetened) and had taken to itself a new name and habitation.[20]

But this is only half the truth. The idea of salvation through death or of life through death is paradoxical. Likewise the image of houses is paradoxical. Grass because it is alive is subject to destruction, it is in a state of dying; whereas hay, once it has withered and sweetened, has passed beyond destruction and has a new and permanent value, it is in a state of living. These same descriptions can be applied to Wickham Place and Howards End—but only *after* death and the transformation which it brings has touched Howards End and given it permanent life. In the early part of the novel this has not happened or at least it has not happened for Margaret and Helen. We first see Howards End in the summer haying season, that is to say, at the beginning of harvest time. But our strongest impression, though largely an imaginative one, is associated with Mrs. Wilcox's invitation to Margaret to come and see her house and meadow. It is very late in the fall and Mrs. Wilcox is dying. Here we see Howards End as autumnal and under the aspect of death.

This view is quite transformed when Margaret first comes to the place—it is the moment of her vision of brotherhood—and finds Miss Avery has unpacked the books and arranged the furniture. Now the hedge is "a half-painted picture which would be finished in a few days." Now "Spring has come, clad in no classical garb, yet fairer than all springs" (p. 284). The chapter describing Margaret's next visit to Howards End—Henry has set a trap for Helen—opens this way:

One speaks of the moods of spring, but the days that are her true children have only one mood: they are all full of the rising and dropping of winds, and the whistling of birds. New flowers may come out, the green embroidery of the hedges increase, but the same heaven broods overhead, soft, thick, and blue, the same figures, seen and unseen, are wandering by coppice and meadow. The morning that Maragret had spent with Miss Avery, and the afternoon she set out to entrap Helen, were the scales of a single balance. Time might never have moved, rain never have fallen, and man alone, with his schemes and ailments, was troubling Nature until he saw her through a veil of tears. (p. 301)

Howards End now exists for Margaret and Helen under the permanent aspect of spring. Like the hay and like Mrs. Wilcox it is seen as unalterable in its value and unchanging in its living reality. For this reason it is appropriate that Margaret does not go with Mrs. Wilcox to see Howards End in its autumnal aspect. And it is appropriate that Mrs. Wilcox is connected with Wickham Place, that the living but temporary house which must suffer destruction should offer a parallel to the mortal woman who must die. Wickham Place, says Helen in retrospect, "was a grave" (p. 317).

Grass and flowers, the life and gaiety of a rented house, all have within them the seed of the death that destroys through time and change and flux. But hay and the house and property of Howards End have incorporated death and mastered it. They have passed through death into a condition of permanence and eternal promise. The concept of salvation through the idea of death has been broadened and enriched by the house image which is a physical symbol of the continuity between past and future generations. And participating in that continuity, the individual is for ever the point of juncture through which death and the past are transformed into new life and the future. That is why the idea of the moment, of "now," is so important, and why this idea is linked with the wych-elm, the most universal of all the symbols.

The tree: "every westerly gale might blow the wych-elm down and bring the end of all things" (p. 355). Here then is the Tree of Life. It is under this tree that Helen and Paul Wilcox kiss. It is under it that Helen and Margaret find peace when Helen returns, carrying Leonard Bast's child. Their conversation at this time develops the implications of one of the minor aspects of the tree but one of its most fascinating, namely the pigs' teeth in its bark.[21] Helen has been speaking of her night with Leonard:

> "Oh, Meg, the little that is known about these things!"
> She laid her face against the tree.
> "The little, too, that is known about growth! Both times it was loneliness, and the night, and panic afterwards. Did Leonard grow out of Paul?"
> Margaret did not speak for a moment. So tired was she that her attention had actually wandered to the teeth—the teeth that had been thrust into the tree's bark to medicate it. From where she sat she could see them gleam. She had been trying to count them. "Leonard is a better growth than madness," she said. "I was afraid that you would react against Paul until you went over the verge." (pp. 330–31)

The tree endures the injury of the teeth, absorbing them into its growth. According to legend, the teeth have a medicinal effect. Similarly, Helen has endured the injury of her brief moment with Paul, and through Leonard she has been able to escape negative reaction and to incorporate the injury into her life. This incorporation, as the further course of the story shows, has its medicinal or beneficent effect. And this not simply psychologically or spiritually, but also physically. As Leonard grows out of Paul, so the unborn child grows out of Leonard. Helen, like the tree and like life itself, embodies the alien and the injurious and transforms them to beauty and promise.

The power of the wych-elm to absorb and transmute the incidental or individual injury strengthens our impression that the significance of the tree is vast and universal. Forster confirms this impression by his statement that the tree is "symbolical," it is "the genius of the house."[22] The genius of a man is his psyche or other self or spirit, which sustains his life. Similarly, the genius of a place is the spirit which sustains the life of the place—precisely the significance Forster attributes to the wych-elm at Howards End.

The tree, like much else about Howards End, comes very directly from Forster's personal experience. Writing many years later of his childhood and his mother, he says: "The truth is that she and I had fallen in love with our Hertfordshire home and did not want to leave it. . . . The garden, the overhanging wych elm, the sloping meadow, the great view to the west, the cliff of fir trees to the north, the adjacent farm through the high tangled hedge of wild roses were all utilised by me in *Howards End,* and the interior is in the novel too."[23] These words, which reach back through more than sixty years of Forster's experience, are charged with a sense of ecstasy. The same sense of ecstasy gets into the novel where it is more subdued and diffused so that without the sounding of trumpets or the banging of drums it touches everything to life at Howards End. In the process the wych-elm—far from conveying an abstract conception of Life—is transformed and expresses the sense of a living totality.

A great tree is both organic and enduring, for in its living it outlives the generations of man. Its development as a traditional life symbol is a reflection of the natural inclination of the image. It is not surprising that Forster personally encountered such a tree and that he came to apprehend it as a life symbol. Nor is it surprising that his conception of the wych-elm was enriched by tradition. I will restrict myself to three possible examples of such enrichment. From his friend Syed Ross Masood he may have learned that in India the "tree, with its spreading branches and leaves, is the Universe itself." In editing the *Aeneid* he may have been impressed by Virgil's ancient oak cleaving to the rocks, "and as high as it shoots up to the top in the ethereal regions, so deep it descends with its root toward Tartarus." And almost certainly he was influenced by the image in Lowes Dickinson's Sonnet XXV:

> Thou knowest, love, of love's immortal tree
> Strength in the root and tenderness the flower,
> And more luxuriant sweet the bloom will be
> The deeper drawn from elemental power.[24]

Forster ignores the heroic aspect of the symbol. Virgil relates his mighty oak to the unmoved heroic mind, and Dickinson in a letter refers to his sonnet in connection with Wagner's heroic love.[25] Forster says that Howards End is English and that the wych-elm is an English tree. It is "neither warrior, nor lover, nor god; in none of these rôles do the English excel." Rather its special attributes are comradeship and the peace of the moment.

"It was a comrade, bending over the house, strength and

adventure in its roots, but in its utmost fingers tenderness, and the girth, that a dozen men could not have spanned, became in the end evanescent, till pale bud clusters seemed to float in the air. It was a comrade. House and tree transcended any similes of sex. . . . to compare either to man, to woman, always dwarfed the vision. Yet they kept within limits of the human" (p. 218). With this compare Margaret's visit to Miss Avery's farm home, which like the surrounding country gives promise of comradeship and the brotherhood of man. Comradeship is the highest and most universal form of human love.

The second meaning of the wych-elm as a symbol is established in the scene between Helen and Margaret during their first evening at Howards End. They are sitting under the tree.

> The present flowed by them like a stream. The tree rustled. It had made music before they were born, and would continue after their deaths, but its song was of the moment. The moment had passed. The tree rustled again. Their senses were sharpened, and they seemed to apprehend life. Life passed. The tree rustled again.
> "Sleep now," said Margaret.
> The peace of the country was entering into her. It has no commerce with memory, and little with hope. . . . It is the peace of the present, which passes understanding. Its murmur came "now," and "now" once more as they trod the gravel, and "now," as the moonlight fell upon their father's sword. (pp. 332–33)

The sisters can apprehend life and know the peace of the present because in their relations they have achieved comradeship and, consequently, are secure in the knowledge that their lives at this moment are contained in a meaningful, that is to say connected, oneness of human life stretching unbrokenly from past to future. Like Stephen Wonham, they guard the paths between the dead who have evoked them and the unborn whom they will evoke. They are the point, the juncture, the living "now" wherein the past lodges against the future. And from such an awareness comes the full acceptance of the moment that is always the present. The wych-elm encompasses all human life. It symbolizes general salvation or comradeship and individual salvation or the peace of the moment. Both are implicit in the idea of death and in the strength of love.

Hay, house, and tree: these great archetypal symbols—life-giving, wholly significant, conveying a sense of totality—are not the result of one or two great moments of ecstatic apprehension but arise from a continuing series of less intense visionary insights. The extraordinary sense of aliveness and wholeness does not adhere to these moments of insight or to the characters who experience them; rather the nouminous quality attaches itself to and remains permanently with the objects. Thus liberated, the power and significance of the symbols can be freely deployed to strengthen and expand the role of Mrs. Wilcox. Such is their destiny, to find unity in her and her love for Howards End.

Mrs. Wilcox is a Great Mother figure. In her highly developed state the Great Mother has two forms or aspects which are often symbolized as separate persons, but in Mrs. Wilcox they are combined. The simpler of the two forms is that of the Earth-Mother or Demeter. She presides over birth and death and all growth and decay. Mrs. Wilcox in her garden and in her devotion to grass and flowers assumes the role of Demeter.

As well as being the source of life, the Great Mother is the source of transformation. At the level of the earth and the womb her power of transformation is both obvious and mysterious. At a higher level—the level that best defines the role of Mrs. Wilcox—her power of transformation is spiritual and encompasses the highest wisdom. Her spirituality is stressed when we speak of the anima (of which more will be said in a moment), her wisdom when we speak of Sophia, the most transcendent of all archetypal feminine figures. Mrs. Wilcox in her meadow and in her devotion to hay assumes the role of Sophia.[26]

At Howards End the tree bends over and sometimes enshadows the house. At other times the house enshadows the tree. But during the night that Helen and Margaret slept at Howards End after hearing the whisper of "now" in the rustling leaves, the house and tree under the moon's light "disentangled, and were clear for a few moments at midnight. Margaret awoke and looked into the garden. How incomprehensible that Leonard Bast should have won her this night of peace! Was he also part of Mrs. Wilcox's mind?" (p. 333) The reader's answer will be affirmative. Leonard sought what Mrs. Wilcox had found, "a real home" (p. 151). Leonard, whom she never knew, is included. Ruth Wilcox's mind is able to connect—"connect without bitterness until all men are brothers." Her symbols are the house and the tree, which between them signify her inclusiveness. The wych-elm by its organic nature enforces her role as Earth-Mother; the house, symbolic of the ancestral wisdom of the past and the joyous promise of the future, her role as Sophia. The two roles complement and support each other. For a moment, at the witching hour, Margaret has an insight into their dual nature.

The wych-elm kept within limits of the human. So does Ruth Wilcox in her Demeter aspect. Otherworldliness is no more than an echo. References to life beyond the grave are attributed to a character or, if Forster's own, are poetically ambiguous. Consider the following: Margaret "knew that out of Nature's device we have built a magic that will win us immortality. . . . We are evolving, in ways that Science cannot measure, to ends that Theology dares not contemplate. 'Men did produce one jewel,' the gods will say, and, saying, will give us immortality. Margaret knew all this . . ." (pp. 254–55). And Forster knows it too. But he is not saying that man will gain immortality in another world or, literally speaking, in this world. Love will win us immortality. When all men are brothers, the individual man will live for ever in the connected continuity of mankind. The "one jewel" may refer to Jesus, not as redeemer of a fallen world, not as dying god, but as a man of love who, like Ruth Wilcox, reveals the promise of human brotherhood.

The death of Ruth Wilcox helped Margaret to see "a little more clearly than hitherto what a human being is, and to what he may aspire. Truer relationships gleamed. Perhaps the last word would be hope—hope even on this side of the grave" (pp. 108–9). Later as Margaret contemplated Howards End and the tree which is a comrade, she understood that their "message was not of eternity, but of hope on this side of the grave. As she stood in the one, gazing at the other, truer relationship had gleamed" (p. 218).

In addition to her role as Demeter, Ruth Wilcox is an anima figure, the feminine image of transformation which in its most transcendant form appears as Sophia. The anima, in keeping with its spiritualized and idealized character, has usually an odd relationship to time and frequently appears as immortal or outside time. Mrs. Wilcox alive is "this shadowy woman" who asks once and will never ask again (p. 89). She is a figure in long trailing skirts who moves slowly, almost automatically, and certainly irresistibly—toward what? And death places her image forever beyond time. Of the dead Forster has written: "their personal yearnings are stilled and so they can help us, as the living cannot; their hatreds and fears are over, their lust for possessions quelled. . . ."[27] And of Mrs. Wilcox he writes: "To her everything was in proportion now . . ." (p. 257). Proportion is the final secret of the inner life that says "I" and the final secret of the outer life that achieves comradeship; it is the establishing of harmony between love, our attachment to things as they are, and truth, our passion for things as they ought to be. Proportion is the union of Demeter and Sophia. Margaret says to her sister: "I feel that you and I and Henry are only fragments of that woman's mind. She knows everything. She is everything. She is the house, and the tree that leans over it. People have their own deaths as well as their own lives, and even if there is nothing beyond death, we shall differ in our nothingness" (p. 331).

Through Mrs. Wilcox all the polarities are reconciled: grass and hay, tree and house, body and soul, matter and spirit, Wickham Place and Howards End, love and truth, Demeter and Sophia. All the polarities are reconciled except one. The city of London is not included in the vision of England, for it negates every value that Howards End and Mrs. Wilcox stand for.

London is a realm of chaos and greyness. That is its insistent image. But on one occasion it is seen in the image of hell. Margaret is returning from her shopping expedition with Mrs. Wilcox and is feeling desolate after refusing the invitation to see Howards End. The exceptional nature of the imagery here is intended to suggest—through Margaret—what London and its way of life mean to Mrs. Wilcox. "The city seemed Satanic, the narrow streets oppressing like the galleries of a mine." It was not the fog that harmed, but a "darkening of the spirit which fell back upon itself, to find a more grievous darkness within." Margaret sees Mrs. Wilcox passing through the glass doors of the lift and, imprisoned, going up heavenward. "And into what a

heaven—a vault as of hell, sooty black, from which soots descended!"
When Margaret rushes to the station to join Mrs. Wilcox in her
expedition to the country, we are told that "the clock of King's Cross
swung into sight, a second moon in that infernal sky" (pp. 89-90).

The clock of King's Cross has already appeared at the beginning of the novel and the difference between Margaret's view of it
then and her view of it now confirms that in the present case the
vision reflects the experience of Mrs. Wilcox. Her own vision is of
railway terminals as gates to sunshine and the unknown (p. 12). "To
Margaret . . . King's Cross had always suggested Infinity. . . . Those
two great arches, colourless, indifferent, shouldering between them
an unlovely clock, were fit portals for some eternal adventure . . ."
(p. 13).

The adventure will at last take Margaret to Howards End.
And Howards End is private and personal and makes possible the
experience of the unseen. "It is private life that holds out the mirror
to infinity; personal intercourse, and that alone, that ever hints at a
personality beyond our daily vision" (p. 86). On the other hand the
city is public and offers a false infinity. When Helen, back from Germany, refuses to meet Margaret and instead fades into London's vast
indifference, Margaret has a true and desolating vision: "The mask
fell off the city, and she saw it for what it really is—a caricature of
infinity. The familiar barriers, the streets along which she moved, the
houses between which she had made her little journeys for so many
years, became negligible suddenly. Helen seemed one with grimy trees
and the traffic and the slowly-flowing slabs of mud. She had accomplished a hideous act of renunciation and returned to the One" (p.
296).

The One is characterized by flux, "eternal formlessness; all
the qualities, good, bad, and indifferent, streaming away—streaming, streaming for ever" (p. 193); and by greyness, "the grey tides of
London" which rise and fall in continual flux (p. 113). Nothing escapes. Even Wickham Place in its quiet backwater falls before the tide
and is "spilt . . . back into the grey" (p. 721). One visualizes London
"as a tract of quivering grey." It lies beyond humanity. "It lies beyond
everything" (p. 114).

One of the committed denizens of this grey realm, one of the kings of chaos,[28] is Henry Wilcox. He has suffered a characteristic fate of the successful man. His conscious mind has lost touch with the emotional, intuitive, and unconscious resources of his nature. The result is isolation, and "Isolation means death."[29] Its outer manifestation is rigidity; its inner manifestation, chaos.

Rigidity is unflagging, unthoughtout, hence meaningless, devotion to the norms of society. "Henry treated a marriage like a funeral, item by item, never raising his eyes to the whole, and 'Death, where is thy sting? Love, where is thy victory?' one would exclaim at the close" (p. 232). Were he to raise his eyes to the whole, the result would be panic and emptiness. For behind rigidity lies chaos. Henry Wilcox has lost the capacity for growth and transformation. When he cannot fall back on conventional formulas he collapses into panic and emptiness. Then begins the process of evasion and muddle until reality is reduced to a kind of grey porridge. "Outwardly he was cheerful, reliable, and brave; but within, all had reverted to chaos . . ." (p. 197).

In this reversion to chaos he is one with the condition of the great city which lies beyond humanity. We know who is responsible for this condition and we know that it spreads far beyond London. Henry Wilcox did indeed buy a house at Oniton. "But the Wilcoxes have no part in the place, nor in any place. It is not their names that recur in the parish register. It is not their ghosts that sigh among the alders at evening. They have swept into the valley and swept out of it, leaving a little dust[30] and a little money behind" (p. 264). Because the Wilcoxes have no part in any place they make no distinctions. And because they make no distinctions, they are "levelling all the world into what they call common sense" (p. 252). The threat is summed up by Helen: "London is only part of something else, I'm afraid. Life's going to be melted down, all over the world" (p. 358).

Though this insight is fearful and oppressive, it is not the controlling vision of the novel. Margaret recognizes that "either some very dear person or some very dear place seems necessary to relieve life's daily grey, and to show that it is grey" (p. 154). Her desire for personal attachment is fulfilled *through* Mrs. Wilcox who, like a great wave, "flowed into her life and ebbed out of it for ever. . . . the wave had strewn at her feet fragments torn from the unknown. . . . Her friend had vanished in agony, but not, she believed, in degradation. Her withdrawal had hinted at other things besides disease and pain" (p. 108). The things hinted at, truer relationships, hope this side of the grave, love of England, all come to Margaret during the course of the story.

For Howards End remains—that is the great fact. There Margaret forgets the phantom of bigness with its continual flux as she recaptures "the sense of space, which is the basis of all earthly beauty." Starting from Howards End, she awakes to unexpected love of the whole island (p. 216). The whole island is alive, for like Howards End it is still a part of nature. Along the entire south coast the rising tides pressed inland "and over the immense displacement the sun presided. . . . England was alive, throbbing through all her estuaries, crying for joy through the mouths of all her gulls, and the north wind, with contrary motion, blew stronger against her rising seas" (pp. 185–86).

In this ecstatic vision of a land embraced by the immense displacement of the tides the vast metropolis of London has no part. The city with its quivering grey reaches is the hell which cannot be included for it is a hideous amorphous monster with a mindless drive to devour the whole island.

Some readers and critics think that, because London and what it stands for cannot be included, the novel is a failure and, in particular, that the happy ending is faked. This way of thinking about the novel ignores two important facts. The first fact is that the terrible monster, the dragon of myth and legend, is never finally destroyed, though it is frequently defeated. Like the goblins of Beethoven's symphony, it rises up again and again, and must be contended with over and over. Psychologically this is a true perception. It is naive to think the goblins can be tidied out of existence. The second fact is that comedy expresses the triumph of light over darkness. Again it is Beethoven's symphony which gives us the best insight into the novel's intention and achievement. For here, more cogently than anywhere else in his fiction, Forster speaks about himself as artist.

Our equation reads: let Beethoven be Forster. After the goblins had twice insinuated their message of despair, Beethoven took them in hand. "He appeared in person. . . . he blew with his mouth and they were scattered!" But Beethoven knew the goblins were real and "might return—and they did!" Thus Beethoven's wisdom is affirmed. After describing the reappearance of the goblins, Forster begins the next paragraph emphatically: "Beethoven chose to make all right in the end" (p. 35). Here then is our image of the personal artist —of the narrator who stands openly at the center of his narrative— personal not to the end that he may indulge in egoistic exhibitionism, but that he may manipulate and comment on his creation, making of it a truthful and meaningful representation of life. For this reason we can trust Forster even though we may disagree with him.

It was also his hope that we could trust him for another reason:

> Beethoven chose to make all right in the end. He built the ramparts up. He blew with his mouth for the second time, and again the goblins were scattered. He brought back the gusts of splendour, the heroism, the youth, the magnificence of life and of death, and, amid vast roarings of a superhuman joy, he led his Fifth Symphony to its conclusion. But the goblins were there. They could return. He had said so bravely, and that is why one can trust Beethoven when he says other things (pp. 35–36).

The novel, like the symphony, ends in joyous splendor—and for the same reason. Forster chooses to make all right in the end. But the goblins are there. Panic and emptiness, squalor and tragedy—they may return, indeed, they will. And they have a place in the splendor and triumph.

Forster many years later notes his conviction that in the *Fifth Symphony* and the other works in C minor Beethoven "is engaged in the pursuit of something outside sound—something which has fused the sinister and the triumphant."[31] In his last two novels, Forster sought an effect not unlike this. His words remind us of Elizabeth Bowen's account of the sense of evil in his novels, "the sense of conscious life's being built up over a somehow august vault of horror." This is the sinister echo of panic and emptiness which lies behind the triumphant joy of the final scene of *Howards End*. The happy ending is a fact of comedy, and its permanence is enforced by art. But when the artist has said the thing that is true, he has earned our confidence. Beethoven and his symphony symbolize not simply Forster and his novel but symbolize as well the trust we may place in both.

Everything has within it an indication of its possible plenitude. An open and noble soul will feel the ambition to perfect it, to help it, so that it may reach this plenitude. This is love—the love for the perfection of the beloved object.

—Ortega y Gasset, *Meditations on Quixote*

Such love is aspired to by Professor Godbole, and by Forster himself. What I wonder is, may it not be aspired to by the literary critic? The willing suspension of disbelief is a minimal and grudging concession. Having made it and having found the writer worthy, may we not expect the critic to help the writer and his reader to reach this possible plenitude? The critic is not asked to gloss over defects or to glorify beyond reason; but when that which is admirable in a writer's work is found to predominate, he is asked to look to its perfection, to discover through love and in face of all its defects how its object was perfection and how, in its less than perfect state, that perfection is none the less adumbrated. It seems to me this is the least one can do for a writer whose considerable achievement is beyond dispute and whose love for the perfection of the beloved object has been unfailing. In Forster's own words, "I would not suggest that our comprehension of the fine arts is or should be of a nature of a mystic union. But, as in mysticism, we enter an unusual state, and we can only enter it through love."

6
Novel as Archetype

The archetype or image of totality has been approached in a number of different ways in the preceding chapters. I propose now to take these ways of approach and apply them to a single work, *A Passage to India,* and to a single episode, the trial scene. The discussion is intended to provide a recapitulation of earlier approaches and at the same time an assessment of the ways *A Passage to India* differs from the four earlier romances. It is intended also to introduce the conception of the novel as archetype, a conception which will serve as the basis for our subsequent analysis of the whole novel.

A brief review of the story's pattern of development may help put the trial scene in perspective. The novel is composed of three sections: "Mosque" serves as prelude, touching lightly upon serious issues; "Caves" represents a physical and spiritual wasteland; "Temple" offers escape from the wasteland and promise of spiritual achievement. This structure may be viewed as symbolic of three stages in the spiritual history of the individual and of mankind.

The first stage is one of superficial optimism. The shallow arcades of the mosque, the verbal gymnastics of the ninety-nine names of God, the narrowness of Christianity, and Mrs. Moore's simple-minded belief in oneness with the universe, all these betoken man's immaturity, his blindness to the strenuous realities of the human situation. Our central image is the mosque, symbolic of the religion that "doesn't carry us far through the complexities of matter and spirit" (p. 287). Our representative human being is Aziz who, through all his experience, remains both young in heart and unenlightened in spirit.

The second stage is one of disillusionment. Earth is a wasteland, God is absent, and every meaning and value is lost in nightmarish mumbo-jumbo. The human wasteland is reflected in the soullessness of the British officials, the debilitating rationalism of Cyril Fielding and Adela Quested, and in the futility and unreality of Aziz's trial. Both wastelands, the human and the physical, are crystallized in the image of the Marabar. Next in importance to the Marabar is Mrs. Moore, who is aware of its implications and is plunged into a "double" disillusionment.

The third stage is one of qualified spiritual achievement. The physical and human wasteland fades into the background and God is no longer totally absent. Temple as religious image and Godbole as human image indicate a hope for man in his quest for the unattainable.

If we wish to look at these three stages—represented by Aziz, Mrs. Moore, and Godbole—as phases in the development of one person, it is to Mrs. Moore we must turn for our example. In the beginning she and Aziz are alike in their spiritual naivety and optimism. The great charm of the scene in the mosque when they first meet is the charm of two children discovering each other in an enchanted place. For Mrs. Moore, the discovery helps confirm her feeling of oneness with the universe. Then the Marabar strikes and hope, human and divine, is shattered. Finally in "Temple" Mrs. Moore, in part through the spiritual force of Godbole, attains to oneness with the universe.

In approaching the trial scene itself, we may begin with the ideas discussed in Chapter 1, taking as our starting point the summary of those ideas as they related to Forster. I wrote that he agreed with the students of myth on essentials: on the oneness of man and universal nature, on the importance of a deeper self and its close ties with a higher self, on the necessity of myth to convey the paradox of man's unchanging yet evolving nature, and on the continuing value of life-oriented art as the vehicle of new insights and new myths. These ideas will now be taken up in order.

The oneness of man and universal nature. It is here that *A Passage to India* contrasts most sharply with the earlier fiction. The novel is set in India, a land reflecting admirably all the world and all its peoples. "Perhaps," says Forster, the word of doubt signifying the uncertain comprehension of Fielding and Adela Quested—"Perhaps the hundred Indias which fuss and squabble so tiresomely are one, and the universe they mirror is one" (p. 274). The extraordinary character of this mirrored universe can most clearly be shown by means of a comparison. In *Howards End,* Forster takes as his theme the conflict of matter and spirit. But the earth of growing things that might logically be viewed as a part of the material universe is represented as an exception. It still exercises a binding force on the character of man. This idea, which has meant so much to Forster in the past, is entirely rejected in *A Passage to India.* Earth becomes the image now for a dead universe of matter. Earth becomes the Marabar Hills: "flesh of the sun's flesh," "older than anything in the world," "older than all spirit" (pp. 129-30). Some bits of life—a tank, trees, and plants—appear in the midst of the humps and ravines. But the tank is reduced to a puddle (p. 153), and the little plants are shrivelled to ashes by the boiling heat of the sun (p. 157). The Marabar is a universe of physical death.

India, however, has other landscapes. The countryside at Mau, where the great Hindu festival of "Temple" takes place, offers lush green jungle, an overflowing tank, and radiant skies. Yet in comparison with the religious festival and the little dramas of human interest, this scenery seems oddly unimpressive. The following passage, referring to Aziz, may help us to understand the reason: "the great Mau tank . . . lay exposed beneath him to its remotest curve. Reflecting the evening clouds, it filled the netherworld with an equal splendour, so that earth and sky leant toward one another, about to clash in ecstasy. He spat, cynical again, more cynical than before. For in the centre of the burnished circle a small black blot was advancing—the Guest House boat" (pp. 318-19). In earlier novels the beauty and power of the earth-sky image would not have been canceled out by emotions arising from the human situation. A little later we find an outright statement of Forster's attitude. Aziz has been speaking of the day when India will free herself from the English: "He paused, and the scenery, though it smiled, fell like a gravestone on any human hope" (p. 334). Clearly, man's salvation is not to be found in nature. Indeed, Forster, having once believed in the power of earth to sustain man's life and spirit—a theme that runs through all his earlier fiction—now seriously accepts the inverse proposition that man must sustain and give life to the earth. The physical universe becomes part of man's spiritual burden. And like the universe of T. S. Eliot's poem, its characteristic aspect is that of a wasteland.

The wasteland also invades man's sense of the beautiful, robbing him of the grace and dignity and formality of art. In India one retreats "from the source of life, the treacherous sun, and no poetry adorns it because disillusionment cannot be beautiful. Men yearn for poetry though they may not confess it; they desire that joy shall be graceful and sorrow august and infinity have a form, and India fails to accommodate them" (p. 219). India also fails to accommodate architecture. Fielding, visiting Europe, is staggered by the contrast between Venice, where harmony and reasonable form prevail, and that monstrous and extraordinary land where all is muddle (p. 293). In India even religious ritual—as ritual—fails to achieve beauty. The festival of Gokul Ashtami is a muddle, "a frustration of reason and form" (p. 297).

Deprived of nature's support and art's solace, the Indian must create in his own person a microcosm of order and beauty: "when the Nawab Bahadur stretched out his hand for food or Nureddin applauded a song, something beautiful had been accomplished which needed no development" (p. 261). In such manner unaccommodated man is driven to rely wholly on his own spiritual resources.

Forster now understands that earth's power to sustain is a power given to it by man. And he understands that the oneness of man and nature is to be interpreted in two opposing ways. Man may return to mindless matter and thereby become one with a material universe which insofar as it has life at all has life ruled over by death. Or man may through his own mind and spirit give significance and human reality to the universe around him. To do so he must be outgoing and must love that which is not himself. Put this way the difference in outlook between the earlier novels and *A Passage to India* is not so great as it at first seemed. The awareness of one universe and the experience of oneness with that universe have become ideals more difficult to attain than they were in the past, but they remain the central preoccupation of the fiction.

Adela Quested has been shattered by her confrontation with the Marabar. With a school-mistressy manner, a determination to acquire knowledge, and a tendency now and then to take a note, she has moved through India without knowing love for either the place or its people. The Marabar caves would be another such experience. How could they be otherwise when she was so preoccupied with her own little affairs and in particular with her prospective marriage to Ronny Heaslop? But something about the Marabar, something about the way it seemed to epitomize the futility and emptiness and deathlike materiality of the whole universe broke through the retaining wall and into the shallow reservoir of her common-sense mind. Because she has been thinking about love (she does not love Ronny) and marriage (has Aziz more than one wife?), this psychic disaster expresses itself as an hysterical delusion that she has been assaulted. The form of the delusion signifies that her extreme self-preoccupation engulfs both mind and body.

Mrs. Moore is the only person Adela loves. And in all the troubles that follow the episode in the cave, Mrs. Moore is the only one who seems to do her any good. Mrs. Moore is herself in a state of despair and refuses to help anyone, but Adela's feelings toward her remain unchanged. When Mrs. Moore's name is mentioned at the trial and is carried through the court by waves of emotion and is caught up by the crowd outside who turn it into a chant for a Hindu goddess, Esmiss Esmoor, Adela remembers her love and is taken out of herself.

> She didn't think what had happened, or even remember in the or-
> dinary way of memory, but she returned to the Marabar Hills, and
> spoke from them across a sort of darkness to Mr. McBryde. The fatal
> day recurred, in every detail, but now she was of it and not of it at
> the same time, and this double relation gave it indescribable splen-

dour. Why had she thought the expedition 'dull'? Now the sun rose
again, the elephant waited, the pale masses of the rock flowed round
her. . . .

> Her vision was of several caves. She saw herself in one, and
> she was also outside it, watching its entrance, for Aziz to pass in.
> She failed to locate him. (pp. 236–38)

This moment has been foreshadowed early in the novel when Adela
speaks of Ronny Heaslop at the same time as she contemplates the
Marabar Hills: "How lovely they suddenly were! But she couldn't
touch them. In front, like a shutter, fell a vision of her married life"
(p. 50). Her failure to love Ronny and her spiritual dishonesty in pre-
tending that she may love him isolate her and cut her off from the
physical universe. At the trial, love for Mrs. Moore takes her outside
herself and enables her to see herself in relation to all else instead of
seeing all else in relation to herself. For a moment she enters into, gives
life and significance to, and so becomes one with the universe epitomized by the Marabar Hills.

In discussing Forster's idea of oneness with the universe and
the particular development of the idea in *A Passage to India,* we have
already encroached on the second area in which Forster found himself
in essential agreement with the students of myth.

*The importance of a deeper self and its close ties with a
higher self.* It is this deeper and higher self which momentarily takes
over at the trial. Then Adela sees the truth and is able to break the
chain of evil that has stretched inexorably from the Marabar caves to
this courtroom in Chandrapore. Forster's point is that for Adela this is
a moment of vision. It is beyond the normal range of her experience
and understanding.

Adela's limitations are underscored in the earlier part of the
novel. Through a subtle repetition of plot[1] and symbol, they are given
fresh emphasis as Adela enters her fateful cave. The plot recalls us to
that moment when Adela and Ronny, having broken off their engagement, are taken for a drive in the Nawab Bahadur's car. It grew
dark as they moved down the Marabar road. Their hands touched, a
thrill passed between them, "and a spurious unity descended on them."
"It would vanish in a moment, perhaps to reappear, but the darkness

is alone durable. And the night that encircled them, absolute as it seemed, was itself only a spurious unity, being modified by the gleams of day that leaked up round the edges of the earth, and by the stars" (p. 92).

An accident follows, the result apparently of the car being attacked by an animal. As Adela and Ronny search for the tracks, "Adela in her excitement knelt and swept her skirts about, until it was she if anyone who appeared to have attacked the car" (p. 94). This curious detail foreshadows her later confusion as to what attacked her in the cave. Now, however, it is agreed the animal is a hyena. Everything is plain, including the fact that Ronny and Adela will marry.

But when they mention the accident to Ronny's mother, "Mrs. Moore shivered, 'A ghost!'" (p. 101). Mrs. Moore is right, though the secret is communicable by blood rather than speech and is unknown to the other English. Nine years previously the Nawab Bahadur had driven his car over a drunken man and killed him, "and the man had been waiting for him ever since" (p. 103). His hyena-like form is in the tradition of the jackal, another animal of the dog kind: "Anubis, the jackal (a beast still dreaded as a ghost by the Egyptians), is explained as 'the circle of the horizon,' or 'the portals of the land of darkness,' the gate kept, as Homer would say, by Hades, the mighty warden."[2]

The engagement of Adela and Ronny is instituted by an agent outside their comprehension. At a later time as Adela toils over the rocks of the Marabar congratulating herself that she and Ronny have "abundance of common sense" and thinking "What about love?" her attention is caught by a double row of footholds. "Where had she seen footholds before? Oh yes, they were the pattern traced in the dust by the wheels of the Nawab Bahadur's car. She and Ronny—no, they did not love each other" (pp. 158–59). Such is Adela's state of mind as she enters a cave alone. She finds herself surrounded by its dark horizon and thinks she sees "a sort of shadow, down the entrance tunnel" (p. 202). The ghost hyena (a sort of shadow), the encircling night, and the gate or "portals of the land of darkness" become for Adela the entry into a terrifying rite of passage which her "well-equipped mind" (p. 142) can neither comprehend nor endure. Faced with this deeper reality, she breaks down.

Even after her moment of vision in the courtroom, Adela has no essential understanding of herself or of what has happened to her. In this lack of insight she is closely associated with Fielding. During their final meeting before Adela leaves India their shared inadequacies are stressed. "A friendliness, as of dwarfs shaking hands, was in the air. Both man and woman were at the height of their powers—sensible, honest, even subtle. . . . Yet they were dissatisfied. . . . Not for them was an infinite goal behind the stars, and they never sought it. But wistfulness descended on them now, as on other occasions; the shadow of the shadow of a dream fell over their clear-cut interests, and objects never seen again seemed messages from another world" (pp. 274-75).

In the cave Adela encounters a range of experience which evades her well-equipped mind, but which tempts her this once to take a wild plunge into a reality not understood but guessed at. Her action is, spiritually, a parody of the activity at the religious festival: "the human spirit had tried by a desperate contortion to ravish the unknown" (p. 300). Adela indulges in a continuing act of evil in torturing Aziz (p. 214). Through love of Mrs. Moore she attains to an act of good. But one contact with good and evil, one plunge into the realm of spirit, one blind sortie into the reaches of the deeper and higher self is all that she is capable of. Her rationalist mind will never permit her to understand her experience and she will never have another like it.

When Adela confronts an experience which requires resources extending above and below the narrow preoccupations of the ego, she finds herself no longer examining life but being examined by it. She fails this examination. The horrifying consequence is a flood of evil and misery which inundates others as well as herself. Thus in a negative way Adela illustrates the supreme importance of the deeper and higher self. The relationship between the two will be clearer if we go on now to the next point in our summary of the ideas Forster shared with the students of myth.

The necessity of myth to convey the paradox of man's unchanging yet evolving nature. We begin with the paradox and with the unchanging side of man's nature. This leads us to one of the most memorable features of the great trial scene, the physically god-like Indian, born of the city and its rubbish heaps, who pulls the punkah at the trial. He is the first person Adela notices; and the only one who remains when the court is finally deserted. We are told three things about him. First this: "When that strange race nears the dust and is condemned as untouchable, then nature remembers the physical perfection that she accomplished elsewhere, and throws out a god—not many, but one here and there, to prove to society how little its categories impress her." Thus he signifies nature as against society. Second this: "Pulling the rope towards him, relaxing it rhythmically, sending swirls of air over others, receiving none himself, he seemed apart from human destinies, a male fate, a winnower of souls." Thus he signifies the impersonality and inevitability of fate. Third this: in contrast to the little assistant magistrate who symbolizes the ego and is cultivated, self-conscious, and conscientious, "The punkah wallah was none of these things; he scarcely knew that he existed and did not understand why the Court was fuller than usual, indeed he did not know that it was fuller than usual, didn't even know he worked a fan, though he thought he pulled a rope." Thus he signifies the unconscious. His placing in the scene and his function are also suggestive of the unconscious. Though he is at the back of the court his importance is asserted in relation to the crowded proceedings by his sitting alone on a raised platform, and his pulling of the rope which moves the overhead fan is a lowly but transcendent activity (p. 226).

Faced with this being, Adela responds intuitively to his otherness: "Something in his aloofness impressed the girl from middle-class England, and rebuked the narrowness of her sufferings. In virtue of what had she collected this roomful of people together? Her particular brand of opinions, and the suburban Jehovah who sanctified them— by what right did they claim so much importance in the world, and assume the title of civilization? Mrs. Moore—she looked round, but Mrs. Moore was far away on the sea . . ." (pp. 226–27). The courtroom and the ideas that activate its proceedings become for the moment simply a projection of Adela's ego. But two things stand outside her ego, the aloofness of the Indian, and Mrs. Moore far away on the sea (a traditional symbol of the unconscious). The petty world of her consciousness is humiliated by contact with the other-than-ego.

Here is the beginning of Adela Quested's one and only experience of profound insight. The confidence of her ego is shaken, its energy weakened so that for once images from the unconscious may emerge. For once her whole nature is in harmony and the past re-emerges, transformed into beauty and truer than anything the conscious mind has known. Wafted on by the airs of the punkah, she has her moment of truth. Fielding who has known nothing like this in his experience thinks she is having a nervous breakdown. He cannot understand that it is a psychic breakthrough; and indeed, once the experience is past, Adela cannot understand this either.

But why does Forster attribute a three-fold significance to the nameless Indian? What connection does he intend between nature, fate, and the unconscious?

Since the unconscious by definition is outside the comprehension or control of the ego, its influence will have the quality of fate and its images, when they emerge into consciousness, a quality of givenness. For Adela, the Indian has these qualities. But what is of particular interest is that he has no special relation to the girl from middle-class England, he is apart from *all* human destinies, and he sends swirls of air over everyone, though receiving none himself. He images not simply Adela's unconscious but a collective unconscious. This universal symbolism reinforces his character as fate.

The connection of the unconscious with nature and the body is just as appropriate as its connection with fate, but it is not quite so obvious. The superb body is a symbol of man's primordial psychic nature. The body is a reflection of the harmony and power of the human organism when the psyche operated at an entirely unconscious and intuitive level. Contrariwise, when a narrow and angular rationality controls the psyche, the body loses harmony and beauty. Adela recognizes that neither she nor Ronny has physical charm. And she notes with an honesty both courageous and wistful that it "does make a difference in a relationship—beauty, thick hair, a fine skin" (p. 160). The absence of physical charm parallels absence of connection with the unconscious and the intuitive. But under the influence of the god-like

Indian in the court, Adela experiences in visual and dramatic form a moment of intuitive insight. Her experience is connected with memories of Mrs. Moore whose most remarkable characteristic has been intuitive understanding of others.

We may learn from this episode how impossible it is to separate the intuitive, even at its most highly developed or spiritual, from the unconscious. Thus the splendid body of the Indian and his absolute detachment make their appeal both to Adela's unconscious and to such higher resources of the spirit as she can muster. This connection of the nameless Indian with the higher development of the psyche is symbolized by his notable resemblance to Professor Godbole.

The old Hindu teacher, like the young Indian, is imperturbable and suggests harmony (p. 76). He remains detached from all the human fuss that surrounds him: he misses the train to the Marabar, and slips away as the trial approaches. He accepts the world of matter but does not dissipate his physical or mental energies by giving it unnecessary attention. Indeed he is so tranquil that at times he gives the impression that all is swallowed up in a tranquility as complete as the unconsciousness of the Indian in the court (p. 82). And like his lowly counterpart who does not know why he pulls a rope and scarcely even knows he pulls it, Godbole eats and eats and never looks at the hand that reaches for the food (p. 76). His interest lies elsewhere, as we see during the religious festival of Part III. There we are told that he has "developed the life of his spirit" (p. 302). He has cultivated the inner life of intuitive or spiritual insight, and has taken it to a higher level than any other character in the novel.

The stillness of the old Hindu and the abstractedness of his physical gestures indicate his oneness with the superb and fateful figure of the courtroom. Intuition and the higher development of the psyche are founded in the permanent wellspring of the unconscious. The nameless Indian, expressive of the primordial unconscious, is the base of a spiritual pyramid that culminates in Professor Godbole. The highest consciousness, transcending the ego, asserts its kinship with the unconscious. Godbole and the god-like Indian (nameless of necessity[3]) symbolize the importance of the deeper self and its close ties with the higher self; and they symbolize the paradox of man's un-changing yet evolving nature.

The necessity of myth to convey this paradox is implicit in Forster's practice of employing archetypal symbols. It is especially interesting to recall Westcott's assertion: "The myth is the unconscious growth of a common mind. . . ." This is precisely what the god-like Indian symbolizes—the unconscious growth of a common mind. And Godbole symbolizes the growth in its evolving aspect. Together they form an archetypal image of the union of the subliminal and supra-liminal.

The continuing value of life-oriented art as the vehicle of new insights and new myths. This is the last in our summary of the ideas Forster shared with the students of myth. If it is assumed that *A Passage to India* is life-oriented, an assumption most of Forster's critics and readers appear to make without hesitation, all we need do is establish that the novel is a vehicle of new insights and new myths. This can only be effectively demonstrated with reference to the whole work. However, when we come to discuss the novel as archetype and have placed Godbole and the god-like Indian in the context of cave, temple, and religious festival, we may feel justified in saying that these great archetypal symbols are the vehicle of a new myth.

Meanwhile we turn to romance, the subject of Chapter 2. I suppose that, of all Forster's works, *A Passage to India* seems least like romance fiction. Yet it shares with the earlier works the essential characteristics of romance. In the first place it is thematic fiction. What has already been said about the trial scene makes sufficiently obvious Forster's intense moral seriousness and his decisive inclination to judge his characters. His evaluation of them may have a wistful quality, for they are honest and they honestly try to keep up their end of things, but they are nonetheless judged.

In the second place *A Passage to India* employs the romance division of character with all that is implied by that division, including the absence of individual responsibility on the part of the characters. But there is one surprising development in the presentation of the characters. On the side of evil are all the important local officials of Anglo-India, no one of whom is especially important to the story as a whole. On the side of good are Mrs. Moore, who is dead before the story is half told, and Godbole, who on first reading may seem to be rather a minor character. Caught between these two groups are the major characters, Aziz, Fielding, and Adela, who are decent and honorable, but in terms of any higher standard are finally inadequate. What surprises us is that Adela, however inadequate she may be, also expresses within herself the conflict between the forces of good and evil.

We already know from a study of the short stories that Forster has little talent for the inner drama of psychological conflict. He gets round the difficulty in *A Passage to India* by continuing to keep the two sides of the conflict separate even though they find expression within a single character. It is true that between the affair of the cave and the affair of the trial Adela exists in a state of utter confusion, a kind of limbo in which her inner life is a no-man's land of incertitude. And it is true that certain questions trouble the honest and efficient surface of her mind as she enters the court. But at the trial, truth emerges as a spectacular revelation, not as an insight acquired through long and merciless probing of her experience. Her delusion, convincing her that she was attacked in the cave, and her momentary vision, showing her that nothing had happened and that the Marabar had a beauty she had never guessed, are presented by Forster as powerful visual images and as symbolic moments of good and evil. And so, after all, the traditional romance separation of good and evil remains almost as decisive as ever.

The character's responsibility for good and evil remains much the same also. Adela's moment of deepest evil when she believes she has been attacked by Aziz simply overtakes her. And her moment of vision, her moment of highest good, is simply given. She may appear unworthy or worthy but she is never represented as criminally responsible for her evil act or as sublimely responsible for her good act. Here, for instance, is the final comment on her good act: "Something that she did not understand took hold of the girl and pulled her through. Though the vision was over, and she had returned to the insipidity of the world, she remembered what she had learnt. Atonement and confession—they could wait. It was in hard prosaic tones that she said, 'I withdraw everything' " (p. 239).

Were Adela a responsible character of a typical novelistic kind, she would be in a state of intense conflict and conscience-ridden suspense during the trial, and this is what the novelist would be busy analyzing. Forster can avoid such analysis because good and evil are represented as transcending the individual or as taking their rise from sources beyond the range of the character's consciousness. They are shown as independent of each other and as operating *through* the character. Thus it is that when good and evil are found in the same character, they need not, like water colors, run together but may stand out separately as the ultimate black and white.

Forster is deeply interested in the sinister or transcendent evil of which we get more than a glimpse in the Marabar Hills. We get more than a glimpse because for the first time in the novels a leading and good character knowingly experiences a total confrontation with evil. In doing so, Mrs. Moore resembles Michael of "The Point of It" and Giuseppe of "The Story of the Siren." She does not resemble Adela because Adela does not *know* she is experiencing a confrontation with evil.

Forster's deep interest in both good and evil is apparent in another way. For the first time he provides an analysis of their nature and gives a kind of philosophical status to their independent existence. He does this through Godbole who takes the affair of the Marabar as an occasion for exegesis: "All perform a good action, when one is performed, and when an evil action is performed, all perform it. . . . When evil occurs, it expresses the whole of the universe. Similarly when good occurs." He adds that good and evil "are not what we think them, they are what they are, and each of us has contributed to both" (pp. 185–86). These observations are later confirmed. Fielding felt that "the evil was propagating in every direction, it seemed to have an existence of its own, apart from anything that was done or said by individuals" (p. 195). And Adela, in her misery, felt that "Evil was loose . . . she could even hear it entering the lives of others" (p. 203).

Evil is not transcendent in the sense that its source is beyond man. But because all contribute to evil, it is universal and so transcends the individual. And because the individual performs all evil acts and all perform each evil act, the responsibility for evil is universal rather than individual. Similarly when good occurs. We may now rephrase the statement first made in Chapter 2 and say that the individual is responsible for a good or evil act to the same degree that every man is responsible for it. Or we may put it another way, that the individual acts for all men and expresses the whole of the universe when he performs a good or an evil act; in so doing he is totally responsible, but totally responsible in his capacity as universal or archetypal man rather than as individual.

However we rephrase the matter, the artistic implications remain the same. Forster has still got his decisive romance conflict based on the firm separation of good and evil and he is still free to manipulate his characters to the end that he may develop this conflict of good and evil and so enforce his moral theme.

In other words—as we saw in Chapter 3—Forster the narrator is responsible not to his characters but to the total order of experience in which they participate. What interests him is not Adela's inner suffering but her confrontation with the image of the god-like Indian and with the memory of Mrs. Moore, a confrontation which takes her outside herself and—from the reader's point of view—places her experience in a larger context.

Forster's capacity to judge his characters and to subordinate them to his total vision is most strikingly illustrated in his treatment of Aziz—who is modeled on Forster's "greatest Indian friend," Syed Ross Masood.[4] Of Masood he later wrote: "He . . . showed me new horizons and a new civilisation and helped me towards the understanding of a continent. . . . He made everything real and exciting as soon as he began to talk, and seventeen years later when I wrote *A Passage to India* I dedicated it to him out of gratitude as well as out of love, for it would never have been written without him."[5] That is Forster's evaluation of Masood. But his evaluation of Aziz is like his evaluation of Fielding and Adela. He is grouped with them, he is judged, and he is found wanting. Mrs. Moore and the god-like Indian and Godbole represent something deeper and truer than he can either be or know.

215

Yet Aziz is the leading character, and would be the hero if the novel had a hero. We are given more of his point of view than of anyone else's, he is the only one to figure prominently in all three sections, and Forster presents him with a kind of throw-away heroic gesture by associating him with "his" six ancient Mogul Emperors. But he is not allowed to be the hero.[6] Indeed, in *A Passage to India,* no character is allowed even so much as a dominant role in the narrative. Only India dominates, and the characters must share such spotlight as is left. In particular, Aziz must share the spotlight with Fielding, whose importance is reinforced by the narrative point of view. The storyteller is a non-Indian, an outsider, in fact an Englishman, so that to some degree Fielding has in common with the storyteller his intimate inside view of India seen through English eyes. Of course Fielding's outlook and Forster's perspective by no means coincide, but they resemble each other enough for Fielding to acquire weight and significance beyond what might be expected from the nature of his role. For this reason he seems almost as important in the narrative as Aziz.

Next in prominence comes Adela, who is no more like a heroine than Fielding and Aziz are like heroes. Adela's confrontation with the god-like Indian provides a measure of her heroic stature. She and her suburban Jehovah do not measure up.

And what of Mrs. Moore? Absence implies existence, says Godbole of his god. The same saying is true of Mrs. Moore. Though no one in Chandrapore knows it yet, Mrs. Moore on the morning of the trial is dead as well as absent. Yet her existence is asserted and her influence is more useful than anyone else's in ending the horror and futility of the caves and the courtroom. Finally, however, Mrs. Moore is not the all-pervasive character we saw in Mrs. Wilcox. All the symbols and characters do not meet in her. In fact her role in the total narrative is beautifully symbolized in the trial scene. Her role is supremely influential but it does not encompass or even dominate the whole scene or the whole novel. Precisely the same assessment could be made of the role of Godbole who, through the nameless Indian, is also present at the trial.

This presentation of the characters is of a piece with everything else. No character, no event, no symbol provides an entry to or a focus for the whole novel. In the trial scene the most important object as archetypal symbol is the Marabar. It is also the most important archetypal symbol in the novel. But it is balanced by and must be understood in relation to the "Temple" of Part III. The most important event of the trial scene is Adela's vision. And as in much of the earlier fiction it is indeed a *moment* of vision. We have noted, however, that later in the scene its effect is diffused and deliberately dissipated. Moreover, Adela's moment of truth balances her moment of delusion in the cave, just as the religious festival and Godbole's impelling of Mrs. Moore to that place where completeness can be found balance the Marabar and Mrs. Moore's experience of desolation. Neither the moment of vision nor the moment of desolation becomes central to or dominates the narrative.

Having exhausted all the other possibilities, we may now turn to the narrator with the confidence that his overmastering perspective will dominate the novel. In one sense of course it does. But in the most important sense—the way it immediately strikes the reader—we get a quite different impression, an impression that even the narrator is swallowed up or subsumed in the vastness of India. To understand why this is so, it is necessary to look briefly at Forster's way of telling the story, and, in particular, at his way of presenting the characters.

In important respects the trial scene is like Forster's earlier fiction. Dialogue continues to be the staple ingredient, with comment and judgment added to taste, and the scene is dominated by the consciousness of a single character. But precisely at this point *A Passage to India* differs from the earlier work in two respects. Frequently in the novel the scene is not dominated by the consciousness of a single character, and when it is so dominated—as here—the inner life of the character is presented without any sense of intimacy. Inside information is treated like public fact. The entering of a character's mind seems almost entirely to be a matter of narrative necessity or convenience and not at all an expression by the narrator of any special attitude or relationship to the character. This impression is fortified by the fact that some of the novel's most impressive moments center around Mrs. Moore and Godbole at times when we do not enter their consciousness. All of which means that Forster's detachment from his characters is greater than ever before. His detachment is further emphasized by the fact that characters like Adela and Aziz are judged through comparison with Godbole and the god-like Indian and Mrs. Moore who is an oriental. It is India which appears to provide the basis for judgment.

Where then is the overmastering perspective of the narrator? Insofar as it is apparent at all, it is chiefly to be found in the general accounts of India and Indians. It is to be found in the description of the god-like figure who presides at the back of the court, and in the description of India which opens the trial chapter: "The annual helter-skelter of April, when irritability and lust spread like a canker, is one of her comments on the orderly hopes of humanity. . . . men try to be harmonious all the year round, and the results are occasionally disastrous. The triumphant machine of civilization may suddenly hitch and be immobilized into a car of stone, and at such moments the destiny of the English seems to resemble their predecessors', who also entered the country with intent to refashion it, but were in the end worked into its pattern and covered with its dust" (pp. 219–20).

Yet even here the perspective, though it transcends that of the characters, fails to master. India, the hundred Indias frustrate the orderly hopes of the narrator. Our sense of anticipated form seems to be out of his control, it seems to depend on India itself rather than on the narrator's knowledge of India. This effect is only possible because we sense that the narrator is, like ourselves, an outsider confronting a reality greater than he or anyone can be expected wholly to comprehend.

The sense of the narrator as an outsider is reinforced by the theme of God as the unattainable. In a work of fiction, the reader naturally associates the author-narrator with the ultimate theme. This is one of the reasons the author-narrator usually achieves a kind of centrality and an absolute status in the work. But when the ultimate theme is an ideal which is unattainable, the narrator seems only to glimpse the theme rather than to have some substantial and vested interest in it. And so he does not *seem* to offer an overmastering thematic perspective which might be used to interpret the novel's oneness of effect. Oneness of effect, if it exists at all, appears to be inherent in

India itself. And India, if it is contained at all, is contained only within the bounds of the whole novel.

In each of Forster's works it has been possible to identify the primary source of archetypal power, that is to say, the principal vehicle through which is conveyed to the reader the sense of a living totality. In the short stories that source or vehicle was the eternal moment itself; in the Italian romances it was the narrator; in *The Longest Journey* it was the hero; and in *Howards End* it was a place and its guardian spirit. In *A Passage to India* the source is none of these. The source is neither more nor less than the whole novel. For the first time in Forster's work the total order of the fiction, rather than simply embodying the ecstatic or visionary, is itself visionary.[7]

In *A Passage to India* then, we encounter the novel as archetype, the novel itself in its every detail and in its ultimate completeness as the source of our experience of totality and mythic unity. The significance of this conception, and in particular its esthetic implications, will be explored more fully at the end of the chapter. For the present we may note that the idea of the novel as archetype takes us back where we began, in connection with the short stories, to an emphasis on the thematic nature of Forster's fiction. For the one thing more allpervading than India itself, the one thing that can unify *A Passage to India* is the vast subcontinent's promise of universal significance. Only in the light of such a theme can India be seen as One and everything be caught up in the net of the universe and imaged in the symbolic unity of the novel.

A Passage to India

The vision is difficult to describe. For how could anyone relate it as "other," not seeing it as other when he beheld it, but as one with himself?

—Plotinus

"At the end of it Godbole said, 'May I now take my leave?'—always an indication that he had not come to his point yet" (p. 183). And earlier at Fielding's tea party, as Adela and Mrs. Moore were saying goodbye and Adela was saying to Godbole, "It's a shame we never heard you sing," he replied, "I may sing now." And did (p. 83). This strange song echoes through the next hundred pages of the novel. It is one of those things about India that defy the Western notion of order. "At times there seemed rhythm, at times there was the illusion of a Western melody. But the ear, baffled repeatedly, soon lost any clue, and wandered in a maze of noises, none harsh or unpleasant, none intelligible" (p. 83).

Godbole explains his song: "I place myself in the position of a milkmaid. I say to Shri Krishna, 'Come! come to me only.' The god refuses to come. I grow humble and say. . . . 'Multiply yourself into a hundred Krishnas, and let one go to each of my hundred companions, but one, O Lord of the Universe, come to me.' He refuses to come. . . . I say to Him, Come, come, come, come, come, come. He neglects to come." To emphasize the importance of the song and its meaning, the next paragraph—the last paragraph of the chapter—reads: "Ronny's steps had died away, and there was a moment of absolute silence. No ripple disturbed the water, no leaf stirred" (p. 84).

It would take too long to rehearse here the many ways this song echoes through the following incidents and especially through Adela's relations with Ronny. But at least we should note the way

220

Godbole and his god serve as a standard by which to judge three creatures: an Anglo-Indian, a Moslem, and the sun. Ronny has a servant named Krishna who should bring the office files, but fails to come. Though he is not seriously angry, Ronny makes a terrific row. He storms and shouts, and "Krishna the earth, Krishna the stars replied, until the Englishman was appeased by their echoes" (p. 102). This is more than a parody. It indicates precisely the spiritual level of the young Englishman in relation to the old Hindu. Similarly, when we read concerning the poem recited by Aziz that "it was a passing reminder. . . . Less explicit than the call to Krishna, it voiced our loneliness nonetheless, our isolation, our need for the Friend who never comes yet is not entirely disproved" (p. 111), we have an assessment of the Moslem's spiritual level in relation to Godbole. And when we read: "The sun was returning to his kingdom with power but without beauty. . . . He was not the unattainable friend, either of men or birds or other suns, he was not the eternal promise, the never-withdrawn suggestion that haunts our consciousness" (p. 120), we understand that the answer to Godbole's call will not come from the universe of matter. "The Friend" is "a Persian expression for God" (p. 288).

When Godbole is asked to describe the Marabar caves he can find nothing to say about them, yet he cannot agree with Aziz that their fame is an empty brag (p. 79). His song which follows in no way describes the Marabar, but in a curious way it prepares Adela and Mrs. Moore for their experience of that unspeakable region. It prepares them by insinuating that God is absent from his universe, and this notion takes them a little way toward an understanding of the Marabar's message. "Ever since Professor Godbole had sung his queer little song, they had lived more or less inside cocoons . . ." (p. 139).

Such is the suspended mental state of the visitors as they approach the Marabar, moving on the half-asleep train through the darkness before dawn, moving through the plain of the Ganges that "encroaches" on the Hills "with something of the sea's action," so that the Hills "are sinking beneath the newer lands. Their main mass is untouched, but at the edge their outposts have been cut off and stand knee-deep, throat-deep, in the advancing soil. There is something unspeakable in these outposts. They are like nothing else in the world, and a glimpse of them makes the breath catch. They rise abruptly, insanely, without the proportion that is kept by the wildest hills elsewhere, they bear no relation to anything dreamt or seen" (pp. 129–30). As one approaches the Hills, they are seen to plunge "straight into the earth, like cliffs into the sea" (p. 147). And the mighty Kawa Dol shoots up in a single slab. But behind it, "recumbent, were the hills that contained the other caves, isolated each from his neighbour by broad channels of the plain" (p. 143). These reclining, leaning, wildly sprawling hills may rise, but they do not stand.

As Aziz's party entered the Marabar, "nothing was to be seen on either side but the granite, very dead and quiet. The sky dominated as usual, but seemed unhealthily near, adhering like a ceiling to the summits of the precipices. It was as if the contents of the corridor had never been changed" (pp. 147–48). The sky that connected the precipices was "bland and glutinous" (p. 153). And when the expedition was over, "they got on the elephant and the picnic began to unwind out of the corridor and escaped under the precipice towards the railway station" (p. 166). Here they are met by the train, "pushing its burning throat over the plain." With shutters closed and electric fans running, they ride back to Chandrapore on this twentieth century dragon. "In the twilight, all resembled corpses, and the train itself seemed dead though it moved—a coffin from the scientific north which troubled the scenery four times a day. . . . The expedition was over. And as it ended, as they sat up in the gloom and prepared to enter ordinary life, suddenly the long-drawn strangeness of the morning snapped" (p. 168).

Obviously this is a journey through dream or nightmare, a journey through a sea of darkness and twilight to a strange other world. But on this journey there is no hero and no goal. The chapel perilous—Forster does not mention so orderly a Western concept—is a cave, an absolutely empty cave.

The Marabar Hills, torn from the sun, boiled and bubbled and (we guess) as they cooled the bubbles froze into stillness. Before all life, even the livingness of the bubbles died. If the Hills epitomize the universe of matter, inanimate and inert, what do these bubbles,

222

these perfectly polished, perfectly empty caves epitomize? I suggest that they epitomize the universe of man, isolated, turned in upon itself, spiritually dead.

This significance of the caves can best be approached through the significance of the echo; and the echo can best be approached through Professor Godbole's little lecture on the nature of evil:[8] "Good and evil are different, as their names imply. But, in my own humble opinion, they are both of them aspects of my Lord. He is present in the one, absent in the other, and the difference between presence and absence is great, as great as my feeble mind can grasp. Yet absence implies presence, absence is not non-existence, and we are therefore entitled to repeat, 'Come, come, come, come,'" (p. 186). "The original sound may be harmless," thinks Fielding, "but the echo is always evil" (pp. 286–87). The echo expresses the absence of the original sound and at the same time implies its existence. The echo symbolizes precisely the situation pertaining in the case of evil which expresses the absence of God but implies his existence. And that is why the echo is always evil.[9]

"Everything echoes now," reflects Fielding (p. 286).[10] The reason: "the countryside was too vast to admit of excellence. In vain did each item in it call out, 'Come, come.' There was not enough god to go around" (p. 92). A similar call of "Come" is implied in the demand for kindness. Aziz says, "no one can ever realize how much kindness we Indians need. . . . Kindness, more kindness, and even after that more kindness. I assure you it is the only hope" (p. 122). Later, when Adela fails during the trial to feel any emotion of love or contrition at the moment when she realizes her mistake, Forster comments: "Truth is not truth in that exacting land unless there go with it kindness and more kindness and kindness again, unless the Word that was with God also is God" (pp. 254–55). The Word that was with God is truth, the Word that is God is kindness or love. Thus to ask for kindness is to call to God. This call is first heard in the novel in Mrs. Moore's echoing plea that we should love our neighbors: "Good will and more good will and more good will" (p. 55).

The call of "Come" echoing through India signifies the absence of God in the natural universe, just as in Godbole's religious song and in the overmastering need for kindness it signifies the absence of God in the world of man. But these echoes of India, implying by analogy the existence of God, are suggestive of hope, however distant. Not so the echo of the Marabar caves, which sounds the negation of every hope. Since caves, as we shall come to see, are symbolic of man devoid of spirit, man isolated and turned inward upon himself, a study of characters thus isolated may offer the best approach to the symbol.

We can quickly dispose of the British officials, the Turtons and the Burtons, who have no inner life and are treated simply as pawns in the narrative. If they visited a Marabar cave they would experience nothing, hence nothing can be said about them. Much more interesting are the three characters of intelligence and some insight: Fielding, Adela Quested, and Aziz.

Fielding is a rationalist who believes, not in God, but in fellowship helped on by "good will plus culture and intelligence . . . (p. 65). Significantly, he omits love. Thus, reflecting on his relations with Aziz, he recognizes that he cannot be intimate with anyone (p. 123). His isolation and narrowness of sympathy are exposed in Forster's comment on his reaction to the death of Mrs. Moore: "It's only one's own dead who matter. . . . How indeed is it possible for one human being to be sorry for all the sadness that meets him on the face of the earth, for the pain that is endured not only by men, but by animals and plants, and perhaps by the stones?" (p. 257). He is, however, strongly aware of his inadequacy: he "had developed his personality, explored his limitations, controlled his passions," yet in a moment of insight "he felt he ought to have been working at something else the whole time—he didn't know at what, never would know, never could know" (p. 199).

Commenting on the episode in the cave, Adela says to Fielding, "It's as if I ran my finger along that polished wall in the dark, and cannot get further. I am up against something, and so are you." Forster comments: "She was at the end of her spiritual tether, and so was he. . . . Perhaps life is a mystery, not a muddle; they could not tell. . . . They had not the apparatus for judging" (pp. 273–74). As we have already seen, Adela is clearly associated with Fielding as a spiritual cripple. Having come to examine the country, and having "no real affection for Aziz, or Indians generally" (p. 270), she sees "India always as a frieze" (p. 50). The frieze reminds us of the mosque, symbol of the religion of Aziz.

——Like Christianity, Mohammedanism is pathetically deficient. Fielding is not alone in missing the significance of the echo; "the mosque missed it too. Like himself, those shallow arcades provided but a limited asylum." It is ironic that the mosque should miss the significance of the echo. "There is no God but God" is only, as Forster notes, a religious pun; and a pun is only, as we may note, a verbal echo (p. 287). Through the symbolism of mosque and echo, Aziz is associated with Fielding and Adela. He differs from them in having a highly emotional nature and a capacity for moments of true affection and intimacy. But he has a capacity also for suspicion and meanness, the grossest example of which is his notion that Fielding may be planning to marry Adela and may therefore have a personal interest in reducing the amount of compensation she should pay Aziz. He admits that this suspicion was "as bad a mistake as the cave itself" (p. 331). Aziz, like Adela, has been guilty of self-deception and the denial of his human brother. The connection of all three characters is summed up by Fielding: "You and I and Miss Quested are, roughly speaking, not after anything. We jog on as decently as we can, you a little in front—a laudable little party" (p. 331).

Such an understanding is possible only to those who have glimpsed a greater reality and are able to "place" themselves. These glimpses on the part of Fielding and Adela offer us a profound insight into the nature of the human spirit in action.

Fielding has a vision of the Marabar Hills expanding until the whole universe is a hill. As he watches, their nasty little cosmos leaps suddenly into beauty. It is transformed momentarily by the power of his feeling "that we exist not in ourselves, but in terms of each other's minds" (p. 259). Yet the experience has, for Fielding, a kind of unreality, a quality that reminds us of Adela's statement about living at half pressure. "Lovely, exquisite moment—but passing the Englishman with averted face and on swift wings. He experienced nothing himself; it was as if someone had told him there was such a moment, and he was obliged to believe" (p. 199). We recall that much the same thing happened to Adela when she contemplated the Hills, until in front, "like a shutter, fell a vision of her married life" (p. 50). However, what needs emphasis here is not the essential failure of these Western rationalists but the character of their limited achievement. The beauty they behold is not the beauty of nature, but nature transformed and rendered beautiful by the human spirit.

This is apparent in Adela's ecstatic vision at the trial. She relinquishes her presence in the courtroom and, returning to the Marabar Hills, places herself inside and outside the cave. This parallels, in an elementary way, Godbole's religious practice in which he alternately places himself in the position of supplicant and the position of the God. As Adela turned back to the Marabar and the many events of that fatal day, she experienced an extraordinary detachment, she was both present and absent: "she was of it and not of it at the same time, and this double relation gave it indescribable splendour" (pp. 236–37). The Marabar is transformed by her vision. Adela's ecstatic experience stands in absolute contrast to Mrs. Moore's experience of desolation with its "double" vision of the horror and smallness of the universe. To Adela, the universe of the Marabar is "all beautiful and significant" (p. 237).

The insight attained momentarily by Adela and Fielding, and the outflowing of love achieved from time to time by Aziz provide a basis for judging the fixed and ordinary nature of each of these characters. So judged, it is apparent that each is subject to the feeling that he exists in himself. Christians call this the sin of pride. Forster does not give it a name, but its symbol is the cave. The association is hinted at in Mrs. Moore's cynical remark that after she has married off her children she will retire into a cave of her own (p. 209). And it is implicit in Aziz's dilemma when he loses Adela in the caves. "How am I to know which contains my guest? Which is the cave I was in myself?" (p. 161) When the individual is isolated he finds it impossible to locate himself for he lacks connection with other things. Later Adela says, "I shouldn't mind if it had happened anywhere else; at least I really don't know where it did happen" (p. 208). What this confused statement means is that the evil event at the cave occurred within herself, that she is not conscious of the fact, and that consequently she does not know where it did happen. The parallel between

Adela (the isolated individual) and the cave is decisively confirmed by the echo mentioned immediately after, which, like the echo in the cave, once it has started in her head, goes on reverberating endlessly.[11]

The phenomenon of pride or narcissistic isolation, symbolized in the cave image, is not restricted to individuals. It is manifest in every human organization. A series of vast caves—personal relations, formal religion, government, and race—arch ominously over the spirit of man.

Personal relations, which Forster had valued so highly in the past, are here severely questioned (pp. 141, 205). For a meaningful association to exist between two persons, there must be a spiritual bond, "that link outside either participant that is necessary to every relationship" (p. 331). Mrs. Moore in her wasteland vision of "Caves" perceives the absence of this outside link and the presence, only, of "centuries of carnal embracement" (p. 141). A personal relationship implies exclusion; it is a double image of the individual in isolation. But a spiritual relationship reveals what one man has in common with another man, and with all men; it is a microcosmic image of the brotherhood of man.

Organized religion, tending always to narrowness and exclusion, is exposed in many ways, in Aziz's religious snobbery, in the fuss over shoe-removal at the mosque, and in the reluctance of the Christian missionaries to extend salvation to all. Obviously, a religion based on exclusion is a contradiction in terms. Turning inward upon itself, it narrows toward zero and the perfect circle of isolation.

The Mau festival, by contrast, is an example, not of organized religion, but of the religious spirit in action. Here no one and no thing is excluded. Even the representatives of the West, bringing with them unexpected confusion as their boats are swept into the midst of the last act of the ritual, are unhesitatingly included. Nor is their presence an accident. Aziz maneuvers his boat nearer in response to Ralph Moore's friendship; Fielding, in response to his wife's love. Ralph and Stella are moved by spiritual sympathy with Hinduism; Fielding and Aziz—great though their limitations may be—are moved by love. Hence, the plunge of all four into the ritual close of the festival is spiritually appropriate.

We turn next to the organized state and to that British

227

colonial government which accords so perfectly with the image of the Indian universe as a wasteland. The India of officialism, materialistic and lifeless, is built on sand and echoes interminably. It is a cave, or perhaps a series of caves. Who can tell? At least, the officials cannot tell, for they have created an India in their own image. And through that image we behold this darker truth: authority inevitably divides the governors and the governed, it moves always toward bureaucratic isolation and spiritual negation. Thus the state stands revealed as a vastly magnified image of man void of spirit.

Racial distinction often allies itself with state authority and the exclusiveness of religion. But in its own right it creates barriers separating man from man and group from group, a fact horrifyingly illustrated by the aftermath of the episode in the caves. To the English, the native appears monstrous not by reason of religious or national entity but by reason of his skin coloring which sets him apart and enables the English to regard him as outside humanity. On the other hand, the Indian distrusts and hates the white man. But at the same time, racial distinctions lead him to distrust his Indian neighbor. Race then is one more instance of man in isolation, man turned inward to behold his own image in those of his own blood. The opposite image, the ideal, is—as usual—embodied in Godbole. He is an internationalist (p. 306), who believes literally in the obliteration of national and racial barriers.

To sum up in Forster's own words, "where there is officialism every human relationship suffers" (p. 220). For every type of human organization is based on exclusiveness and tends toward spiritual emptiness. Such organizations are magnified expressions of the novel's negative theme: the nature of individual isolation and soullessness. We should note, however, that spiritual negation, whether individual or organizational, is not absolute. Though there are hints of God's nonexistence (to be discussed later), it is his absence that is asserted. Thus Adela's head, Ronny's footsteps, the Indian earth, the Indian nation, everything echoes—everything, that is, except the region of the Marabar.

Since echo implies the existence of God, the failure of the Marabar Hills to echo implies the nonexistence of God. And the "boum" of perverted reflections of sound in the caves offers ominous confirmation. In the hills and caves of the Marabar, echo, like arch, has a significance totally at variance with its implications in the world beyond the Marabar. Thus, we know that the echo is always evil, but we also know from Forster's comment on Mrs. Moore's experience that "Nothing evil had been in the cave" (p. 154). The reason is implied in the account of the expedition party as it enters the Marabar: "a new quality occurred, a spiritual silence which invaded more senses than the ear. Life went on as usual, but had no consequences, that is to say, sounds did not echo or thoughts develop. Everything seemed cut off at its root, and therefore infected with illusion" (p. 147). This is the most conclusive indication that the journey to the Marabar is a journey to a world apart whose significance is "other." But the symbols of arch and echo and the phenomenon of silence are used to suggest that the universe of the caves has implications which are felt beyond the Marabar.

Thus, after Fielding's announcement that he feared the dead would not live again and Adela's agreement, "There was a moment's silence, such as often follows the triumph of rationalism" (p. 250). And at the East-West Bridge Party, after Ronnie's condescending talk about the Indians grouped on the other side of the tennis court, "There was a silence when he had finished speaking, on both sides of the court; at least, more ladies joined the English group, but their words seemed to die as soon as uttered. Some kites hovered overhead, impartial, over the kites passed the mass of a vulture, and with an impartiality exceeding all, the sky, not deeply coloured but translucent, poured light from its whole circumference. It seemed unlikely that the series stopped here. Beyond the sky must not there be something that overarches all the skies, more impartial even than they? Beyond which again . . ." (p. 42). And a little later we read, with reference to Mrs. Moore's experience: "Outside the arch there seemed always an arch, beyond the remotest echo a silence" (p. 56). The invisible arch, deathlike and appallingly impartial, and the ominous silence beyond the remotest echo are signs or premonitions of a godless or soulless universe, "of the world as a series of concentric circles vanishing into a non-human horizon."[12]

This spiritual void in its absolute form is symbolized by the perfectly intact cave, the "bubble-shaped cave that has neither ceiling nor floor, and mirrors its own darkness in every direction infinitely" (p. 131) and knows a silence without end, for it "can hear no sound but its own" (p. 161); "if mankind grew curious and excavated, nothing, nothing would be added to the sum of good or evil. . . . If the boulder falls and smashes, the cave will smash too—empty as an Easter egg" (p. 131).[13]

This empty egg is under no circumstances to be confused with the one conjured up by Forster in 1952 to describe the narrative role of the Marabar caves. Then he said that they "represented an area in which concentration can take place. A cavity. They were something to focus everything up: they were to engender an event like an egg."[14] Forster was, of course, familiar with the Indian myth of the egg or womb which engenders the universe. He knew and admired the works of E. B. Havell and there he read that the "first comprehensible and expressible manifestation of the Unknowable, before creation itself, was conceived by ancient philosophers as the Egg, or Womb of the Universe."[15] Forster may also have understood that the primordial feminine, the vessel of the world and life, can be a vessel of death as well, can be cave or coffin, tomb or urn.[16] Such a conception integrates death into the life cycle. But no such idea is implied by Forster's caves, which are empty. "Nothing, nothing attaches to them . . ." (p. 130).

While writing *A Passage to India* Forster was interested in the status of nothingness or nonexistence in art. He tells us in a 1920 review that Loveliness and Beauty are "the two divine children that Imagination has created out of Fact." They are sharply distinguished. Loveliness is lovable and accessible, whereas Beauty is strong and ruthless like her father. "Beauty is the elder of the pair and the less popular. Her head is in the sky, her feet in the mire. She comprises all existence, even the remote and the loathsome, and all non-existence also."[17] Since Forster has evinced this interest in the place of non-existence in art, and since he has gone out of his way to suggest that nothing was in the caves, and since he has even parodied the traditional dragon or terrible mother in the image of "the serpent of eternity made of maggots" (p. 217), it seems a little perverse of readers and critics to turn the caves into wombs. Worse still, it misses the point Forster would make. The cave is not the womb, it is not the closed circle of the undivided primal parents, it is not the unconscious, it is not the terrible mother. Rather—and this is the point—it is the absolute negation of all these things which it might be.

Man's confronting of ultimate negation is symbolized by his entry into the cave with a tunnel. Life is represented by light and sound, though in the first account of the caves at the beginning of Part II only light is introduced—a match is struck:

> Immediately another flame rises in the depths of the rock and moves towards the surface like an imprisoned spirit: the walls of the circular chamber have been most marvellously polished. The two flames approach and strive to unite, but cannot, because one of them breathes air, the other stone. A mirror inlaid with lovely colours divides the lovers, delicate stars of pink and grey interpose, exquisite nebulae, shadings fainter than the tail of a comet or the midday moon, all the evanescent life of the granite, only here visible. Fists and fingers thrust above the advancing soil—here at last is their skin, finer than any covering acquired by the animals, smoother than windless water, more voluptuous than love. The radiance increases, the flames touch one another, kiss, expire. The cave is dark again, like all the caves.

Here is the horror and attraction of narcissism: supreme isolation in all its insidious charm and deathlike beauty. The human spirit ravishes the known self, and the lost soul momentarily reflects its own glimmerings—then endlessly reflects its own darkness.

From description, Forster proceeds to drama, showing us the reaction of those characters who enter the caves, that is, who come face to face with the illusory reality of a world without spirit. Fielding notices the echo but fails to apprehend its significance. Adela does likewise—until the evil event in the second cave (her evil event) sets the echo going in her own head. She fails to understand the echo because she lacks insight into her isolation and self-regarding love. Mrs. Moore cannot explain to her that she is suffering from the reverberations of her own hollowness (p. 208). Yet her agonizing awareness of the sound indicates some resources of spirit, and prepares us for her moment of insight at the trial.

Mrs. Moore is the one character among the visitors to the

Marabar who has the spiritual capacity to grasp the full horror of its meaning. Hence the description we have is essentially an account of her experience. She finds the echo of the cave is not like the other echoes of India: "Whatever is said, the same monotonous noise replies. . . . Hope, politeness, the blowing of a nose, the squeak of a boot, all produce 'boum.' Even the striking of a match starts a little worm coiling, which is too small to complete a circle, but is eternally watchful. And if several people talk at once, an overlapping howling noise begins, echoes generate echoes, and the cave is stuffed with a snake composed of small snakes, which writhe independently" (p. 154).[18]

The horror here is not so much in the confusion as in the terrifying revelation that the echoes and the snakes of light are self-perpetuating and take on a violently chaotic and multiple independence. They cease to have reference to any origin, for in a valueless universe no distinction or relationship is meaningful. This vision, suggestive of insanity and nightmare, cannot offer even the empty consolation of a dark and silent void. Mrs. Moore in her spiritual aliveness must undergo the full horror of perceiving the nonexistence of the spirit as a point-by-point negation or perversion of the spirit's life.

With Mrs. Moore we approach the thematic center of the novel. She and Godbole represent the extremes of spiritual apprehension. Mrs. Moore has an overwhelming awareness of the absence of God, an awareness of evil; Godbole of the presence of God, of good. But the existence of God is as much asserted by the one as by the other.

The theme of death is closely associated with the theme of the absence of God. If we looked at the narrative exclusively from Mrs. Moore's point of view, we might justly say that the theme is death and the subject Mrs. Moore's initiation into death. The novel asks, are the dead nonexistent or only absent? The answer will depend on whether God is nonexistent or only absent, and the answer to that question must wait on Part III of the novel. Meanwhile Mrs. Moore's initiation into death is effectively begun by India and particularly by Godbole's song.

When Mrs. Moore comes to India she believes, as she always has, that God is love. And because she intuitively knows whether she likes a person (p. 26) and whether he is her friend (p. 324), she can love and respond to love instantly, freely, and without calculation. This is the basis of her spiritual strength, her influence, and her final salvation. There is no easy triumph, however. She must undergo the darkest of all journeys. Even at the beginning of her visit, India subtly undermines her confidence. The naming of God becomes less and less efficacious (p. 56). She experiences "a new feeling, half languor, half excitement" (p. 73). The feeling grows under the strange influence of Godbole's song and, as Mrs. Moore approaches the caves, becomes one of apathy and hypersensitivity.

When the Marabar strikes, Mrs. Moore comes "to that state where the horror of the universe and its smallness are both visible at the same time—the twilight of the double vision" in which "a spiritual muddledom is set up for which no high-sounding words can be found" (p. 216). The horror is visible in a perception of the universe as void of spirit, as meaningless and death-ridden; the smallness is visible in a perception of the universe as a closed system, as no more extensive than the isolated individual turned inward upon himself, the cave eternally mirroring its own darkness.

If Mrs. Moore's vision were complete, both horror and smallness would be swallowed up in darkness. Instead her vision induces a twilight state. Twilight, paralleling echo in structure, is a state in which light is absent but the existence of light is implied. The same principle is at work in the conception of "spiritual muddledom." The meaningless disorder of the caves might be called a muddle. But Forster avoids the word in that context, reserving it for a higher end. Muddledom is a state in which order is absent but the existence of order is implied. In these ways we know that hope, however distant, is implicit in Mrs. Moore's despair. She may be evil, as she says herself (p. 214), she may be unable to assert God's presence through love, but at the approach of death she begins to emerge from the twilight of horror and disillusionment. As she leaves India the palm trees of Bombay wave to her, laughing, mocking her thought that an echo—the echo of the Marabar—was India (p. 219).

Mrs. Moore's visit to the Marabar cave is the principal event in her initiation, the central act in her rite of passage from life into death. After this act she must participate in that state of withdrawal during which the initiate prepares himself for his new condition so that when at last he emerges he is, in essence, reborn. As Mrs. Moore plunges toward Bombay and the sea, there are hints of such a rebirth. The mighty fortress of Asirgarh reappears (here is no echo, nor was meant to be) and seems to say "I do not vanish" (p. 218), and the coconut palms of Bombay laugh and say "Good-bye" (p. 219). And after her body is "lowered into yet another India—the Indian Ocean" (p. 266), her continued vitality is asserted in the lives of others.

She becomes herself one of the echoes of India. Absent, her name is chanted at the trial where the echoed assurance of her existence and her love enables Adela to escape her subjective involvement and to see the caves again and to speak the truth.

This same vitality is the source of her final "experience" at the Mau festival. As the culmination of the ceremony approaches we are told that the singers "loved all men, the whole universe, and scraps of their past, tiny splinters of detail, emerged for a moment to melt into the universal warmth. Thus Godbole, though she was not important to him, remembered an old woman he had met in Chandrapore days. Chance brought her into his mind while it was in this heated state, he did not select her, she happened to occur among the throng of soliciting images, a tiny splinter, and he impelled her by his spiritual force to that place where completeness can be found. Completeness, not reconstruction" (p. 298). In the one word "reconstruction," Forster dismisses Christianity with its notions of redemption and resurrection. In the one word "completeness," he sums up the spiritual aim of Godbole. "That place where completeness can be found" is that which the singers love, it is "all men, the whole universe." Through Godbole's spiritual force, his love—he is imitating God—Mrs. Moore achieves oneness with the universe.

Forster has subtly prepared us for this event. Four passages will serve as demonstration. The first relates to Mrs. Moore's opening days in India: "In England the moon had seemed dead and alien; here she was caught in the shawl of night together with earth and all the other stars. A sudden sense of unity, of kinship with the heavenly bodies, passed into the old woman and out, like water through a tank,

234

leaving a strange freshness behind" (p. 32). As she leaves India, this experience is glanced at: "when she saw the water flowing through the mosque-tank . . . or the moon, caught in the shawl of night with all the other stars, it seemed a beautiful goal and an easy one. To be one with the universe!" (p. 216)

After the trial we learn that Mrs. Moore is dead. That evening Aziz and Fielding lie on the roof of the Nawab Bahadur's mansion, "gazing through mosquito nets at the stars. Exactly above their heads hung the constellation of the Lion, the disc of Regulus so large and bright that it resembled a tunnel, and when this fancy was accepted all the other stars seemed tunnels too" (p. 260). We may not think of the shawl of night, but we are certain to think of the tunnels into the caves, recognizing in the thought a contrast between the universe of life and the universe of death. Up to this moment Aziz has not been told of Mrs. Moore's death. His evening of triumph is to be unmarred by sadness. But suddenly he announces to Fielding that he will consult Mrs. Moore. What is Fielding to answer? "Opening his eyes, and beholding thousands of stars, he could not reply, they silenced him" (p. 263). The stars deny that Mrs. Moore is dead: she is one with the universe of which they are the symbol. Fielding experiences the fact without in any way comprehending it. This corroborates the reality of Godbole's religious activity. At the same time it shows that Mrs. Moore's spiritual destiny is not dependent on Godbole alone, but on all whom she has loved, all who have loved her, and all who have loved their fellow men and the universe in which we dwell. Godbole has his small part.

Mrs. Moore's attainment of oneness with the universe is prefigured from the beginning by her association with the moon. We first meet her at the mosque which stands in full moonlight. Like a ghost she moves from behind the pillars into the moonlight (p. 22). In the next scene the moon, at first caught in the shawl of night, soon becomes part of a more ominous image. The Ganges, the plain, the whole of the dark world is pictured as "the streaming void" on which is burnished a radiance that belongs neither to water nor moonlight, "a luminous sheaf upon the fields of darkness." Soon the sheaf will be gone and a bright circlet, itself to alter, will take its place (pp. 34–35).

Thus even in this early and optimistic phase of the story, Mrs. Moore's moon slips from the shawl of night into the streaming void and reveals its transitory and changing nature.

Much later, as Mrs. Moore left Chandrapore, "the moon, full again, shone over the Ganges . . . then veered and looked into her window" (p. 217). In the middle of the night she woke "for the train was falling over the western cliff. Moonlit pinnacles rushed up at her like the fringes of a sea . . ." (p. 218). Finally, on the roof of the Nawab Bahadur's house, Fielding tried to persuade Aziz that Mrs. Moore was dead. "He had tried to kill Mrs. Moore this evening . . . but she still eluded him, and the atmosphere remained tranquil. Presently the moon rose—the exhausted crescent that precedes the sun— and shortly after men and oxen began their interminable labour, and the gracious interlude, which he had tried to curtail, came to its natural conclusion" (p. 265). In the wasteland world of "Caves," Mrs. Moore, like the moon, is an exhausted form. And like the moon she appears briefly and departs.

But why, if it is her symbol, does the moon not reappear in "Temple"? The answer is simple. The moon is another echo symbol. The moon asserts the absence of the source of light but implies the existence of the source, the sun. Such an echo symbol would be out of place in Part III. Of course Mrs. Moore reappears, but she is represented quite directly by her son Ralph, who can always tell whether a stranger is his friend and so is an Oriental like his mother (p. 324), and by her daughter Stella who "found something soothing, some solution of her queer troubles" in the Hindu religious festival (p. 332). She is represented too in the heart and memory of Aziz. Her "eternal goodness" did not in any practical way amount to much, "yet she had stolen to the depths of his heart, and he always adored her" (p. 325). And so at the culmination of the religious festival, in the midst of repeated chanting, "he heard, almost certainly, the syllables of salvation that had sounded during his trial at Chandrapore": Esmiss Esmoor (p. 327). Here is one more indication of Mrs. Moore's vitality and universality and one more corroboration of the validity of Godbole's religious activity at the Mau festival.

It is to "Temple" and to this festival that we must now turn

236

if we are to understand how Mrs. Moore escapes the horror of the Marabar and becomes one with the universe and how the innumerable calls of "Come" and the interminable echoes of India are answered by Krishna, the god of love. Like so much else in India, the god's answer is not without its ambiguity. Hence the festival and its final word of love must be approached with caution. It is the purpose of the style of Part III to encourage such caution. The style is urbane and often ironic, as in the opening paragraph which discovers Professor Godbole and God at opposite ends of the same strip of carpet. This opening also indicates the sense in which Godbole is to be the center of our attention. It could be someone else standing on the strip of carpet. But it happens to be Godbole and the narrative happens to find this convenient. We, in turn, will find it convenient to follow the narrative and deal first with Godbole's idea of love and with the limits of his personal achievement. Then we will expand our focus to show the many ways the religious festival contrasts with and mocks the Marabar. Finally we will observe the way the ideal of universal love is brought within bounds of the human by its being unattainable.

In Part II the essential nature of the caves was presented first in the abstract and then as it impinged on the individual life. A similar division prevails in the account of the religious ritual. We may begin with the ultimate spiritual reality. "All spirit as well as all matter must participate in salvation . . ." (p. 301). Thus at midnight, "Infinite Love took upon itself the form of SHRI KRISHNA, and saved the world. All sorrow was annihilated, not only for Indians, but for foreigners, birds, caves, railways, and the stars; all became joy, all laughter; there had never been disease nor doubt, misunderstanding, cruelty, fear" (pp. 299–300).

We turn now to Godbole's actual experience. At the height of the religious ceremony he happened to recall an old woman from Chandrapore days: "It was his duty, as it was his desire, to place himself in the position of the God and to love her, and to place himself in her position and to say to the God, 'Come, come, come, come'" (p. 303). With a love that looks outward always, he is imitating God. And in so doing he impels Mrs. Moore "to that place where completeness can be found. . . . His senses grew thinner, he remembered a wasp seen he forgot where, perhaps on a stone. He loved the wasp equally, he impelled it likewise, he was imitating God. And the stone where the wasp clung—could he . . . no, he could not, he had been wrong to attempt the stone, logic and conscious effort had seduced . . ." (p. 298). With this we may compare the response of the Maharaja of Chhatarpur when Forster asked him if, while meditating, he could forget his troubles: "Oh no, not at all, they come in with me always unless I can meditate on love, for love is the only power that can keep thought out."[19] For Godbole as for the Maharajah love is the ecstatic experience of union with the other-than-self. It has nothing to do with logic or conscious effort.

The casually remembered old woman, the wasp, and the stone define the goal to which Godbole aspires, the goal of salvation for all spirit and all matter. Godbole commands our respect because he aspires to this goal, and also because from our first encounter with him he has appeared to be a profound and contemplative character, as inscrutable as "Ancient Night" (p. 80)—"no eye could see what lay at the bottom of the Brahman's mind, and yet he had a mind and a heart too, and all his friends trusted him, without knowing why" (p. 183). He conforms to Shelley's requirements for the greatly good man: "A man, to be greatly good, must imagine intensely and comprehensively; he must put himself in the place of another and of many others; the pains and pleasures of his species must become his own."[20] Godbole's outgoing nature is best symbolized when, at the height of the festival, "he threw up his hands and detached the tiny reverberation that was his soul" (p. 298). Yet Godbole enters into the pains and pleasures of no more than a few fragments of the universe. To compare his very modest achievement with the ultimate goal of universal salvation is to see how wide is the gap between attainment and aspiration.

The same gap is revealed in other phases of the Mau festival. "When the villagers broke cordon for a glimpse of the silver image, a most beautiful and radiant expression came into their faces, a beauty in which there was nothing personal, for it caused them all to resemble one another during the moment of its indwelling, and only when it was withdrawn did they revert to individual clods" (p. 296).[21] And as the ceremony moves toward its climax we read: "Mixed and confused in their passage, the rumours of salvation entered the Guest House. . . . The bronze gun up on the fort kept flashing, the town was a blur of light, in which the houses seemed dancing, and the palace waving little wings. The water below, the hills and sky above, were not involved as yet; there was still only a little light and song struggling among the shapeless lumps of the universe" (p. 323).

These references to individual clods and shapeless lumps of the universe, by directing attention to that which is as yet unattained, help clarify the final incident of the novel. Fielding and Aziz have ridden out to view the country. As they return, Fielding exclaims:

"Why can't we be friends now? . . . It's what I want. It's what you want."

But the horses didn't want it—they swerved apart; the earth didn't want it, sending up rocks through which riders must pass single file; the temples, the tank, the jail, the palace, the birds, the carrion, the Guest House, that came into view as they issued from the gap and saw Mau beneath: they didn't want it, they said in their hundred voices, "No, not yet," and the sky said, "No, not there."

The conclusion has been foreshadowed with great care. As characters in the human drama, the two men are incapable of deep spiritual union; and symbolically, so little light and song informs the universe that it cannot be expected to do more than struggle with shapeless lumps of clay. But at least there is *some* light and song and there *is* a struggle.

Here we can see one of the many contrasts with the Marabar. These contrasts increase our awareness of the gulf that divides the positive nature of the Mau festival and the ultimate negation of the Marabar. Fielding and Aziz cross this gulf when they come under the benign influence of Mau. The evil of the Marabar, leaving behind it an unexplained residue which corrupts relations between them (p. 292), is obliterated as they plunge into the water at the end of the festival. They "went back laughingly to their old relationship as if nothing had happened" (p. 330).

This event is preceded by a sacred meal for those participants in the ceremony who feel worthy. The food is partaken of beside the great Mau tank which is in flood. In contrast we think of the Tank of the Dagger in the Marabar, "the puddle of water" (p. 153) beside which the expedition from Chandrapore indulge in their English-style picnic. On that expedition, Aziz acted as Mrs. Moore's guide; now at Mau it is Ralph Moore, his mother's surrogate, who acts as guide and brings Aziz into the heart of the Hindu festival. And whereas before, under Aziz's conduct, an accident sent evil spouting after Adela and spreading like a flood into the lives of others, now under Ralph Moore's conduct an accident brings harmony, warmth, and friendly union out of muddle and confusion.

The contrasts are not limited to the human drama, but extend beyond the individual characters and encompass the total India which is the universe of the novel. As the ceremonial procession nears the water, a woman praises God without attributes. Others praise him in "this or that organ of the body or manifestation of the sky" (p. 327).[22] Here the body is redeemed from the ugly lumpy imagery of the Marabar's fists and fingers, and the sky is redeemed from the imagery of glutinous ceilings. However, it must be recalled that there is "still only a little light and song struggling among the shapeless lumps of the universe," and that water, hill, and sky are not as yet participants in salvation. But at least they are not heralds of negation as in the Marabar where the water has contracted to a mudhole and the sky has shrivelled to a ceiling and both have compounded with the Hills to form the sinister corridors of a nightmare wasteland. The contrasting sense of space at Mau is impressive. As the sun shone forth and flooded the world with color, "pink and green skeins of cloud" seemed "to link up the upper sky" (p. 318). And as the festival neared its end, lightning flashed, producing "little red scratches on the ponderous sky" (p. 326); "and high above them a wild tempest started, confined at first to the upper regions of the air" (p. 327). The oppressive sense of the sky sitting on top of one and of the cave "stuffed with a snake composed of small snakes" yields to a sense of space and freedom.

Sound too becomes tolerable and meaningful. The silence of the Marabar Hills, the desolate identity of every word and meaning in the echo of the caves, and the absolute isolation inside the cave (for it can hear nothing outside itself) give way at Mau to a rich muddle of sound. Inside the palace the many sources of music blend mysteriously into a single mass and penetrate outside to unite with the thunder (p. 296). The effect is furthered by the singers, who sound "every note but terror" (p. 327). This one note they omit is the "boum" of the Marabar cave, the note of empty reverberation, of ultimate negation. The climax of the festival is marked by a tornado of noise. "Artillery was fired, drums beaten, the elephants trumpeted, and drowning all an immense peal of thunder, unaccompanied by lightning, cracked like a mallet on the dome" (pp. 328–29).

The thunderstorm symbolizes the marriage of Heaven and Earth.[23] It nullifies the silence beyond the remotest echo, the invisible arch beyond all arches, and the Marabar caves in which these pale images of infinity become self-perpetuating snakes of light and echoes of sound. The sky is now a dome of imaginable proportions. Sound, not echoing but single, not restricted but as a mallet striking the dome from the outside, now penetrates from highest heaven to earth. For the moment Heaven and Earth attain to union.[24]

The Mau festival ends in a mighty muddle, possibly a mystery. The significance of muddle and mystery and their connection with the theme of the "unattainable" may be interpreted in the light of Forster's attitude to order. Order is a state of coherence which man may find in things or may impose on things. Forster does not find such a state of coherence in our universe. He has said that in *A Passage to India* he "tried to indicate the human predicament in a universe which is not, so far, comprehensible to our minds."[25] This is simply a much later echoing of the statement in the novel that the universe had never been comprehensible to Mrs. Moore's intellect (p. 157). What is said in the novel is not a statement about Mrs. Moore's personal limitations but rather a reflection of the general human predicament.

The corollary of the statement is that the discovering of any precise order or comprehensibility will be suspect. In a number of ways Forster has shown his profound distrust of the neat and tidy. Natwar-Singh reports him as saying: "Some of my best friends have been Muslim. I have been attracted to Islamic culture, but I do not like the orderliness of Islam."[26] In the novel this orderliness is represented not by Aziz himself but by his poetry and his mosque. Aziz is personally untidy and his inner life is emotional and volatile. He does, however, lead "a steady life beneath his mutability" (p. 64). When this steady life makes contact with the Muslim tradition an easy and illusory coherence steals over things. Aziz recites poetry to his friends while "India—a hundred Indias—whispered outside beneath the indifferent moon," but to them at that moment "India seemed one and their own" (p. 17). "Mosque" ends on a similar note. And in case there is any doubt about the overneatness of Islam, the point is reiterated near the close of the novel: " 'There is no God but God'; that symmetrical injunction melts in the mild airs of Mau . . ." (p. 308).

The temple stands as a contrast to the order and harmony of the mosque. In an interesting article published in 1919 Forster says that "the general deportment of the Temple is odious. It is unaccommodating, it rejects every human grace. . . . No one could love such a building. Yet no one can forget it. It remains in the mind when fairer types have faded, and sometimes seems to be the only type that has any significance. When we tire of being pleased and of being improved, and of the other gymnastics of the West, and care, or think we care, for Truth alone; then the Indian Temple exerts its power, and beckons down absurd or detestable vistas to an exit unknown to the Parthenon."[27]

The contrast here between East and West is the same contrast that pervades *A Passage to India*. The account of Adela's return to Europe notes that the clean sands of Egypt "seemed to wipe off everything that was difficult and equivocal" (p. 276). And the account of Fielding's visit begins: "Egypt was charming—a green strip of carpet and walking up and down it four sorts of animals and one sort of man" (p. 292). This witty description, conjuring up an image of the members of Noah's Ark on parade—and parodied at the beginning of the next chapter where Godbole and God stand at opposite ends of the same strip of carpet—should warn us that Fielding's raptures about Mediterranean harmony as the human norm are a reflection of his own limited and too orderly outlook (p. 293).

Forster himself, unlike Fielding, was able to confront the muddle of India and Gokul Ashtami, he was able to accept the frustration of reason and form. He was neither overwhelmed nor driven to reject what he found. To read Lowes Dickinson's comments on

India is to appreciate more fully Forster's achievement. In 1913 Dickinson wrote to Forster: "India, as it glimmers in a remote past, is supernatural, uncanny, terrifying, sublime, horrible, monotonous, full of mountains and abysses, all heights and depths, and for ever incomprehensible." And in *Appearances* he refers to India as "this terrible country, where the great forces of nature, drought and famine and pestilence, the intolerable sun, the intolerable rain, and the exuberance of life and death, have made of mankind a mere passive horde cowering before inscrutable Powers."[28] Forster experienced the impact of this terrible India with its cowering hordes. He also experienced the appeal of its mysterious life. But he always insisted, as Dickinson did not, on seeing the human reality which hid just beneath the surface of the grand and gross appearances.

To see the human reality, Forster found he must establish some degree of detachment. The urbane and too facetious tone of the letters he wrote home from India and later published in *The Hill of Devi* are one sign of his efforts to stand back from his experiences of India. That his purpose in standing back was to achieve a deeper insight is attested by the novel. In the account of the Hindu festival, the facetiousness of the earlier description is transformed by an irony and wit which become part of an extraordinarily complex and convincing human reality.

Something of this same reality can be found in Alfred Lyall's *Asiatic Studies* of 1882 and 1899. Comparison with Lyall, who writes with insight and intelligence, shows Forster's true achievement: the mastery with which he has captured the confusion and multiplicity, the popular enthusiasms and spiritual refinements in the actual practice of Hinduism as it expressed itself in the many levels of Indian society. Sacred Indian texts and elaborate expositions of Hindu mythology and theology are quite the wrong approach to the novel. The novel does not offer a judicious and historically balanced analysis, but something much better—an immediate and, as comparison with *The Hill of Devi* shows, an imaginatively transmuted impression. It captures the multiplicity of India and at the same time its oneness, which is finally a mystery.

E. B. Havell has, in another context, effectively described that spirit of oneness which the novel conveys through the Mau festival: "Even now, on the ghats of Benares, all Indian men, women, and children, forgetting for once sectarian and racial differences, daily join together in worship of the One God, in similar rites to those which the Aryan people used in the same spot three thousand years ago. There we may see, if we have eyes to see, that all India is one spirit, however diverse in race and in creed."[29]

"Perhaps life is a mystery, not a muddle. . . . Perhaps the hundred Indias which fuss and squabble so tiresomely are one, and the universe they mirror is one" (p. 274). The muddle of the hundred Indias expresses the absence of order. The mystery of the one India expresses a supreme order which is wholly unlike the order understood by Fielding and Adela. Their Western rationalist conception of order does not fit with anything in the vast subcontinent. "India is the country, fields, fields, then hills, jungle, hills, and more fields. . . . How can the mind take hold of such a country?" (p. 142) The answer is, it cannot. India defies man's orderly hopes (p. 219) and his itch for the seemly (p. 153). If it could be seen from the moon it might have a definite outline—but it cannot be so seen (p. 104). The peoples who dwell around that charming lake called the Mediterranean share an idea of order which, in its stress on perspective and proportion, is irrelevant to the vastness and confusion of India, for India—as a true image of the universe—cannot be comprehended by the intellect.

"How can the mind take hold of such a country? Generations of invaders have tried, but they remain in exile. The important towns they build are only retreats, their quarrels the malaise of men who cannot find their way home. India knows of their trouble. She knows of the whole world's trouble, to its uttermost depth. She calls 'Come' through her hundred mouths, through objects ridiculous and august. And come to what? She has never defined. She is not a promise, only an appeal" (pp. 142-43).

Why has India never defined? Why does she remain an appeal? Why is Godbole understood to say that in his songs God never comes, so that each song remains an appeal? And why does the voice of the hundred Indias say "No, not yet" to the friendship of Fielding and Aziz? And why does the sky, referring to the universe of the hundred Indias, say "No, not there" to the appeal for friendship? The answer to all these questions is the same. If God were present, friendship possible, and one India a reality, they would all of them fall under the rule of time and become slaves of order and be reduced to the sterile categories of rational thought and mechanical organization.

Forster's profound distrust of supposedly rational order is shown in a 1919 review in which he quotes with warm approval this statement by Romain Rolland. "By its very definition the state belongs to the past. No matter how new the forms of life it represents, it arrests and congeals them. It is its function to petrify everything with which it comes into contact, and turn living into bureaucratic ideals."[30] Indeed, every form of organization is stultifying and soulless and every form of arbitrarily imposed order is negative. Even the kindly missionaries are condemned by their own rationality. Someone must be excluded from Heaven, they argue, otherwise there would be no telling whether everyone was in or whether everyone was out, there would be no way of knowing whether Heaven was all or nothing (p. 41). A logical dilemma, the product of rational conformity, forces the missionaries into an act of exclusion and negation.

We can now see the thematic significance of the discussion of the mystic's dilemma. As soon as he thinks he has been with God, the event becomes history, it falls under the rules of time, it congeals and petrifies (p. 300). And along with the event, God too falls under the rules of time and becomes fossilized. Yet God transcends process and cannot be accommodated to the stultifying demands of the rational mind. That is why he is and must forever remain unattainable. One of the most powerful and significant passages in the novel gives expression to this idea immediately before the mighty climax of the festival:

> Gusts of wind mixed darkness and light, sheets of rain cut from the north, stopped, cut from the south, began rising from below, and across them struggled the singers, sounding every note but terror, and preparing to throw God away, God Himself, (not that God can be thrown) into the storm. Thus was He thrown year after year, and were others thrown—little images of Ganpati, baskets of ten-day corn, tiny tazias after Mohurram—scapegoats, husks, emblems of

245

passage; a passage not easy, not now, not here, not to be apprehended except when it is unattainable: the God to be thrown was an emblem of that. (pp. 327–28)

In an article published in 1914, Forster distinguished between the Eastern and Western view of religion. Of the Eastern view he said: "And the promise is not that a man shall see God, but that he shall be God. He is God already, but imperfectly grasps the mystery."[31] This idea is given full and extended representation in *A Passage to India*. God is the universe, he is all men united in love and informing all matter with life. But the goal of universal oneness is to be attained only through love, for love begins as individual participation but aspires to universal participation. It is not to be attained through any system of rational thought or social organization, nor is it to be derived from the sensible tidying up of a muddle. Oneness is a mystery. It is apprehended only *through* individuals and only insofar as the individual is able to transcend time and space and ego and is able, by utilizing the furthest reaches of the subconscious and supraconscious, to achieve identity with the universe that is not himself.[32] But because the experience of ecstatic identity is fleeting as well as timeless, oneness with the universe cannot be instituted in the world of reason and social order. In that sense it is forever unattainable. But it can be apprehended momentarily.

The experience of oneness need not arise from a vision of ecstasy, it may arise from a vision of desolation. Then the other-than-self is a negative reality like the death-ridden universe apprehended by Giuseppe in "The Story of the Siren." As Mrs. Moore leaves India, Forster asks: "What had spoken to her in that scoured-out cavity of the granite? What dwelt in the first of the caves? . . . the undying worm itself. . . . the serpent of eternity made of maggots . . ." (p. 217). The cave does not symbolize death, but Mrs. Moore sees death as implicit in her vision. She sees life as an endless process of dying in which oneness is identity with a dead universe of matter. This is oneness with the universe experienced as total negation. And the individual, mirroring this negation, is turned inward and undergoes identity with the narcissistic limits of the isolated self. When, however, the eternal moment is ecstatic, when it involves a positive and outgoing union with the other-than-self, the universe is to some degree redeemed and given life, and the dead who are part of its materiality are also redeemed and given life. It is in this way—and in part through Godbole—that Mrs. Moore becomes one with a living universe.

In *A Passage to India,* Forster for the first time in the novels gives extended representation to the vision of desolation. It dominates the whole of Part II, which is half the novel. In Part III, as Forster has noted, he needed a balance, a vision of ecstasy. We might express this structural situation in the terms of Godbole's philosophy. The first two parts of the novel establish the difference between God's absence and his nonexistence. But the very idea of nonexistence symbolized by the Marabar must be balanced by an interval of presence. "Temple" is the architectural lump that provides this balance and this presence. The temple and the Marabar Hills are antithetical in the extreme, for they symbolize the presence and the nonexistence of God. That is why Forster has said that the Hindu festival represents the same thing as the scene in the cave "turned inside out."[33]

This narrative interdependence of good and evil, being and not-being, Temple and Marabar is essential to Forster's success in rendering his entire novel archetypal. The key to his achievement is Mrs. Moore and her vision of desolation. In the earlier works there is a decisive separation of good and evil. And as well, there is a qualitative distinction: the good is visionary; the evil is not visionary, though behind it we glimpse a transcendent horror. Archetypal unity and totality transmute only those persons and objects which are eminently good. All that is evil or indifferent remains outside the circle, though it is firmly contained within the total order of the fiction. As a result of this qualitative disparity, the good attains dominance in our minds, even though it may be defeated as in "The Machine Stops," and the evil serves as counterpoint to underscore its special character. (All of which is right and proper in works of romance comedy; the good and the true should have the edge.)

It is only when we reach *Howards End* that a change is perceptible. The note of the sinister—a note that is caught in all Forster's successful fiction and that echoes the horror lurking just beneath the smooth-functioning surfaces of his evil people—the note of the sinister becomes insistent like the goblins of Beethoven's symphony walking over the universe from end to end. In the symphony and in Margaret's perception of London as Hell, evil is rendered visionary.

With *A Passage to India* this process reaches its culmination. For the first time in the novels good and evil are closely matched. (This is intended as a statement of fact. The writer's choice as to whether he will match his moral forces or give one or other of them pre-eminence is a prerogative of his art. It is not, in itself, a criterion for assessing the truth or value of his work.) Through Mrs. Moore's experience of desolation, evil becomes an object of vision. The earlier experiments in this line, "The Point of It" (Part III), "The Story of the Siren," and Beethoven's symphony are now carried to a triumphant conclusion. Mrs. Moore experiences both the joyful love of oneness with the universe and the twilight horror of identity with a distinction-less world of matter. Good and evil lodge side by side in her person. More important, they appear qualitatively equal in that they are both visionary. In this way Mrs. Moore provides the human center for that narrative interdependence of good and evil which reaches out to include being and not-being, Temple and Marabar.

This takes us some way toward an understanding of Forster's success in rendering the whole of *A Passage to India* archetypal. The universe of India and the nasty cosmos of the Marabar are seen as the objects of Mrs. Moore's positive and negative vision. Many other elements in the novel are similarly caught up in the vision of one or another of the characters. Mrs. Moore herself takes on an unmistakable quality of transcendence in the eyes of Adela, Aziz, and even Fielding; the nameless Indian at the back of the court appears strangely "other" to Adela; the wasp is transmuted in the perception of Mrs. Moore and Professor Godbole; and so the catalogue might be extended. But at the last there remain significant portions of the novel, including the greatest scenes of the Mau festival, in which the narrator ceases to rely on the insight of his characters. Such scenes are presented by the narrator as the object of his own vision. It is directly through him that they are rendered archetypal.

There is nothing remarkable in this per se. The same technique can be seen from time to time even in the earliest fiction. The remarkable feature is the inclusiveness, the narrative capacity to extend the sense of archetypal unity and totality to every aspect of the story. How this came about is made comprehensible by Forster's analysis of the experience of visionary novelists. "Everything comes to them in a rush, their arms are filled at once with material for a life's work, and their task is to sort and re-sort what they have rather than to seek fresh experiences." In the discussion of this point in Chapter 2, it was noted that the youthful experience of insight and revelation will be attached to specific persons and events, and further that at a future time this youthful sense of vision may enter into a new domain, thereby taking on a fresh body of imagery. This is precisely the situation in *A Passage to India*. The author's permanent vision has entered into the vast subcontinent and found there a new set of symbols in which to express itself. But the endeavor was not easy, as Forster's prolonged struggle with the novel attests. Never before had youth and the memories of youth permeated a universe so removed in external features from the world of his initial vision. It is significant, as he tells us, that the personal stimulus of friendship was essential to the achievement; and equally significant that his second visit to India turned the novel to ashes and withered his creative impulse. For the India of his novel was not the land of his travels but a new and mysterious universe which only careful waiting and anxious unflagging honesty could render conformable to his permanent vision.

As long as Forster employed material closely related to his earliest insights and revelations, he relied on the eternal moment to express his vision, at first directly and then more indirectly. But he knew from experience that many things in life remained outside the bounds of ecstatic perception. In his earlier novels he drew on these unleavened elements to institute a formal as well as a moral counterpoint and contrast. In *A Passage to India,* however, Forster made contact with a new and alien world which opened to him the possibility of creating a universe wholly conformable to his vision and expressive of its inmost meaning. In this new universe all could be transmuted, even the Turtons and the Burtons could take their place within the purview of negation and evil, and be translated into the desolating vision of hollowly oubouming echoes.

Forster's commitment to his Indian universe is a total engagement of that self whose vision goes back to his youth. Because the self must strive for contact with a land mysterious and intellectually incomprehensible, it does not dominate the fiction but rather takes its place as a part of the whole. And because the self has an independent and visionary status going back to youth and the deepest experiences of youth, Forster is able to represent this engaged self and the Indian world of its involvement as a single liberated object of vision. He is able to transmute all the elements and make of them one universe, total, vast, and archetypal.

The esthetic wholeness of this created world is the outward and visible sign of its inmost meaning. Through its concrete, sensuous, and visionary unity, Forster's mythic India gives immediate and incarnate assurance that the universe is one. And to the individual it gives assurance that in the moment of ecstasy he may, like Godbole, participate in this mystery of oneness and so apprehend his own divinity. For it will be his duty as it will be his desire to strive toward a passage to the universe—a passage to India.

Appendix A

*Forster and the Nineteenth-Century View of
Nature and Symbol*

It was pointed out at the end of Chapter 1 that the recognition
of an indwelling spirit in nature admits of two responses, conscious
identification or unconscious identity with nature; and (following
Jung's definition) that identification with nature is a state in which
one is aware of the relationship whereas identity with nature is a state
in which awareness of relationship is effectively obliterated, for the
self and the object are one. Conscious identification with nature is the
characteristic response of writers throughout the nineteenth century.
The vague pantheism of the Victorians is well illustrated by the mature Arnold:

> The *not ourselves,* which is in us and in the world round us, has
> almost everywhere, as far as we can see, struck the minds of men as
> they awoke to consciousness, and has inspired them with awe. Every-
> one knows how the mighty natural objects which most took their
> regards became the objects to which this awe addressed itself. Our
> very word *God* is a reminiscence of these times, when men invoked
> "The Brilliant on high" . . . as the power representing to them that
> which transcended the limits of their narrow selves, and that by

which they lived and moved and had their being. (*Literature & Dogma* [2nd. ed.; London, 1873], p. 29.)

This passage describes the experience of identification with nature in a very typical way by its emphasis on the insignificance of oneself in relation to the awesome magnitude of the not-oneself. But it is possible to stand in a relationship of approximate equality with nature and to envisage it—in the words of Walter Pater—"as the unity of a living spirit or person, revealing itself in various degrees to the kindred spirit of the observer." (*Greek Studies*, p. 95.)

Compare the serenity of this account, the serenity of the "observer," with Erwin Rohde's description—it belongs to the nineties—of violent participation in the cult of Dionysus:

> In moments of supreme exaltation man felt the presence above him and around him of mighty powers that seemed to express themselves even in his own personal life. These he was no longer to confront in pious and fearful awe, passively confined within the limits of his own separate personality; he was to break down every barrier and clasp them to his heart, making them his own in unconditional surrender. Mankind needed not to wait for that strange product of poetry and thought, Pantheism, before it could experience this instinctive need to lose its own private existence, for a moment, in the divine. (*Psyche,* trans. Hillis, p. 261. First German ed. 1890.)

These accounts by Arnold and Pater on the one hand and Rohde on the other display in extreme form the difference between identification and identity with nature.

The Romantics made conscious identification with nature the cornerstone of life and art. Wordsworth's "Tintern Abbey" describes the poet's youthful response of "dizzy rapture" before the passionate and awesome spectacle of nature's grandeur, and then his mature response of serene wisdom under the guiding spirit of nature's sustaining power. His account of the motion and the spirit "that impels / All thinking things . . . / And rolls through all things" brilliantly interprets an ecstatic experience of oneness with nature. But Wordsworth at no point longs to lose himself in nature. It is quite otherwise with Shelley. His "Ode to the West Wind" is a passionate prayer for identity: "Be thou me, impetuous one!" But it remains a prayer, a self-conscious plea. Like the other Romantics, he values sensation, feeling, and self-awareness too highly to give them up for the sake of participating in a primitive loss of self.

The intense moment of identity with nature, of union with the other-than-self, is an ecstatic experience. At the end of the nineteenth century interest in anthropology and the primitive, in psychology and the unconscious, and in mythology and the unexpressible created an atmosphere in which ecstatic experience was more intensely valued than ever before. This explains why, though ecstatic experiences are as old as civilization, they achieved a special prominence at this time. And it explains why the Romantics, for all that they were prone to ecstatic experiences, were self-conscious and talkative about them, and were given to exploring and interpreting such experiences rather than recreating them.

This can be seen in Coleridge's "Hymn before Sunrise in the Vale of Chamouni" and "The Eolian Harp." In the latter poem we read:

> O! the one life within us and abroad,
> Which meets all motion and becomes its soul,
> A light in sound, a sound-like power in light,
> Rhythm in all thought, and joyance everywhere—

Ethel F. Cornwell describes this passage as "an intellectualization of the ecstatic moment in which the poet has reached the still point and feels unified with the Spirit which permeates all life. One might go so far as to say that the theory of organic unity that Coleridge consistently applies to life and to art is but an intellectualization of what the poet *feels,* and the truth that the poet recognizes in the ecstatic moment." (*The "Still Point": Theme and Variations in the Writings of T. S. Eliot, Coleridge, Yeats, Henry James, Virginia Woolf, and D. H. Lawrence* [New Brunswick, N.J., 1962], p. 79.)

The predilection for interpreting ecstatic experience is deftly illustrated by Shelley, who tells us that as a boy he sought for ghosts and hoped for talk with the departed dead:

> I was not heard—I saw them not—
> When musing deeply on the lot
> Of life, at that sweet time when winds are wooing
> All vital things that wake to bring

News of birds and blossoming,—
Sudden, thy shadow fell on me;
I shrieked, and clasped my hands in ecstasy.

Despite the suspiciousness of the shriek this reads like an authentic experience. The description of the setting and mood which precedes the moment of ecstasy is especially convincing. But what is the shadow which falls on the poet? What is the source of the moment? Who could ever guess it to be what indeed we are told it is—Intellectual Beauty? This and what follows make clear that the poet has transformed the experience from one of identity to one of identification in which he develops his conscious relationship with the object of vision. Consequently the other-than-self is inflated and the self deflated. The source of the ecstasy becomes "O awful loveliness" which "like the truth / Of nature" on his "passive youth / Descended" and bound him "To fear himself, and love all human kind."

René Wellek's well-known and authoritative essay on "The Concept of Romanticism in Literary History" has nothing to say directly on this subject. But by implication it confirms the Romantic stress on identification and interpretation.

> This new view emphasizes the totality of man's forces, not reason alone, nor sentiment alone, but rather intuition, "intellectual intuition," imagination. It is a revival of neo-Platonism, a pantheism (whatever its concessions to orthodoxy), a monism which arrived at an identification of God and the world, soul and body, subject and object. The propounders of these ideas were always conscious of the precariousness and difficulty of these views, which frequently appeared to them only as distant ideals; hence the "unending desire" of the German romantics, the stress on evolution, on art as a groping towards the ideal. Exoticism of many kinds is part of the reaction against the eighteenth century and its self-complacency; the suppressed forces of the soul seek their analogies and models in prehistory, in the Orient, in the Middle Ages, and finally in India, as well as in the unconscious and in dreams. (*Concepts of Criticism* [New Haven, 1963], pp. 165–66.)

This analysis, especially in its conclusion, points very dramatically though indirectly toward developments at the end of the century. But its object is to describe the nature of Romanticism. What is of interest is not the use of the word "identification" but the picture of a consciousness aware of precariousness and difficulty, a consciousness desiring, groping, seeking. Here there can be no stopping to rest in the eternal moment of ecstasy. This is the less surprising when we remember—as Wellek points out in the same essay (p. 185)—that in the writings of the late Coleridge "Nature is consistently interpreted by analogy with the progress of man to self-consciousness."

It is this emphasis on self-consciousness which later in the century turns esthetic and culminates in Walter Pater and his literary heirs. The hard gem-like flame leads Pater to use the word ecstasy, but it is nothing of the kind. Rather it is a late development of Romanticism, a renewed but increasingly narcissistic intensity of self-awareness. The fact that Pater's flame could so readily be confused with accounts of authentic ecstasy shows how difficult it is in this period to keep things straight. We must separate the intense moment of esthetic self-consciousness and the ecstatic moment of identity with the other-than-self, and we must distinguish them both from the moment of revelation engendered by that other great phenomenon of the period, the literary symbol.

A good many writers with a well-mixed babble of voices were asserting at this time the authority and autonomy of the literary symbol and were insisting upon its ineffable power to be and to express not another thing but itself. We can recapture the quality of contemporary commitment to the symbol in these words of Arthur Symons: "Gérard de Nerval . . . had divined, before all the world, that poetry should be a miracle; not a hymn to beauty, nor the description of beauty, nor beauty's mirror; but beauty itself, the colour, fragrance, and form of the imagined flower as it blossoms again out of the page. Vision, the over-powering vision, had come to him beyond, if not against, his will; and he knew that vision is the root out of which the flower must grow. Vision had taught him symbol, and he knew that it is by symbol alone that the flower can take visible form." (*Collected Works*, VIII, 121; and see A. G. Lehmann, *The Symbolist Aesthetic in France, 1885–1895* [Oxford, 1950].)

255

I take this to mean that Nerval had a vision not of a flower but of a truth, namely that the symbol as a whole and sensuous image must be created by the imagination of the poet, for only by such a process could it blossom from the page, only thus could the poem be a miracle. But whatever the poem or the symbol is called, we must not be taken in by the appearance of magical objectivity. What we have here is Romantic self-consciousness taken to its extreme, not its extreme of ego mania which comes early but its extreme of sophistication which comes late. Symbolism is an extension of that estheticism which in England had Walter Pater as its high-priest. And in the England of the nineties, in the England of the generation of poets who had to face their ends when young (Yeats's words), we are (in Frank Kermode's words) "dealing with a tradition which has become fully, not to say histrionically, self-conscious." (*Romantic Image* [New York, 1957], p. 22.) The point is confirmed by Arthur Symons' famous essay "The Decadent Movement in Literature" (*Harper's New Monthly Magazine,* LXXXVII [November 1893], 858) which specifies "an intense self-consciousness" as one of the hallmarks of decadence. The literature of this symbolist-esthetic tradition must be distinguished from the literature of ecstatic experience which is characterized by the absence of self-consciousness.*

The symbolists, of course, had ecstatic experiences. The point is that they made highly self-conscious symbols out of their objects of vision, and sometimes—like the earlier Romantics—they added the spit and polish of interpretation. Arthur Symons' "The Dance" is a good illustration of these tendencies. I have italicized the words which most directly convey the ecstasy.

---

* Richard Ellman in his interesting composite portrait of the Edwardian writer, "Two Faces of Edward," *Edwardians and Late Victorians,* English Institute Essays, 1959, ed. Ellman (New York, 1960), fails to make this distinction. He rightly says: "The central miracle for the Edwardians is the sudden alteration of the self; around it much of their literature pivots" (p. 198). This miracle, redolent of the self-consciousness of the symbolist-esthetic tradition, is perfectly reflected in the alteration or conversion of such diverse heroes as Strether in *The Ambassadors* and Stephen Dedalus in *Portrait of the Artist;* it is not reflected in the conversion of Forster's heroes (Philip Herriton is a partial exception) precisely because their experience is essentially impersonal and rooted in the unconscious.

For the immortal moment of a passionate dance,
Surely our two souls rushed together and were one,
Once, in the beat of our winged feet in unison,
When, in the brief and flaming ardour of your glance,
The world withered away, vanishing into smoke;
The world narrowed about us, and we heard the beat
As of the rushing winds encompassing our feet;
In the blind heart of the winds, eternal silence woke,
And, cast adrift on our unchainable ecstasy,
Once, and once only, heart to heart, *and soul to soul,*
For an immortal moment *we endured the whole*
Rapture of intolerable immortality. (*Collected Works,* I, 305.)

The paradox of the beating, rushing winds and the silence at their heart is impressive and is a guarantee if any were needed that this is an authentic experience of ecstasy. One notices too in the italicized parts the poet's sense of being overtaken by the experience so that he endures rather than wills. The rest of the lines tend to contradict this impression. The speaker's ego exposes itself in "our unchainable ecstasy," he busies himself with interpretation as in line two, and he suggests that the world has withered away in response to his partner's glance ("vanished into smoke" is pure hocus-pocus). The impersonality, the sense of givenness characteristic of ecstatic experience, here collides with the Romantic ego. And because Symons is not a great poet he allows us to see the collision very clearly. Yeats, on the other hand, takes the offered symbol, takes it from what he thought of as the Great Memory, stores it in his own memory, explores it, develops it, and has it ready when the literary occasion offers. And so he may ask: "How can we know the dancer from the dance?"

Romantic self-consciousness dominates nineteenth-century literature and culminates in estheticism and symbolism. Forster breaks with this tradition. He does not have the symbolist's preoccupation with art and image, a preoccupation which led to such extremes as Yeats's assertion that "the laws of art . . . are the hidden laws of the world," and Lionel Johnson's insistence that "life is ritual," and Yeats's more mundane admission—he is speaking of the nineties—that Johnson's phrase "expressed something that was in some degree in all our thoughts."* Nor was Forster interested in that life-in-death death-in-life paradox embodied in the Romantic Image as analyzed by Frank Kermode. He did find death in life, but that came directly from looking at the world around him and more particularly from the ecstatic experience of identity with nature. Forster's symbols are life-oriented not art-oriented. Hence it is not the symbolists but the thinkers discussed in Chapter 1 who present themselves as the most suitable backdrop to his thought and artistic practice.

We can now see, however, that these thinkers are making many of the same assumptions about myth that the symbolists make about images. What is it that embodies our most profound and continuing intuitions and expresses the spiritual essence of the world and man? And what may bring light and instruction to mankind and a profound assurance of the truth? (Symonds) What is it that is unique and indispensable as a way of imparting knowledge and that goes down to the bedrock of human nature where man is more at one with universal nature? (Stewart) What is it that has power in its concrete form and meaning in its literal sense? (Stewart and Westcott) The answer to each of these questions is myth, but it could almost be symbol. Indeed Myers and Stewart at their most interesting make no distinction between the mythic image as such and the literary symbol. Genius, penetrating into or penetrated by the subconscious and the supraconscious, is the true spring of symbolism, and art is the most likely place for its manifestation. Thus the symbol, at once mythic and literary, expresses the hidden concordance between the visible and the invisible, between matter and thought.

I need not stress the degree to which this resembles symbolist theory. Indeed I want rather to stress such differences as there are between the accounts of myth and symbol. These are differences of degree or emphasis and might be summed up in this way. Compared to symbolist theory, mythic theory suggests that the myth is more deeply rooted in the unconscious, more broadly based on a foundation

---

* "The Symbolism of Poetry" (1900), in *The Collected Works in Verse and Prose of William Butler Yeats,* Vol. VI: *Ideas of Good and Evil* (London, 1908), p. 198; and *The Autobiography of William Butler Yeats* (New York, 1953), p. 181.

of universal nature, and hence more generally expressive of the elemental in man and nature.

Here is another way of putting the difference. In the essay "William Blake and his Illustrations to the *Divine Comedy*" (1896), Yeats said, his words almost a copy of those used by Symonds in referring to myth: "A symbol is indeed the only possible expression of some invisible essence. . . ." (*Works*, VI, 138.) The symbolist tends to think of essence as the soul of a thing or as its distillation or quintessence. The mythic theorist tends to think of essence as that which is characteristic and hence shared with all other members of the same class and hence fundamental, which is to say (among other things) elemental.

The implications of this difference can be seen by comparing Pater's view of Plato with Stewart's view. In *Plato and Platonism* (London, 1893) Pater insists that art is finite and that its function is to control the infinite and formless. Plato's theory of ideas is an attempt to enforce a finite definition upon "the infinite, the indefinite, formless, brute matter, of our experience of the world" (pp. 51–52). For Stewart the essence is to be found not in the theory of ideas and the definition of the indefinite and formless but rather in the actuality of the myths and their power to penetrate the depths and express the elemental.

The other difference between the symbolist and the student of myth is more drastic. The symbolist thinks first and most intensely of myth and symbol as art-enhancing;* his counterpart thinks of them first and most obviously as life-enhancing. Again Plato is found to support both sides. Pater says that he "anticipates the modern notion that art as such has no end but its own perfection,—'art for art's sake'" (pp. 244–45). Westcott and Stewart say that through myth he goes down to the bedrock of human nature and thereby expresses truths about ourselves and about our relations with universal nature which

---

* Edward Engelberg holds this view, though he thinks Yeats an exception to it: "for the *symboliste* poet, let us say Baudelaire, the symbol is the end product. . . . The world is used to evoke the symbol. Yeats, I think, came to work in the opposite direction: he would use the symbol to evoke the world, and his interest, ultimately, was less in the symbol than in the things evoked." See *The Vast Design: Patterns in W. B. Yeats's Aesthetic* (Toronto, 1964), p. 110.

could not otherwise be expressed. In this division of emphasis there can be absolutely no doubt that Forster is on the side of Westcott and Stewart, on the side of the new century with its view of myth and symbol as a source of deepest insight and as profoundly life-enhancing.

Though he was on the side of the new century, Forster at first used the traditional mythic symbols of Greece. In doing so he was fully aware both of their power and of their openness to facile criticism. In 1904 he said of Demeter that poets, "generation after generation, have sung in passionate incompetence of . . . the wanderings of the Goddess, and her gift to us of corn and tears; so that generations of critics, obeying also their need, have censured the poets for reviving the effete mythology of Greece, and urged them to themes of living interest which shall touch the heart of to-day." (*Abinger Harvest,* p. 201.) Times have not changed; critics still trumpet their objections, on the misguided assumption that Forster's Grecian myths are in the tradition of nineteenth-century pantheism and are no more than clichéd personifications of nature's awesome or kindred spirit. In the unsuccessful short stories that is what they appear to be. But in the successful short stories and in *The Longest Journey* they are expressive of elemental universal forces; and the hero, in the eternal moment of identity with these forces as embodied in nature or the other-than-self, participates in a total order of mythic power and unity.

Appendix B

The Manuscripts of A Passage to India

The manuscripts of *A Passage to India,* acquired by The University of Texas in 1960 and presently located in the Humanities Research Center of the Main University Library at Austin, consist of the following:

(1) Manuscript A: a holograph of 399 pages numbered A1 through A399, which represents a fairly complete draft of the novel.

(2) Manuscript B: a holograph of 101 pages numbered B1 through B101, consisting in most instances of earlier variants of passages found in MS. A.

(3) Manuscript C: a typescript carbon including title page, dedication page and eighteen pages of text, for the most part unnumbered, corresponding to pp. 5–8, 160, 228 and 310–18 of the first printed edition.

(4) Four large folded sheets of corrections and addenda keyed apparently to the original copy of the typescript.

(Robert Ligon Harrison, "The Manuscripts of *A Passage to India,*" Ann Arbor: University Microfilms, 1965, p. vi. In the discussion that follows, page references to Harrison's typescript edition of the manuscripts are included in the text and are preceded by the letter H. When a passage or incident is found only in the book, the page reference is to the Arnold Pocket Edition of the novel and is preceded by the letter F. In quoting Harrison's edition I have greatly simplified his typographical conventions. Where words crossed out by Forster are included in a quotation, they are placed in parentheses.)

Earlier versions of a literary work belong in the same category as the author's essays and his publicly stated opinions. Whatever merit they may have in themselves, they stand outside the work as it was finally created. They tell us more about the creator and about his ordinary as well as his creative self than they tell us about his creation. Thus discretion and restraint are indispensible when one uses earlier versions of a work to gain insight into its final form.

For this reason it may be some advantage that my chapter on *A Passage to India* was in the hands of the publisher before the manuscript versions of the novel were read. It is a point worth making that my interpretation of the novel was arrived at independent of the manuscripts, and that they tend to confirm this interpretation.

The manuscript variants of *A Passage to India* are extraordinarily interesting not because radical changes have taken place between manuscript and book but because many minor changes have greatly influenced the final effect of the book. These changes will be discussed under three headings: The Major Characters and India, the Marabar and India, the Marabar and the Mau Festival. These headings do not finally indicate three separate topics, for all three converge on a single theme: Forster's development of precise distinctions between the wasteland of India in which God is absent, the negation of the Marabar in which God is nonexistent, and the affirmation of the Mau Festival in which God is present.

The Major Characters and India

The Adela of the manuscripts, variously called Violet, Janet, Edith, and Adela, undergoes more vicissitudes than any other character, but they are vicissitudes of plot. She is loved by Aziz (H, p. 722), physically assaulted in the cave (H, pp. 315–16), and becomes the wife of Fielding (H, pp. 658–59). Through all these versions her character seems to remain very much as it finally appears in the book. Forster's most interesting changes have to do with her experience of vision. In the book Forster adds Adela's important moment of insight as she contemplates the Marabar Hills: "How lovely they suddenly were! But she couldn't touch them" (F, p. 50). What he gives with one hand he takes away with the other. For instance, he deletes the following passage from the book: "Her afternoon at Fielding's had passed in a steady crescendo as if a blare of revelation approached; then Ronny had intervened . . . with the result that the melody had been broken . . ."—broken, like the queer melody of Godbole's song (H, p. 176).

This sense of approaching revelation, of crescendo without culmination, and its parallel with Godbole's song, a revelation equally unfulfilled or broken, is explicitly echoed in the MS B account of the spectacular but finally disappointing Marabar sunrise. It is echoed, too, in Adela's comment: "The sun promises to come and then does not come" (H, p. 275). By omitting these passages, Forster has restricted Adela's experience of vision to the trial scene and to a single direct prelude, the early vision of the Hills. Moreover the trial scene in the book contains notable additions in detail and comment, the effect of which is to make the reader more decisively aware of the unique and visionary character of Adela's experience (H, pp. 498–501; F, pp. 236–38).

Forster's changes in presenting the punkah wallah also work to the same end. A rejected MS A version describes him in much the same terms as the book but, instead of fortifying his significance by contrasting him with the self-conscious little magistrate, the manuscript turns to Adela and her qualified response to him:

The impression he made on Adela was not profound, but he was the first person she saw, and he was almost naked whereas the rest of them wore clothes. He twisted back her mind to that moment on the great notched rock where she had thought 'do I love Ronny,' he was a link in a series that stretched back into mental darkness and had never been properly explored by her.

Turning from him she saw Aziz, and her heart stopped. He hadn't done it. As soon as she saw him, she knew. She had made a mistake. (H, pp. 482–83; compare F, pp. 226–27, 229.)

Though the consequences of Adela's seeing the punkah wallah are memorable, the impression he makes on her is not profound because he is only a link in a sexual chain. The impression takes on depth only when, as in the book, he becomes for her an expression of the collective unconscious in which for one brief moment she participates. (See above, pp. 209–12.)

MS A tells us that Adela, after hearing Mrs. Moore named at the trial, stopped worrying and "made her mind a void" (H, p. 496). Like the material Forster added to the book concerning Adela's vision, these words (which he dropped from the book) show the direction he was moving in. The words express admirably that suspended mental state which precludes entry into the unconscious. They were dropped, I believe, because Forster wished to eradicate any hint of a connection between the mental void of ego-free receptiveness and the ultimate void of the Marabar caves.

As Forster moves from manuscript to book, Adela's moment of vision becomes more isolated and accentuated, but her ordinary character remains essentially prosaic and unchanged. The situation is rather different with Fielding and Aziz. They are treated more critically in the book, and so brought closer to Adela's prosaic level of understanding. In company with her they compose the little jog-along party of which Fielding speaks.

In MS A a flame burnt in the heart of Aziz, "a flame which desired to light up the whole world with good fellowship" (H, p. 12). The book deprives Aziz of this association with the theme of universal love. Later, when Adela makes the mistake of regarding Aziz as "India," the book adds as the manuscripts do not that "his outlook was limited and his method inaccurate" (F, p. 76). These are small touches but they have their effect.

The effect is more marked in the case of Fielding. MS A reads: "The world to him remained a globe of men who are trying to reach one another and can only do so by the help of good will plus emotion: a creed ill suited to Moradpore [i.e. Chandrapore], but he had come out too late to lose it" (H, pp. 110–11). That good will plus emotion was ill suited to Chandrapore suggests that Forster did not intend emotion to mean love. He may, however, have thought the word too open to such an interpretation, for the book substitutes *culture and intelligence* (compare Adela) for *emotion* (F, p. 65). Later, on the occasion of Fielding's visit to Aziz, we read: " 'I shall not really be intimate with this fellow,' Fielding thought, and then 'nor with anyone.' That was the corollary" (F, p. 123). These words, offering one of the book's most decisive comments on Fielding's character, are not present in the manuscripts.

More notable still is the way certain insights about the Marabar are attributed to Fielding in MS B and later transferred to Mrs. Moore in MS A and the book. It was Fielding who learned that the universe is incomprehensible to our reason, that infinity and eternity are robbed of their vastness, and that "Pathos, piety, courage— all are the same; they exist but they are identical. Everything exists, & nothing has value" (H, pp. 336–37). In the book Fielding learns nothing of all this. He is cut down to size and made to jog along with Adela and Aziz.

The transferring of these insights to Mrs. Moore is an important first step in the creation of her mysteriously impressive character. A second step takes place between MS A and the book. In MS A Mrs. Moore busies herself with prosaic and practical details (H, pp. 184–88 and 460 esp.) which have the effect of suggesting that hers is a rather ordinary nature. In the book some judicious cutting produces an astounding transformation in her character. Putting from her everything that is petty and mundane, she stands forth as a powerfully intuitive being.

The manuscripts reveal how greatly Forster's art depended on pertinent elaborations and deletions. It is an art of immense discretion. This discretion in the handling of the major characters has as its object the subtle equating of Adela, Fielding, and Aziz as people of the wasteland, and the more subtle projecting of Mrs. Moore as a wholly memorable and haunting figure who, though caught up in the wasteland, yet makes contact with the negation of the Marabar and the affirmation of the Mau festival.

The Marabar and India

At some point in the middle portion of *A Passage to India,* Forster bogged down. The manuscript versions indicate the expedition to the Marabar was almost certainly that point. Harrison notes that "at one time many of the pages of MS. A belonged wholly or in part to MS. B. In other words: MS. A constitutes essentially a draft of the book; MS. B is what was left over" (p. ix). Of the 101 pages of MS B, half are devoted to the expedition to the Marabar. Forster's difficulties were about plot (was Adela actually assaulted?), about character (was Fielding or Mrs. Moore to receive the message of the Marabar?), and above all about the significance of the Marabar.

In MS B the Marabar, rather than expressing its unique and terrifying message of negation, conveys the message of the Indian wasteland. When the echo of the caves is heard by Aziz and Adela, a reference to Hindus decisively associates the repeated "boum" of the caves with the repeated "come" of Godbole's song (H, p. 310). And when Fielding enters on the scene, the whole point of his encounter with the Hills and caves is that they concentrate the message of India. "One tree, a raw and raging green," speaks to him: " 'You want a mystery,' it waved: 'human beings do, but I announce no mystery, only a muddle; the universe, incomprehensible to your reason, shall yet offer no repose to your soul.' " In the next paragraph the speech is repeated: "I am muddle not mystery." And who is the speaker? Forster first wrote "the Marabar Hills," crossed these words out, then wrote "India" (H, pp. 335–36).

MS B also makes it explicit that the message of the Marabar train, "pomper, pomper" (F, p. 142), is the message of India's echoes, the call of "Come, come" through a thousand mouths, through objects ridiculous and august (H, pp. 266, 269). MS B, like the book, presents the journey as a rite of passage into a strange world. In both, the message of the train is to be understood as a recapitulation of the echoes of India (they escape Adela's well-equipped mind), and as a prelude to the echoes of the Marabar. But in MS B the Marabar is a condensed image of India as a wasteland and the echoes of the Marabar are the culminating expression of a land in which order and meaning are persistently absent and the plea that God may "come" is vainly repeated. Whereas in the book, the Marabar is truly an "other" world so that the message of the train, as well as recapitulating the echoes of India, is a premonition of "other" echoes. In the book these echoes of the Marabar cave speak not of absence but of utter negation and the nonexistence of God.

The description of the cave in MS B, with the two flames striving to meet in the depths of the rock, is much like the final version, but with additional material that was later deleted. Of Adela we read: "She thought not of the Myriads of crystals extending into the hills, unseen, (unimagined, but members one with them another,) red and grey roses dropped from the sun among the fields of earth." Moreover, the rough entrances into the polished caves seemed to Adela (or to the author) an afterthought, "a breach to internal perfection" (H, p. 312). At this stage, then, the caves give a hint of beauty and perfection.

As for the Hills, seen close up they are "gods to whom earth is a ghost" (H, p. 275). Perhaps they have a life of their own, thinks Mrs. Moore. "Yes—why not? There are colours and sounds we cannot perceive. There is also life we cannot perceive. Man is not the measure, he can only focus a tiny spot, he cannot define what is remarkable about the Marabar Caves" (H, p. 296). These passages are not conclusive, but conjoined with the cave's hint of beauty and perfection they suggest that in MS B the Marabar had positive spiritual meaning. And even in MS A Forster wrote that Mrs. Moore could forget the crush in the cave, "but not the echo, because in some way it was spiritual" (H, pp. 302–3; see also p. 457). Of course, Mrs. Moore's encounter with the echo is spiritual. But Forster deleted the words from the book because, in its final development, the Marabar echo is not itself spiritual, nor is it the reverberation of a deeper reality. Rather it is the denial of all spirit.

In the book Forster transforms the Marabar and its echoes into an expression of absolute negation. At the same time he adds a few brief but impressive statements to re-inforce the idea that the echoes of India, as distinct from the echoes of the Marabar, imply the existence of spirit, the existence of God. Of the melancholy fields and poor trees along the road to the Marabar, we read: "the whole scene was inferior, and suggested that the country-side was too vast to admit of excellence. In vain did each item in it call out, 'Come, come.' There was not enough god to go round" (F, p. 92). Also added is Aziz's plea for "Kindness, more kindness, and even after that more kindness" (F, p. 122). As I have shown (p. 223 above), this echoing plea is a call to God who is absent. It becomes one with the hundred echoing voices of India.

Forster also takes care in the book not to associate the echoes of India and the echoes of the Marabar. In MS B we read of the caves: "Make a noise, any noise, and a sound forms above your head and falls over it like a ring, strikes the ground, rises up, falls again, and is finally reabsorbed into the roof. Even the striking of a match produces an echo, a little coiling worm too small to complete a circle but eternally watchful" (H, p. 306). In MS A and the book the image of rings of sound is obscured; but the image of coiling snakes of light as echoes mingling with the echoing "ou-boum" retains its vividness (F, p. 154). Later in the story, when Fielding notes that in India everything echoes and that the echo is always evil, we read: "This reflection about an echo lay at the verge of Fielding's mind" (F, p. 287). At this point in MS A Forster inserts and then crosses out the words: "The uncoiling echo" (H, p. 609). This reference back to the caves is neat but inadmissible.

The many changes from manuscript to book confirm beyond doubt Forster's deliberate intention of making a sharp and meaningful distinction between the Marabar as a symbol of absolute negation implying the nonexistence of God or spirit, and the India of Parts I and II as a symbol of the wasteland in which God is absent but not on that account nonexistent. The fact that this was not his original intention almost certainly means that small and unobtrusive vestiges of the old conception of the Marabar as the essence of the Indian wasteland still linger in the book. This may explain why the distinction, so essential to an understanding of the novel, has evaded many of Forster's critics.

(It is only fair to add that MS B gives hints of Forster's later conception of the Marabar, most notably in the statement that nothing was in the caves, "nothing but absolute emptiness, which local report had not even peopled with ghosts" [H, p. 239]. At least two views about such material are possible. One, Forster at this stage had conflicting or confused notions about the significance of the caves. Two, the emptiness parallels Adela's making her mind a void; in other words it is a prelude to revelation or a deeper understanding. I have not found the evidence of MS B sufficient to judge between these possibilities.)

The Marabar and the Mau Festival

The manuscript versions of the expedition to the Marabar four times refer to the Hills and caves as a muddle (H, pp. 280, 303, 336). All four references are eliminated in the book. The manuscripts of "Temple" twice introduce echoes, once as a noun (H, p. 625), once as a verb (H, p. 717). The use of the verb is especially interesting. The last page of MS B ends "and the sky above them said 'No. Not there.'" The last page of MS A ends "and the sky (said echoed) said, 'No. Not there.'" The idea of echo runs through Forster's mind and slips from his pen to the page. It is a neat concluding echo in a novel filled with echoes: neat, but the temptation must be resisted. Just as the full development of the Marabar as meaningless negation precludes the use of muddle with its implication that order exists though it is absent, so the development of "Temple" as spiritually positive, as indicating presence, precludes the use of echo with its implication of absence. In the manuscript treatment of these images we have a glimpse of Forster's hesitations as he moved toward the final version with its decisive contrast between the Marabar and Mau.

These hesitations are of special interest in Forster's treatment of individualism and oneness with the universe. As Fielding and Aziz ride out in the jungle above Mau, Aziz (according to MS B) is disturbed by the Hindu shrines: "the whole effect of the scenery spotty with idolatry oppressed him, he felt in exile" (H, p. 715). In MS A, after writing (as in the book): "great trees with leaves like plates rose among the brushwood," Forster adds and then strikes the following words on the situation of Aziz: "and seemed to have existed before the creation of man. Though born in the country, he was an exile" (H, pp. 713–14). The notion of the trees as incredibly old like the Marabar Hills was untenable at this point in the novel. But what is interesting is the way the notion of exile has been universalized. It is no longer Aziz but man, both corporate and individual, who is alien.

The situation of man in the universe is explored in another way in this same MS B passage: "Man could occupy the whole universe by extending his actual powers grave & gay,—["that is the message of India," adds MS A (H, p. 668)] but in the process he would cease to be man . . ." for he would become the universe he occupied or extended himself into. To use Forster's example: "He would find that the monkeys had occupied it also, that he was a monkey, and that both of them were trees" (H, p. 715). MS A retains the first part of these reflections and transfers them from Aziz to Fielding (H, p. 668). But since neither of them could be credited with such an insight into man's spiritual power, the passage had to be cut from the book. Its deletion, however, had a far deeper motive than change of character. In this part of MS B, man as an individual is an exile (the more so if we take into account the universalizing of the idea in MS A). And man as one with the universe is at once all or nothing. This was the logical dilemma of the Christian missionaries and was an expression of their limitations (F, p. 41; discussed above, p. 245). But here in the earlier version it is the dilemma of the same character who has the insight to recognize that man can be one with the universe. This disturbing fact, conjoined with the sense of exile, suggests that in MS B the vision inherent in the concluding episode was not an expression of the limitations of Fielding and Aziz but was the expression of a general and pessimistic outlook.

We can see how Forster strives toward a more optimistic

vision if we look carefully at the MS A version of that memorable moment when the god of the Mau festival is thrown away (quoted on p. 245): "Thus, year after year, had He been thrown and were others thrown . . . scapegoats, husks, emblems of salvation, a salvation not easy, not now, not here, where the earth says 'be different' from the start of time, not to [supply "be"] apprehended except when it is about to be lost: the God to be thrown was an emblem of that. . . . Why this sacrifice rapid destruction at the heart of creation? To ask this question is sensible, but none who asks it will make passage to India" (H, pp. 699–700). That is, none who asks it will enter into the salvation which is India. The question "Why this sacrifice" is presumably answered by the previous statement. Salvation or passage can be apprehended only when it is about to be lost. Though not stated very clearly this seems to imply that one must lose oneself (and the sense of one's salvation) to save oneself. But since the imagery of sacrifice and destruction is not developed elsewhere in either MS A or the book, Forster deleted it here. What is of more interest is the earth's saying "be different." The individual inevitably stands apart from everything else in creation, including his fellow man. This fact plus the use of the phrase "about to be lost" where the book says "unattainable" reflects some of the pessimism of MS B. On the other hand, the conclusion that no one who asks the hard-headed question will make passage to India reflects a markedly optimistic commitment to the philosophy and experience expressed by Godbole.

According to that philosophy, the individual is not wholly an exile in an alien world. He can through his love give significant life to the universe. And from his "moments" of oneness with the universe, his "moments" of becoming or imitating God, he can return to the world of his individuality with a more developed spiritual life, with a higher self (MS A: H, p. 637; F, pp. 302–3).

The transmutation of "Temple" from the inherent pessimism of MS B to the qualified optimism of the book is of a piece with Forster's other changes. As the Marabar develops into a symbol of negation, so the Mau Festival develops into a symbol of affirmation. And so, for example, Forster in the book adds the powerful description

271

of the villagers as they glimpse the silver image of the god: "a most beautiful and radiant expression came into their faces, a beauty in which there was nothing personal, for it caused them all to resemble one another during the moment of its indwelling . . ." (F, p. 296). As the novel takes on its final form, Mau balances Marabar.

Notes

Introduction

1. Charles Moorman, *Arthurian Triptych: Mythical Materials in Charles Williams, C. S. Lewis, and T. S. Eliot* (Berkeley, 1960), pp. 3–19.
2. T. S. Eliot, "Ulysses, Order and Myth," *The Dial*, LXXV (1923), 485.
3. R. P. Blackmur, *Eleven Essays in the European Novel* (New York, 1964), pp. 109–10.
4. Virginia Woolf, *The Death of the Moth and other Essays* (New York, 1942), pp. 162–75, esp. pp. 168–69. For the point about Mrs. Moore, see p. 169.
5. Compare the epigraph to *The Waste Land* (1922): "Yes, and I myself saw with my own eyes the Sibyl of Cumae hanging in a cage; and when the children cried at her: 'Sybil, what do you want?' she used to reply: 'I want to die'" (Petronius, *Satyricon*, Ch. 48). I have quoted the translation in *English Masterpieces*, Vol. VII: *Modern Poetry*, ed. M. Mack et al. (New York, 1950), p. 123.
6. Wilfred Stone, *The Cave and the Mountain: A Study of E. M. Forster* (Stanford and London, 1966), pp. 216, 185, 215.
7. Robert Penn Warren, "Introduction" to Joseph Conrad, *Nostromo*, Modern Library (New York, 1951), p. xxvi.
8. *Two Cheers for Democracy*, p. 88.
9. F. R. Leavis, *The Common Pursuit* (New York, 1952), p. 274. Here are the exact words: "Once one's critical notice has been fastened on it [the phrase referring to plants and stones] . . . can one do anything but reflect how extraordinary it is that so fine a writer should be able, in such a place, to be so little certain just how serious he is?" The reader who has observed Forster's habit "sees merely the easy, natural lapse of the very personal writer whose hand is 'in.'" By the qualification "in such a place," Leavis may claim that his remarks are relevant to this passage only. That makes them nonetheless narrow. Forster's sentence does two things and does them brilliantly. It catches the mood of the characters, the tone of their response, and it assesses with sympathetic irony their spiritual limitations. Forster's seriousness and poise are no more in question here than they are when Professor Godbole attempts to impel the stone.
10. C. B. Cox, *The Free Spirit: A Study of Liberal Humanism in the Novels of George Eliot, Henry James, E. M. Forster, Virginia Woolf, Angus Wilson* (London, 1963), p. 79.

273

Chapter 1

1. Forster has written at length about the Thornton family in his biography, *Marianne Thornton*, and briefly about them in the essays "Battersea Rise" (*Abinger Harvest*) and "Henry Thornton" (*Two Cheers*).

2. The Stephens and the Stracheys were the two intellectual families most important in the formation of Bloomsbury. Lytton Strachey was one of a large family. His brothers and sisters were well known to Bloomsbury and his first cousin was Duncan Grant. But the Strachey influence was not to be estimated by counting heads; it was incalculable, and it was a match for the Stephen influence. See the Appendix to *The Memoirs of James Stephen: Written by Himself for the Use of His Children*, ed. Merle M. Bevington (London, 1954); C. R. Sanders, *The Strachey Family, 1588–1932* (Durham, 1953); and Noel G. Annan, "The Intellectual Aristocracy," in *Studies in Social History: A Tribute to G. M. Trevelyan*, ed. J. H. Plumb (London, 1955), pp. 241–57.

3. Leonard Woolf, *Beginning Again: An Autobiography of the Years 1911–1918* (London, 1964), pp. 22–24. On the membership of Bloomsbury compare Noel G. Annan, *Leslie Stephen: His Thought and Character in Relation to his Time* (London, 1951), p. 123 n.; Clive Bell, *Old Friends: Personal Recollections* (London, 1956), pp. 25–28, 130–31; and Sanders, esp. pp. 246–55.

4. Alfred W. Benn, *The History of English Rationalism in the Nineteenth Century* (London, 1906), II, 466.

5. Their revolt against the hardening arteries of the late-Victorian intelligentsia into which they were born is especially interesting. See Annan, *Studies in Social History*, pp. 241–87, esp. p. 252. In *Leslie Stephen*, pp. 123–24, Annan gives an admirable account of the similarities between the Clapham sect (the founding fathers of the nineteenth-century intellectual aristocracy) and the Bloomsbury group.

6. Bebel Lang, "Intuition in Bloomsbury," *Journal of the History of Ideas*, XXV (1964), 295–302, demonstrates that Moore's idea of intuition is applied by J. M. Keynes to probability theory and by Roger Fry (and Clive Bell) to esthetic theory. The precision and austere passion with which Moore elaborated his ideas moved Lytton Strachey to exclaim, "The age of reason has come!" (Forster, *Goldsworthy Lowes Dickinson*, p. 110), but Bloomsbury for all it admired the manner and the man largely ignored his emphasis on ethics and instead took only what it cared to take, namely the stress on intuition, personal relations (love pre-eminently), and beautiful objects (art). See J. M. Keynes, *Two Memoirs* (London, 1949), p. 82, and "The Influence and Thought of G. E. Moore: II," *The Listener*, LX (1959), 756. The stress on personal relations might equally well have been taken from McTaggart or Dickinson. See G. Lowes Dickinson, *J. McT. E. McTaggart* (Cambridge, 1931), esp. Ch. 4 by Basil Williams; *After Two Thousand Years: A Dialogue Between Plato and a Modern Young Man* (London, 1930); and *The Meaning of the Good: A Dialogue* (Glasgow, 1901), pp. 177–93. The stress on art was more pre-eminently Moore's, but Dickinson gave it an important place. See *The Meaning of the Good*, pp. 155–66. In *Edwardian England, 1901–1914*, ed. Simon Nowell-Smith (London, 1964), Anthony Quinton's chapter on "Thought" (pp. 251–302) provides a good survey of philosophic developments during the period.

7. Leonard Woolf, p. 22.

8. See J. K. Johnstone, *The Bloomsbury Group: A Study of E. M. Forster, Lytton Strachey, Virginia Woolf, and their Circle* (New York, 1954). As for continuing prejudice, see for example *The Pelican Guide to English Literature*, Vol. VII: *The Modern Age* (2nd. ed.; Harmondsworth, Middlesex, 1963), esp. "L. H. Myers and Bloomsbury" by G. H. Bantock.

9. Leonard Woolf, p. 23.

10. K. W. Gransden, "E. M. Forster at Eighty," *Encounter*, XII (January 1959), 77 n.

11. Leonard Woolf, p. 22.

12. P. N. Furbank and F. J. H. Haskell, "E. M. Forster," in *Writers at Work: The Paris Review Interviews*, ed. Malcolm Cowley (New York, 1958), p. 34. But see *Two Cheers*, p. 183, for a comment on Freud's interpretations in relation to art.

13. *Howards End*, p. 294. Henry Wilcox is so egregious an illustration of this heedlessness that he is almost ingratiating: "I am not a fellow who bothers about my own inside" (p. 197).

14. Wendell V. Harris, "Identifying the Decadent Fiction of the Eighteen-Nineties," *English Fiction in Transition*, V, 5 (1962), 1–13, esp. 10. As the title indicates, he is concerned with fiction, but "Yellow Book" poetry—to which he sometimes refers—is also covered by these categories.

15. Jane Harrison, *Introductory Studies in Greek Art* (4th ed.; London, 1897), p. vii.

16. J. A. Symonds, *Essays Speculative and Suggestive* (London, 1890), II, 34–35. Cf. Lowes Dickinson who in 1896, after condemning art for art's sake because it is "purely subjective in character" and absolutely indifferent to the value of the subject matter chosen, asserts that the theory "arises naturally and perhaps inevitably in an age where national life has degenerated into materialism and squalor, and the artist feels himself a stranger in a world of Philistines." See *The Greek View of Life* (London, 1896), p. 188.

17. *Abinger Harvest*, p. 216.

18. Samuel Butler, *Unconscious Memory* (1880), with introduction by Marcus Hartog (new ed.; London, 1910), p. xiii.

19. L. L. Whyte, *The Unconscious Before Freud* (New York, 1960), p. 170.

20. Butler, p. 178.

21. Butler speaks of "the omnipresence of mind in the universe," in the Appendix, Ch. 2, to the 2nd ed. of *Evolution, Old and New* (London, 1882), p. 399.

22. Andrew Lang, *Myth, Ritual, and Religion* (London, 1887), I, 28.

23. A phrase used by Lang in *Custom and Myth* (new ed.; London, 1893), p. viii.

24. Lang, *Myth*, I, 37.

25. Charles Darwin, *The Descent of Man or Selection in Relation to Sex* (London, 1871), I, 69.

26. I have passed over *The Golden Bough* because it is not especially important as a contribution to anthropological or mythological theory. Its great influence can be dated from the publication of the 3rd ed. (London, 1911–15) and was primarily literary. See John B. Vickery, "*The Golden Bough*: Impact and Archetype," in *Myth and Symbol: Critical Approaches and Applications* by Northrop Frye, L. C. Knights, et al. (Lincoln, 1963), pp. 174–96.

27. Sir Alfred C. Lyall, *Asiatic Studies, Religious and Social: Being a Selection from*

Essays Published Under that Title in 1882 and 1889 (London, 1907), p. 128; and see Ch. 7, pp. 110–31.

28. Symonds, II, 129.

29. Lang, *Myth,* I, 38. In this he follows Edward Tylor who asserts that the development of legend is so "uniform . . . that it becomes possible to treat myth as an organic product of mankind at large, in which individual, national, and even racial distinctions stand subordinate to universal qualities of the human mind"—*Primitive Culture: Researches into the Development of Mythology, Philosophy, Religion, Art, and Custom* (London, 1871), I, 376. Though modern research indicates that much of the uniformity of myth and legend is the result of cultural diffusion, this takes nothing away from Tylor's assertion and Lang's supposition as important influences in the development of the idea of myth as a profound and universal product of the human mind.

30. Arthur Waite, *Lives of Alchemical Philosophers* (London, 1888), pp. 36–37. For a survey of the occult at this time see John Senior, *The Way Down and Out: The Occult in Symbolist Literature* (Ithaca, 1959).

31. "The Decay of Lying," *The Prose of Oscar Wilde* (New York, 1916), p. 47.

32. Avis M. Dry, *The Psychology of Jung* (London, 1961), p. 7. For the relation of psychical research to other developments of the period, see L. S. Hearnshaw, *A Short History of British Psychology, 1840–1940* (London, 1964). He includes material on social psychology, social anthropology, psychical research, and their relation to philosophical developments in the last half of the nineteenth century.

33. F. W. H. Myers, *Human Personality and its Survival of Bodily Death* (London, 1903), II, 280–81.

34. Symonds, *Essays Speculative,* II, 143–44.

35. Myers, I, 277.

36. Myers, I, 100–1.

37. Jane Harrison, *Mythology & Monuments of Ancient Athens . . . with Introductory Essay and Archaeological Commentary* (London, 1890), p. iii.

38. Harrison, *Introductory Studies,* pp. 53–54, 231.

39. J. A. Stewart, *The Myths of Plato,* ed. G. R. Levy (London, 1960), Introduction by Levy, p. 4. This place of honor might be given to Westcott, who will be quoted later. When Jane Harrison discovered Stewart's second work four years later, she showed "immediate recognition of his part in a movement of which she was the centre" (Introduction, p. 4).

40. *The Letters of John Keats,* ed. M. B. Forman (4th ed.; London, 1952), p. 67.

41. Stewart, pp. 44–45, 59, 345.

42. B. F. Westcott, *Essays in the History of Religious Thought in the West* (London, 1891), pp. 4, 5, 12, 48. According to the Preface, the essay on Plato was first published in *Contemporary Review* (1866). The passage from p. 4 is quoted by Stewart.

43. Stewart, p. 236.

44. *Early Essays by John Stuart Mill,* ed. J. W. M. Gibbs (London, 1897), pp. 208–9.

45. M. H. Abrams, *The Mirror and the Lamp: Romantic Theory and Critical Tradition* (New York, 1953), pp. 173, 209–13.

46. Whyte, *The Unconscious Before Freud,* pp. 169–70.

47. *Two Cheers,* p. 275. Cf. Arthur Machen, *Hieroglyphics: A Note Upon Ecstasy in*

Literature (1902) (London, 1960), p. 120: "I am strangely inclined to think that all the quintessence of art is distilled from the subconscious and not from the conscious self."

48. *Two Cheers*, pp. 83–84. See also p. 114 where he says (1947) that the artist "lets down . . . a bucket into his subconscious." As early as 1912 he argued that inspiration, which alone makes good work possible, is not controlled by the writer's normal consciousness. See "Inspiration," *The Author*, XXII (July 1912), 281–82.

49. *Two Cheers*, p. 227.

50. *G. L. Dickinson*, p. 121.

51. *Two Cheers*, p. 88.

52. *Two Cheers*, p. 117.

53. Arthur M. Hocart, *The Life-Giving Myth and other Essays* (New York, n.d.), Introduction by Lord Raglan, p. 7.

54. For a psychological elaboration of these definitions see Carl G. Jung, *Psychological Types, or the Psychological of Individuation*, trans. H. G. Baynes (New York, 1933), pp. 551–53.

Chapter 2

1. Lionel Trilling, *The Liberal Imagination: Essays on Literature and Society* (New York, 1950), p. 212.

2. *Two Cheers*, p. 246. He said the same thing in 1925—*Abinger Harvest*, p. 127.

3. José Ortega y Gasset, *Meditations on Quixote*, trans. E. Rugg and D. Marín (New York, 1961), p. 132.

4. See Northrop Frye's "Four Forms of Prose Fiction," now incorporated in his *Anatomy of Criticism* (Princeton, 1957), pp. 302–14, in which he discusses the four forms: novel, romance, confession, and anatomy. On epic, romance, and novel see also Ortega, esp. pp. 118–34.

5. Elizabeth Bowen, *Collected Impressions* (New York, 1950), p. 121. This sense of evil distinguishes Forster from Bloomsbury. Maynard Keynes notes that the devotees of G. E. Moore, among whom he numbers himself, were the victims of a rationality which led to superficiality. They repudiated the notion of there being "insane and irrational springs of wickedness in most men." They "were not aware that civilisation was a thin and precarious crust erected by the personality and the will of a very few, and only maintained by rules and conventions skillfully put across and guilefully preserved." See *Two Memories*, pp. 99–100.

6. *Abinger Harvest*, pp. 21–22.

7. Bowen, p. 125.

8. *Aspects of the Novel*, p. 132. Forster's freedom from a niggling conscience is well expressed in this 1959 statement: "I never had much sense of sin and when I realized that the main aim of the Incarnation was not to stop war or pain or poverty, but to free us from sin I became less interested and ended by scrapping it. . . ." The point is vividly underscored in the same speech when he analyzes the coolness of his response to Christ. In Christian art he is confronted by a figure whose "sufferings, we are told, are undergone for our sake." And he thinks to himself: "I hope none of this has been undertaken for my sake, for I don't know what it's about." See "A Presidential Address to the Cambridge Humanists—Summer 1959," *University Humanist*

Federation Bulletin, No. 11 (Spring 1963), pp. 4, 7. These statements indicate an important characteristic of Forster's psychology and one that explains why the conflict of good and evil in his fiction is decisive and why his characters are notably free of feelings of guilt. Their creator is equally decisive and equally free.

9. *Abinger Harvest,* p. 36; see also *Aspects,* pp. 102–4. Forster uses the phrase in distinguishing between fantasy where there is no right and wrong and those works into which the soul has entered and which, though they still treat the unusual, treat it mystically or humanistically. On his own definition, then, Forster's fiction is not fantasy. This is one of my reasons for avoiding the term. The other reason is that the word has so frequently been used as a term of condescending disparagement that it has lost any objective value it might have had in the analysis of Forster's work.

10. Frye, p. 306.

11. This diffidence and modesty is still apparent in a statement Forster made in 1959: "One further note on the subject of Salvation. I used to be very keen on this and it figures in most of my early short stories, and a little in my novels up to *A Passage to India,* from which it has almost disappeared. It has now disappeared from my thoughts, like other absolutes. I no longer wish to save or be saved, and here is another barrier that has interposed between myself and revealed religion whether Christian or Pagan." Because it has disappeared from his thought, Forster is all the more likely to underestimate the role of salvation in the novels. The salvation he speaks of is not theological, for he had fallen away from believing even before writing the short stories. Salvation is very nearly synonymous with the insight of the eternal moment. What has been said above about the eternal moment applies here. The portrayal of salvation is more diffused in the novels but it is nonetheless decisive. See "A Presidential Address" p. 8, and note 8 above.

12. " 'Amis and Amiles' at Weybridge," *Athenaeum,* July 25, 1919, p. 662. The phrase is used in praising the achievement of a play, put on by children, which was "deeply emotional because it did not mimic emotion." In this connection see also "Break-Up Day—New Style," *The Manchester Guardian,* December 8, 1920, p. 8. Another review, "*The White Devil* at Cambridge," *New Statesman,* March 20, 1920, pp. 708–9, shows Forster's dislike of the slickness used on the stage to gain what is supposed to be an illusion of realism. Such an illusion make impossible the direct communication of any deeper reality the play might have. This attitude to realism in the theater indicates some of the grounds for his rejection of realism in fiction.

13. C. G. Heilbrun, *The Garnett Family* (London, 1961), pp. 139–40. He must have disagreed with other friends, including Lowes Dickinson and Virginia Woolf. See *G. L. Dickinson,* p. 216 and *The Death of the Moth,* pp. 169–70.

14. The letters of Forster and T. E. Lawrence indicate the existence in 1927 of one unpublished novel and the existence in 1928 of one unpublished short story. The dedication of *The Eternal Moment* (1928) is apparently only a half-statement and might be expanded to read: "To T. E. in the absence of anything else" *it is possible to publish or to publicly dedicate.* Whether there is more unpublished work is not known. But however much there is, I do not think it likely to invalidate the argument which follows. ("Arctic Summer" will be mentioned later). See *Letters to T. E. Lawrence,* ed. A. W. Lawrence (London, 1962)—Forster's letters of December 16, 1927 (p. 66), August 6, 1928 (p. 69), and December 16, 1929 (p. 73); and *The*

Letters of T. E. Lawrence, ed. David Garnett (London, 1938)—to Forster September 8, 1927 (p. 537), and April 16, 1928 (p. 593). Stone, *The Cave and the Mountain,* p. 347, specifies that an "unpublished novel dealing with the subject of homosexuality was produced after *Passage.*" He adds that "those who have read the novel generally consider it a failure." Stone's valuable book was published too late for me to benefit from it, except by way of notes. See note 20 below.

15. *Abinger Harvest,* pp. 97–98. The essay is dated 1919.

16. Furbank and Haskell, *Writers at Work,* pp. 32–33; see also Forster's Introduction to *The Longest Journey,* World's Classics (London, 1960).

17. "Literary Eccentrics," *Independent Review,* XI (October 1906), 108.

18. *Abinger Harvest,* p. 289.

19. *Collected Tales,* Introduction, pp. v–vi; *The Longest Journey,* World's Classics, Introduction, pp. x–xi.

20. *Collected Impressions,* p. 123. With this judgment I entirely concur. For the contrary view see *The Cave and the Mountain,* which argues in immense detail that the attempt at self-discovery is at the heart of Forster's fiction and that he develops painfully and slowly before reaching maturity with *A Passage to India.* This psychological approach entails the down-grading of all Forster's earlier fiction, including *Howards End.* Readers who value the earlier fiction will, for this reason alone, find the approach untenable. I am glad, however, to have Stone's support for the general proposition that Forster, like Lawrence, is "primarily interested in the mythic and the unconscious" (p. 382). Our profound disagreement is over the interpretation of this interest.

21. Furbank and Haskell, p. 35.

22. Introduction to the novel, p. ix.

23. After writing these words I read Alan Wilde, *Art and Order: A Study of E. M. Forster* (New York, 1964) in which the following perfect illustration of the point is found: "There are no heavenly agents here to bring the great moment about . . . no fantastic other kingdoms to provide a permanent refuge from the inadequacies of personal relations or from the encroachments of old age. The two worlds of the other stories appear now not as discrete and polar entities but as different, though coexistent, levels of the mind. Consequently, Miss Raby is more fully realized than any of her fellow protagonists, while the narrator, for once, is less concerned with pointing facile morals than with probing psychological and moral complexities" (pp. 92–93).

24. Something of the effect Forster was aiming for can be seen in his account of the influence on him of an episode in one of William de Morgan's novels: "a little tune is introduced, and words are put to it, a tune by Beethoven. The tune floats out of upper windows and is heard by Mr. de Morgan's characters when they are feeling depressed. They are cheered by the sound of the piano; they pull themselves together as the pianist's left hand passes over her right, and as she hits the upper G successfully they leap towards the happy ending which their kindly creator has destined for them" (*Abinger Harvest,* p. 121). If only Forster's story had been as effective as this description!

25. For a very different evaluation see Robert B. Heilman (ed.), *Modern Short Stories: A Critical Anthology* (New York, 1950), pp. 310–11.

26. Winifred Lynskey (ed.) suggests this in *Reading Modern Fiction: 29 Stories with Study Aids,* (rev. ed., New York, 1957), p. 208.

27. See "Dante," *The Working Men's College Journal,* X (April 1908), 301. The paper was read November 21, 1907.

28. This episode may have been influenced by George MacDonald's fantastic romance *Lilith* (London, 1895), esp. p. 64. The hero several times crosses a dreadful plain, a kind of arid sea where horrible worm-like monsters writhe beneath the surface and emerge wriggling into the moonlight. The pearl-colored mist which Forster describes (p. 176) is also reminiscent of scenery in *Lilith.*

29. Carl G. Jung, *Collected Works,* Vol. V: *Symbols of Transformation,* trans. R. F. C. Hull, Bollingen Series, XX (New York, 1956), pp. 355, 357.

30. Preface to *The American,* in Henry James, *The Art of the Novel: Critical Prefaces,* ed. R. P. Blackmur (New York, 1935), p. 33.

31. The idea for this part of the story (published January 1908) is hinted at in *The Longest Journey* when Rickie Elliot is thinking about the secluded dell near Madingley: "If the dell was to bear any inscription, he would have liked it to be 'This way to Heaven,' painted on a sign-post by the high-road, and he did not realize till later years that the number of visitors would not thereby have sensibly increased" (pp. 25–26).

32. Stewart C. Wilcox, "The Allegory of Forster's 'The Celestial Omnibus,' " *Modern Fiction Studies,* II (Winter 1956–57), 191–96, covers the allegorical ground admirably but obscures the essential quality of the story.

33. *Abinger Harvest,* p. 218; the essay "Gemistus Pletho" was first published in 1905.

34. "Albergo Empedocle," *Temple Bar,* CXXVIII (December 1903), 667–68.

35. *Temple Bar,* p. 674.

36. *Temple Bar,* p. 684.

37. *Collected Tales,* Introduction, p. v.

38. Compare the sexual overtones of a similar scene in a very different mood in *The Longest Journey.* Ansell grabs Rickie by the ankle and tumbles him to the grass (pp. 76–77).

39. *Collected Tales,* pp. 129, 194.

40. See Cyril Connolly, *The Condemned Playground: Essays 1927–1944* (New York, 1946), pp. 255–56 for an excellent analysis of the opening paragraphs.

41. Jane Harrison, *The Myths of the Odyssey in Art and Literature* (London, 1882), pp. 149–50.

42. Giuseppe di Lampedusa, *Two Stories and a Memory,* trans. A. Colquhoun, introduction by E. M. Forster (New York, 1962), p. 15.

43. Lampedusa, pp. 155–57.

44. Kerényi, in discussing the Earth-Mother worshipped under the name of Ge and Themis at Delphi, notes "that even a rocky landscape can appear in the mythology of the Primordial Child [or child-god] as the world of the Mother." The beautiful grottos of the story confirm such an interpretation: the Siren is exiled from her rightful home. He also notes, in exploring the Primordial Child's relations with Apollo of Delphi, that we are driven to think of "a more general, primary connexion that existed before all specific names: the connexion of water, child, and music." To this we may add that Plato and Milton associate the song of the Sirens with the

music of the spheres. For anyone interested in archetypal symbols this story is eminently rewarding. See C. G. Jung and C. Kerényi, *Essays on a Science of Mythology: The Myth of the Divine Child and the Mysteries of Eleusis,* trans. R. F. C. Hull, Bollingen Series, XXII (New York, 1949), pp. 70, 79.

Chapter 3

1. Richard Jefferies, *The Story of My Heart* (London, 1906), p. 76.
2. Marghanita Laski, *Ecstasy: A Study of Some Secular and Religious Experiences* (Bloomington, 1962), p. 47.
3. In this last example from *The Longest Journey,* the object of ecstatic experience comes directly from the perceiver's own mind and emerges in dream or vision. W. T. Stace, in *Mysticism and Philosophy* (Philadelphia, 1960), argues that a phenomenon of this kind is not a mystical (ecstatic) experience (pp. 47–55). It may be noted that Rickie's vision has an ironic point, and that his earlier dream in which his mother speaks to him also had an ironic point. On the evidence, Forster would appear to confirm Stace's judgment, though at the same time he demonstrates the remarkable similarities between dream visions and mystical experiences.

   Stace's term mysticism includes Laski's ecstasy. Stace stresses the profound introvertive experience, Laski the extrovertive. In the conclusions they reach there are serious differences which cannot be gone into here. Stace's book is the more important as a theoretical study, but Laski's is more helpful in exploring the kind of experience represented by Forster's fiction.
4. Laski, pp. 106–7.
5. Laski, esp. pp. 162–63.
6. I conclude from Miss Laski's book that Forster's visionary moments are, without exception, authentic; they have not been faked, or tricked out in fancy dress. Even the false note in "Albergo Empedocle" does not touch the moment of vision but only its later interpretation. I conclude, too, that Forster experienced a mild form of ecstasy in the act of writing. Miss Laski is tentatively of the opinion that ecstatic states are extreme or heightened forms of more normal states known to all, such as various forms of creativity. Forster's insistence that he enjoyed writing, that it was no agony, suggests that in the act of creation he experienced a mild but more than usually marked sense of ecstasy. This joy in the act of creation comes through in his work.
7. Laski, pp. 241–43, 127.
8. Angus Fletcher, *Allegory: The Theory of a Symbolic Mode* (Ithaca, 1964), pp. 355–56.
9. S. T. Coleridge, *Biographia Literaria,* ed. John Shawcross (London, 1907), II, 12.
10. *Two Cheers,* p. 43.
11. D. H. Lawrence, "The Novel," *Reflections on the Death of a Porcupine and Other Essays* (Philadelphia, 1925), pp. 109–10; reprinted in *Discussions of the Novel,* ed. Roger Sale (Boston, 1960), p. 96.
12. Joseph Conrad, *Heart of Darkness,* in *Youth: A Narrative and Two Other Stories* (London, 1902), p. 55.
13. See Forster's discussion of this in *Two Cheers,* p. 115.

14. James Joyce, *A Portrait of the Artist as a Young Man* (London, 1918), p. 252.
15. *Meditations on Quixote*, p. 100.
16. Wayne C. Booth, *The Rhetoric of Fiction* (Chicago, 1961), p. 272.
17. Suzanne Langer, *Feeling and Form: A Theory of Art Developed from* Philosophy in a New Key (New York, 1953), p. 273.
18. Henry James, *The Art of Fiction and Other Essays*, ed. Morris Roberts (New York, 1948), pp. 12–13, 207.
19. *Meditations*, pp. 130–31; Philip Rahv, "Fiction and the Criticism of Fiction," *Kenyon Review*, XVIII (Spring 1956), 295.
20. Langer, p. 265. Her italics do my work for me. Mrs. Langer says the art lover "enters into a direct relation not with the artist, but with the work" (p. 394). I would say when the work is narrative a direct relation with the work inevitably brings one into relation, direct or indirect, with the artist-narrator.
21. *The Death of the Moth*, p. 166; *The Art of Fiction*, p. 21; *Aspects*, p. 41. Compare Robert Scholes: "Quality of mind (as expressed in the language of characterization, motivation, description, and commentary) not plot, is the soul of narrative." See Scholes and Robert Kellogg, *The Nature of Narrative* (New York, 1966), p. 239. And see Booth, pp. 213 ff. for a discussion of the assertion made by both H. W. Leggett and Paul Goodman that we identify with the author or narrator.
22. For a discussion of "The Novel as Unmediated Reality" and the theory of Sartre who rejects the point of view of order because it is the point of view of the absolute, see Booth, pp. 50–53. The phrase "the ultimate man of order" is from an unpublished poem by Stuart MacKinnon.
23. *Aspects*, p. 41.
24. For a general discussion of this point see Paul Goodman, *The Structure of Literature* (Chicago, 1954), esp. Ch. 4.
25. Forster's position in this matter should not surprise us. When E. K. Brown published an article stressing his ideas and values, Forster wrote to say: "It is a great novelty to be written about like that. I have been praised for my character drawing, sense of social distinctions, etc., but seldom for the things which really interest me, and which I have tried to express through the medium of fiction." Quoted by Brown, "The Revival of E. M. Forster," in William Van O'Connor (ed.), *Forms of Modern Fiction* (Minneapolis, 1948), p. 174.
26. A fixed character *can* change. But as Richard Chase points out, "if characters change in a romance, let's say as Captain Ahab in *Moby-Dick* or the Reverend Dimmesdale in *The Scarlet Letter* change, we are not shown a 'development'; we are left rather with an element of mystery, as with Ahab, or a simplified and conventionalized alteration of character, as with Dimmesdale." See *The American Novel and its Tradition* (New York, 1957), p. 22.
27. *Chase*, p. 39. Forster has said that the kind of opera he would have made of *Peter Grimes* shows his love of melodrama (*Two Cheers*, p. 185).
28. This splendid scene has a remarkable and amusing origin: ". . . at the beginning of the present century. . . . I go to *Lucia di Lammermoor* at Florence. The soprano is not well known. Her name is Tetrazzini. I put her and her opera into a novel I am writing, and later on she becomes famous and makes the whole world of coloratura ring. Shall I send her a copy of the novel? Would she be pleased? She

would not. No soprano, however great, likes to be called ugly and fat." See "My First Opera," *Opera,* XIV (June 1963), 374.

29. For an excellent discussion of the nature of the autobiographical in fiction see Louis D. Rubin Jr., "The Self Recaptured," *Kenyon Review,* XXV (Summer 1963), 393–415.

30. Charles Morgan, "The Nature of Dramatic Illusion," *Essays by Divers Hands, Being the Transactions of the Royal Society of Literature of the United Kingdom,* N. S., XII (1933), 70–71.

Chapter 4

1. In phrasing and conception this paragraph is indebted to William Whewell's definition of type. See *History of Scientific Ideas* (3rd ed.; London, 1858), II, 121–22.

2. Up to this point my discussion of the novelistic hero and the way he differs from the hero of epic and romance follows Paul Goodman's line of argument in *The Structure of Literature.* A similar position is maintained by Angus Fletcher, though he might not agree that the characters of a primarily mimetic epic like the *Iliad* are unchanging. His distinction is between the characters of mimetic or realistic narrative, who are capable of maturation, and those of allegorical narrative (in which category he includes romance), who are possessed as by a daemon and obey a strict causal necessity. See *Allegory,* pp. 66–67, 286–87.

3. "Arctic Summer (Fragment of an Unfinished Novel)," in *Tribute to Benjamin Britten on his Fiftieth Birthday,* ed. Anthony Gishford (London, 1963), p. 54. The fragment and the two-page comment on it from which I have quoted were read by Forster at the Aldeburgh Festival on June 10, 1951. Passages quoted in Furbank and Haskell, *Writers at Work,* pp. 25–27 indicate that the comment has been somewhat revised for publication.

4. Forster's problems with Ansell and Mrs. Elliot are instructive. Ansell stands for truth, but he is too aware of what he stands for. The image he creates is rather one of knowing than of being. Fortunately, the elaborate symbolism of the novel establishes strong unarticulated connections between Ansell and Stephen, and these give to his role a power reaching beyond his own assertions and understanding.

   Mrs. Elliot's character, in spite of careful presentation at the beginning of Part III, does not quite meet the needs of her symbolic role as Earth-Mother. This is not because the detailed account of her character is inconsistent with her role, but because it is so closely conjoined in the narrative with the projecting of her mythic significance that the realistic details undermine our willingness to believe fully in her symbolic import. In general Forster has avoided overexposure and a too realistic commitment in presenting Mrs. Elliot. His task was made easier because she was dead. But he did not contrive the disposition of his material with quite enough cunning.

5. "Efficiency and Liberty—Great Britain. A Discussion between E. M. Forster and A. M. Ludovici, with Wilson Harris in the Chair," *Listener,* March 9, 1938, p. 498.

6. Joseph Campbell, *The Hero with a Thousand Faces,* Bollingen Series, XVII (New York, 1961), pp. 245–46.

7. *The Longest Journey,* World's Classics, Introduction, pp. xi, xii.

8. Campbell, p. 81.

9. The Egyptian god Ra appears to be another instance. See Jung, *Collected Works,* V, esp. 293–97.

10. The chapter recalls a passage from the end of Book III of Plato's *Republic* concerning the life of the governors who are enjoined to distinguish between "mortal gold" and "the precious metals placed in their souls by the gods themselves" because "the world's coinage has been the cause of countless impieties" whereas the divine species of the precious metals "is undefiled." Forster ends his chapter with a question which implies his rejection of the sharp division between spirit and matter implicit in both Plato and Christianity. "Will it really profit us so much if we save our souls and lose the whole world?" (p. 256) The coinage passage from Plato is quoted by Lowes Dickinson in *The Greek View of Life* (from which I have quoted, p. 92) which is a way of saying that it had been brought specially to Forster's attention.

11. Though I do not wish to emphasize unduly the psychological interpretation of myth, I cannot resist noting the way in which the extremes of Rickie's response to life illustrate the two forms of castration by the father. I quote Erich Neumann's account:

> Patriarchal castration has two forms: captivity and possession. In captivity, the ego remains totally dependent upon the father as the representative of collective norms—that is, it identifies with the lower father and thus loses its connection with the creative powers. It remains bound by traditional morality and conscience, and, as though castrated by convention, loses the higher half of its dual nature.
>
> The other form of patriarchal castration is identification with the father-god. This leads to the possessed state of heavenly inflation, "annihilation through the spirit." Here too the ego-hero loses consciousness of his dual nature by losing touch with his earthly part.

The Origins and History of Consciousness, trans. R. F. C. Hull, Bollingen Series, XLII (New York, 1954), p. 187.

12. James McConkey, *The Novels of E. M. Forster* (Ithaca, 1957), p. 110, has shown the deliberate parallel between the description of the square-within-circle diagram and the description of the Rings.

13. *The Dialogues of Plato,* trans. B. Jowett (3rd. ed.; London, 1892), III, 451, 452.

14. E. Schroeder as quoted by Ananda K. Coomaraswamy, "Symbolism of the Dome," *The Indian Historical Quarterly,* XIV (March 1938), 1–2.

15. Jung and Kerényi, *Science of Mythology,* p. 18. The passage is by Kerényi.

16. Mircea Eliade, *Myths, Dreams and Mysteries: The Encounter between Contemporary Faiths and Archaic Realities,* trans. Philip Mairet (New York, 1960), p. 119.

17. Ansell's symbol has, perhaps, a secondary and highly ingenious relation to the lighted ball of paper. Any reader with a passion for doodling will quickly discover that a roughly drawn square-within-circle series, especially as one looks toward its center, resembles a multi-petaled rose. The mystical rose is the commonest of all symbols representing the ideal of the Maiden-Mother and the Eternal Feminine. Thus for example Ernest Crawley called his scholarly study of primitive marriage *The Mystic Rose* (London, 1902).

18. Howard N. Doughty, "The Novels of E. M. Forster," *The Bookman* (New York), LXXV (October 1932), 545.

19. Erwin Rohde, *Psyche: The Cult of Souls and Belief in Immortality among the Greeks,* trans. W. B. Hillis from 8th German ed. (London, 1925), p. 161.

20. Walter Pater, *Greek Studies: A Series of Essays* (London, 1895), pp. 150–51. For a photograph of the Demeter of Cnidus see the *Cambridge Ancient History,* Vol. of Plates II (Cambridge, 1928), p. 88.

21. *Abinger Harvest,* p. 201. The quotation which follows is from the same page.

22. *Myths, Dreams,* p. 185.

23. *Working Men's College Journal,* X, 302.

24. *The Mystical Hymns of Orpheus,* trans. Thomas Taylor (London, 1896), pp. 30, 29.

25. *Orpheus,* pp. 34, 63, 41.

26. *The Longest Journey,* World's Classics, Introduction, p. xiv.

27. During the writing of the novel Stephen was for a time called Siegfried. In Wagner's opera, Siegfried is raised by the dwarf Mime whose desire to have Siegfried killed reveals his serpent-like nature and shows that for all his masculine form he is a manifestation of the Terrible Mother. Mime is a chthonic god, a cripple, and belongs to a race that has abjured love. The giant-dragon Fafner whom Siegfried fights is also a little reminiscent of Mrs. Failing. His desire is to slumber in his cave. See Jung, *Collected Works,* V, 361–62.

28. Jung and Kerényi, p. 115. The chapter to which I am indebted here is by Jung. Stephen's appearance in this scene bears some resemblance to the apparition of the Radiant Boy who may appear either naked or clothed in white. See John H. Ingram, *The Haunted Homes and Family Traditions of Great Britain* (London, 1901), pp. 43–51.

29. *Greek Studies,* p. 27.

30. *Abinger Harvest,* p. 197.

31. The English first edition and all other editions I have seen contain the repeated misprint in the second last sentence: "even swift, even pure" should read "ever swift, ever pure."

32. *Psyche,* p. 138.

33. *The Bloomsbury Group,* p. 189.

34. Otto Rank, *Beyond Psychology* (New York, 1958), p. 96.

35. For instance, in the epic of Gilgamesh the hero and his friend Enkidu have broken the taboos of the gods. The decision of the gods is revealed in a dream: "Enkidu shall die, Gilgamesh shall not die." When Enkidu tells his friend of the decision of the gods, Gilgamesh says: "My brother, my dear brother, why do they acquit me instead of you?" Or in another translation: "Me they would clear at the expense of my brother!" Here the friend, called brother, must die that the hero may live.

36. We may contrast with this Forster's ideal as stated in his 1907 paper on Dante: "It is only the poet who points upward, and offers humanity the example of the stars. Men, like stars, differ from each other in brilliancy. Let them also imitate the stars' harmonious motion" (*Working Men's College Journal,* X, 301). That they differ in brilliancy signifies their individuality. That they are all brilliant in their degree and harmonious in their motion signifies their shared universal nature. In *The Longest Journey,* published the same year, this harmony gives place to an inherent conflict; Rickie the individualist is sacrificed to Stephen the archetypal star hero.

Chapter 5

1. *Anatomy of Criticism,* p. 99; Leslie Fiedler, *An End to Innocence: Essays on Culture and Politics* (Boston, 1952), p. 146. On symbol and archetype, see also W. K. Wimsatt, *Hateful Contraries: Studies in Literature and Criticism* (Lexington, 1965), "Two Meanings of Symbolism: A Grammatical Exercise," pp. 55–71.

2. The paradoxical character of this formulation does not invalidate the conception of the narrator as archetype. What we need is a distinction between the author-creator and the narrator. Let me make a hypothetical case. In 1901 Forster encountered a former castle in a small Italian town. It became the source of an ecstatic experience which four years later he wrote into a novel. The narrator (omniscient) of that novel stands between the young man of twenty-two and the author of twenty-six. The immediacy of the narrator's experience allies him with the young man; the enriched significance of his experience allies him with the older author. But he is not identical with either. Such being the case, it is neither surprising nor paradoxical that the narrator, placed at the juncture of actual experience recreated and remembered experience reflected upon, should become for his creator an object of vision.

3. Their role is further discussed in note 26 below. Needless to say, in terms of Northrop Frye's definition both sisters would be accounted archetypal.

4. Kenneth Burke, *The Rhetoric of Religion: Studies in Logology* (Boston, 1961), p. 10.

5. Erich Neumann, *Art and the Creative Unconscious: Four Essays,* trans. Ralph Manheim, Bollingen Series, LXI (New York, 1959), p. 175.

6. Hocart, *The Life-Giving Myth,* Introduction, p. 7.

7. But it comes close to paralleling the story, especially with reference to Helen's career. This has been ably demonstrated by Johnstone in *The Bloomsbury Group,* pp. 226–28. For another parallel, between Helen's *synaesthesia* and the novel's theme of *synthesis,* see the lively and perceptive article by Barry R. Westburg, "Forster's Fifth Symphony: Another Aspect of *Howards End,*" *Modern Fiction Studies,* X (Winter 1964–65), 359–65.

8. The reader may have guessed from the style—but certainly not from the meaning—that the quoted remarks are not Forster's. They are from "An Essay in Aesthetics" published in 1909 by Roger Fry and show how precisely Forster's thoughts echo those of another member of the Bloomsbury intellectual aristocracy. See *Vision and Design* (London, 1928), pp. 24, 23.

9. *Abinger Harvest,* pp. 285, 281.

10. I am indebted to Mr. Forster for bringing this fact to my attention. The words do not appear in Vasari or Condivi or in Charles Holroyd's *Michael Angelo Buonarroti* (1903). They appear in the following form in John Addington Symonds, *The Life of Michelangelo Buonarroti* (New York, 1962):

> While still in his seventieth year, Michelangelo had educated himself to meditate upon the thought of death as a prophylactic against vain distractions and the passion of love. . . . "Marvellous is the operation of this thought of death, which, albeit death, by his nature, destroys all things, preserves and supports those who think on death, and defends them from all human passions." He supports this position by reciting a madrigal he had composed, to show how the thought of death is the greatest foe to love:—

Not death indeed, but the dread thought of death
Saveth and severeth
Me from the heartless fair who doth me slay. . . . (p. 502)

Forster may have been influenced by this association of death and love but the use to which he puts the association is the opposite of Michelangelo's.

11. *Working Men's College Journal*, X, 283.

12. *Timaeus, Dialogues of Plato*, III, 451.

13. *Two Cheers*, p. 299.

14. I distinguish in Appendix A between the life-oriented attitude of Forster and the art-oriented attitude of the French symbolists and the English poets of the nineties. One could hardly find a more apt illustration of this distinction than that which comes from setting Forster's treatment of death in *Howards End* over against Arthur Symons' analysis in *The Symbolist Movement in Literature*:

> And so there is a great, silent conspiracy between us to forget death. . . . That is why we are active about so many things which we know to be unimportant; why we are so afraid of solitude, and so thankful for the company of our fellow-creatures. Allowing ourselves, for the most part, to be but vaguely conscious of that great suspense in which we live, we find our escape from its sterile, annihilating reality in many dreams, in religion, passion, art. . . . Each is a kind of sublime selfishness, the saint, the lover, and the artist having each an incommunicable ecstasy which he esteems as his ultimate attainment. . . . But it is, before all things, an escape; and the prophets who have redeemed the world and the artists who have made the world beautiful, and the lovers who have quickened the pulses of the world, have really, whether they knew it or not, been fleeing from the certainty of one thought: that we have, all of us, only our one day; and from the dread of that other thought: that the day, however used, must after all be wasted. (*Collected Works* [London, 1924], VIII, 248–49.)

Here we find an impressive mixture of century's-end pessimism and art-for-art's-sake theory, and a striking contrast with Forster's emphasis on the life-enhancing.

15. Cf. "Dolly raised her faded little face, which sorrow could wither but not steady" (p. 360).

16. As so often in Forster's work, this crucial appearance of the greengage tree has been carefully prepared. See pp. 4, 211.

17. *Psyche*, pp. 172–73. This is better than Forster's own account: "The past is not a series of vanished presents . . . it would exercise no effect if it were. It is a distillation, and a few drops of it work wonders. . . . This is not a private fancy of mine: all races who have practised ancestor-worship know about it, and Ulysses went down into the underworld to acquire better balance for his course in this." See "Recollectionism," *New Statesman and Nation*, N.S., March 13, 1937, p. 405.

18. I. A. Richards, "A Passage to Forster; Reflections on a Novelist," *The Forum*, LXXVIII (1927), 918.

19. In *Marianne Thornton* there is an admirable illustration of how a feeling for place can establish a continuity between past and future generations. See the account of Marianne Thornton's second visit to Paris, and esp. p. 186.

20. Further connection is established in Miss Avery's judgment that Ruth Wilcox should

have married "Some real soldier" (p. 290). The father of Margaret and Helen was a soldier and an idealist. A soldier fights to preserve what now exists, thereby showing his love. But a soldier idealist fights also for things as they ought to be—for truth. Mr. Schlegel, I think, would have satisfied Miss Avery's conception of a real soldier. (See esp. pp. 29–31.) Had Ruth Wilcox married this real soldier, Margaret would have been her physical as well as spiritual heir and Howards End would have been her home always.

21. Pigs, of course, were traditionally associated with Demeter. Images of pigs were found in the holy plot of Demeter at Cnidus. See C. T. Newton, *A History of Discoveries at Halicarnassus, Cnidus, and Branchidae* (London, 1862–63), II, 331–32, 385, 390–91.

22. Furbank and Haskell, *Writers at Work,* p. 30.

23. *Marianne Thornton,* p. 301. Opposite p. 302 there is an excellent photograph of the house as a background to "My mother, pony and self in Hertfordshire (about 1885)."

24. The sources for the three quotations are: E. B. Havell, *The Ideals of Indian Art* (London, 1911), p. 59; *The Works of Virgil,* trans. Davidson, rev. T. A. Buckley (New York, 1877), Bk. IV, lines 441 ff.; [Dickinson], *Poems* (London, 1896), p. 54.

25. *G. L. Dickinson,* p. 227.

26. The immensely articulate Margaret Schlegel and her charming and lively sister, though they are not portrayed as archetypal characters, move toward a full sharing of Mrs. Wilcox's experience and significance. Margaret in her association with grass and in her final understanding of hay is the heir of Mrs. Wilcox. Thus in the novel's closing scene the narrator for the first time refers to her by that name. She may not be the equal of the first Mrs. Wilcox but she follows heroically in her footsteps, and like her predecessor, attains proportion. Helen is related to Mrs. Wilcox more indirectly. She represents the same aspects of the Great Mother that Mrs. Wilcox represents, but at a much more elemental level. As an Earth-Mother figure Helen's role is simply biological. As a feminine figure of transformation her role is also primarily biological. Injury becomes promise. Paul Wilcox is transformed into Leonard Bast who is transformed into the child. Of course Helen's experience has psychological and spiritual implications; but as a figure of transformation she remains, in comparison with Mrs. Wilcox, elemental. Her role is reflected in her character: in her lack of interest in any permanent relationship with a man, in her inclination to attract or be attracted, and in her spontaneity and glad animal spirits.

For the various manifestations of the Great Mother, see esp. Jung, *Collected Works,* Vol. XVI: *The Practice of Psychotherapy* (1954), pp. 173–74; and Erich Neumann, *The Great Mother: An Analysis of the Archetype,* trans. Ralph Manheim, Bollingen Series, XLVII (New York, 1963).

27. "The Function of Literature in War-time," *Working Men's College Journal,* XIV (March 1915), 61.

28. To Leonard Bast, "Mr. Wilcox was king of this world, the superman, with his own morality, whose head remained in the clouds" (p. 253). He is a superman because he never says "I," because he is impersonal and so beyond humanity (p. 248). He is also an imperialist and in the very act of building empires he levels all the world. He is a destroyer (p. 342). In this he resembles death. But the comparison with death, as Helen insists, reveals him for the false emperor he is. "Death's really Imperial," and

the mention of Death strikes panic into the heart of any Wilcox for it reveals that the destroyer and all that he has built will in turn be destroyed (p. 252). Death reveals also that the false emperor worships false gods, of which the novel offers one memorable example, the Porphyrion Insurance Company. This god was a giant. "A giant was of an impulsive morality—one knew that much. . . . But his true fighting weight, his antecedents, his amours with other members of the commercial Pantheon —all these were as uncertain to ordinary mortals as were the escapades of Zeus" (p. 147). Forster is saying again that London and the London way of life is a caricature of infinity.

29. Forster continues: "And isolation sometimes masks itself behind bustle or worldly success or what passes for civilization." See the Introduction to Donald Windham, *The Warm Country* (London, 1960).

30. The dust is thrown up by the motor cars which the Wilcoxes delight to drive. These cars are a prominent symbol of the Wilcox attitude and way of life. The emergence of the automobile on the roads of England during the first decade of the century aroused a degree of consternation and passion that it is not easy for the modern reader to appreciate. I quote from Lowes Dickinson's "The Motor Tyranny," *Independent Review* (October 1906):

> For some ten years the people of this country—as of all countries—have been groaning under a public nuisance which increases day by day until it has reached a malignity and magnitude altogether unprecedented. Their property has been depreciated; their senses offended; their comfort destroyed; their security invaded. . . . And if it is urged that this nuisance is as yet confined to a few main thoroughfares, it must be remembered that we are only at the beginning; and that, according to any reasonable forecast, in ten years' time, unless some drastic measures are adopted, there will not be a country lane in the kingdom free from dust and stench, nor a field or a common undisturbed by that most odious of sounds, the hooting of the motor horn. (p. 15)

31. *Two Cheers*, p. 125.

Chapter 6

1. See Glen O. Allen, "Structure, Symbol, and Theme in E. M. Forster's *A Passage to India*," *PMLA*, LXX (December 1955), 940; Richard R. Werry, "Rhythm in Forster's *A Passage to India*" in *Studies in Honor of John Wilcox*, ed. A. D. Wallace and W. O. Ross (Detroit, 1958); J. B. Beer, *The Achievement of E. M. Forster* (London, 1962), pp. 141–42, 149; and Wilde, *Art and Order*, esp. pp. 142, 155.

2. Lang, *Myth*, II, 123.

3. See Forster's essay, "Anonymity," esp. the last paragraph, and my discussion of it in Ch. 1. Nothing I have said here or elsewhere in this book is intended to suggest that Forster invites or blindly welcomes incursions of the irrational or unconscious. Rather, such incursions must be contained and then integrated into ordered existence. Adela's experience in the cave shows that the violent breakthrough of unconscious elements is an unmitigated disaster. The concluding paragraphs of Forster's obituary note on Roger Fry (1931) in *Abinger Harvest* show with what cautiousness he regarded intuition. It too must be contained and integrated.

4. Forster said this to K. Natwar-Singh in a 1962 conversation recorded in the Intro-

duction (p. xii) to *E. M. Forster: A Tribute, with Selections from his Writings on India*, ed. K. Natwar-Singh (New York, 1964).

5. *Two Cheers*, p. 292.

6. Aziz's career could be seen as a parody of the hero's experience. Mrs. Moore in the mosque is the shadowy figure who must be propitiated. This done, the hero sets out on his journey to the Marabar—with an entourage. The journey culminates in a cave with no markings, in nothing, and in nonunion with a false bride-mother Adela. In attempting to return the hero is captured and imprisoned by the Anglo-Indians, the deities or rulers of the nothing-world. All of which is followed by trial and escape. This does not seem to me a profitable way of looking at Aziz's nature and destiny.

7. For the usual distinction in Forster's work between the total order of the fiction and those parts of it which express visionary order or mythic unity, see the concluding discussion in Ch. 3.

8. Godbole makes two preliminary observations that help both to develop the theme and to confirm his wisdom. The first (when good or evil occurs it expresses the whole of the universe) has already been discussed. The second is a distinction between suffering and evil. "Suffering is merely a matter for the individual. If a young lady has sunstroke, that is a matter of no significance to the universe. . . . If she thought her head did not ache, she would not be ill, and that would end it" (p. 186). Near the close of the novel Aziz meets Mrs. Moore's son, Ralph, who has been stung by bees. When Aziz handles him roughly Ralph says, "Your hands are unkind." Aziz replies that he will not hurt him. And Ralph replies, "I don't mind pain, there is no pain. . . . But there is cruelty" (p. 322).

9. "There are some exquisite echoes in India" (p. 154) is not a contradiction. They are exquisite on account of the faithfulness with which they reproduce the exquisite quality of the original sound, but they are nonetheless evil. Moreover, Forster's object when he says this is to distinguish emphatically between these exquisite echoes and those of the Marabar caves.

10. Keith Hollingsworth notes that any reasonable interpretation of the echo must explain this emphasis on *now* and the deliberate contrast with the eighteenth century "when cruelty and injustice raged" but "an invisible power repaired their ravages" (p. 286). Forster makes another comparison that throws light on this. Commenting on the extraordinary phenomenon of Mrs. Moore becoming a Hindu goddess, he observes that such an event was not uncommon a hundred years ago "when Europeans still made their home in the country-side and appealed to its imagination" (p. 267). During the past century relations have deteriorated between Indians and Anglo-Indians, partly as a result of urbanization and increased organization. Thus it looks as though much of the significance of Forster's "now" is political and social. In another sense, of course, the "now" is perfectly natural. The notion of the universe as a wasteland in the Eliot-Forster sense is a twentieth-century idea. See Hollingsworth, "*A Passage to India*: The Echoes in the Marabar Caves," *Criticism*, IV (Summer 1962), esp. p. 222, who interprets the echoes of India very specifically as suggesting "the technological society" which "introduces a mechanization of human relations."

For the Hindu practice of making Europeans or Hindus into local deities, see

Lyall, *Asiatic Studies,* p. 17 and E. B. Havell, *Benares, The Sacred City: Sketches of Hindu Life and Religion* (London; 1905), p. 31.

11. "And consequently the echo flourished . . . and the noise in the cave, so unimportant intellectually, was prolonged over the surface of her life" (p. 202). We are reminded of the impressive account of the cave's highly polished inner surface which is described as a fine voluptuous skin (p. 131). We think of this when we read that Adela's senses were abnormally inert until the crisis in the cave, after which everything came to a focus on the surface of her body. Adela has severed the connection between her senses and their source of vitality in her instinctive and unconscious nature. Now this source of vitality is transferred to the surface of her body, which begins "to avenge itself, and feed unhealthily" (p. 201). The imagery suggests that Adela is an inverted cave. The outside world has got locked up within the subjective prison of the self while the instinctual inner world has got outside where it shows itself as a diseased hypersensitiveness.

Adela's echo is associated with the sea imagery of the Marabar. After her momentary insight into Aziz's innocence, she "gasped as if she had risen to the surface of the water, then touched her ear." Her echo had got better (p. 211).

12. Stanley Cooperman, "The Imperial Posture and the Shrine of Darkness: Kipling's *The Naulahka* and E. M. Forster's *A Passage to India*," *English Literature in Transition,* VI (1963), 9.

13. Observe that Forster, whose idea is expressed in a visual image, faces the same dilemma as the metaphysician: a void is a logical impossibility for it possesses the attributes of infinity and eternity. He attempts, by imagistic sleight of hand, to evade the dilemma: if the intactness of the cave were violated, if the cave were smashed, its attributes would be revealed as nonexistent.

14. Furbank and Haskell, *Writers at Work,* p. 27.

15. *The Ideals of Indian Art,* p. 58. In a 1920 review of this work Forster says that Havell's books "are the best interpretation of Indian Art that has yet appeared, because they have a profound knowledge of Indian religion." See "The Churning of the Ocean," *Athenaeum,* May 21, 1920, p. 667.

16. See Neumann, *The Great Mother,* p. 45.

17. "Songs of Loveliness," *Daily News,* January 27, 1920, p. 5.

18. "What," asks the narrator as Mrs. Moore leaves India, "What dwelt in the first of the caves?" And the answer, "the undying worm itself," "the serpent of eternity made of maggots" (p. 217). This use of snake imagery to define the significance of the Marabar cave has its counterpart in other novels and indicates that Forster associated the spiritual negation of the Marabar with rationality and abstraction. In *Howards End* Leonard Bast, consumed by remorse on account of his night with Helen Schlegel, lies awake carrying on an inner dialogue as he watches the moonlight gather motion and run up his blanket. "Presently a blue snake appeared; then another, parallel to it. 'Is there life in the moon?' 'Of course.' 'But I thought it was uninhabited.' 'Not by Time, Death, Judgment, and the smaller snakes'" (p. 340). In the Marabar cave the grandeur of Heaven, Hell, Annihilation and the consoling magnitude of eternity and infinity are robbed of their vastness and reduced to the enclosed smallness of the cave and the serpent of eternity is reduced to snakes of light, little coiling worms (pp. 216–17, 156). In *Howards End,* Time, Death, Judgment are the consoling grand

abstractions while the smaller snakes parallel the maggots of the cave, the grubby horror of the everyday reality of these abstractions. The remorse of conscience Leonard experiences derives from these smaller snakes, the lesser abstractions which distort reality for him and make him a lesser man. The snake-dragon imagery associated with Mrs. Failing in *The Longest Journey* has much the same significance. Her cold rationality and artificiality is compounded of petty abstractions and cuts her off from the sources of life. This parallel use of snake imagery in the three novels illustrates Forster's intense distrust of all abstraction.

19. *The Hill of Devi*, p. 47.

20. "The Defence of Poetry," *Shelley's Literary and Philosophical Criticism,* ed. John Shawcross (London, 1909), p. 131.

21. Compare Lowes Dickinson's description of "A Mystery Play" of Krishna and the milkmaids: "The Hindus interpret in a religious spirit this legendary sport of Krishna with the milkmaids. It symbolises the soul's wooing of God. And so these boys interpreted it. Their passion, though it included the flesh, was not of the flesh. The mood was rapturous, but not abandoned; ecstatic, but not orgiastic. . . . and always, on those young faces, even in the moment of most excitement, a look of solemn rapture, as though they were carried out of themselves into the divine." See *Appearances, Being Notes of Travel* (New York, 1914), p. 21.

22. The English first edition and all other editions I have seen read: "She was praising God without attributes. . . . Others praised him without attributes, seeing him in this or that organ of the body or manifestation of the sky." The text should read: "Others praised him with attributes. . . ." MS A so reads (Harrison, p. 698; see Appendix B for a discussion of the manuscripts).

23. This is a traditional meaning. See Coomaraswamy, "Symbolism of the Dome," *Indian Historical Quarterly,* XIV (March 1938), 56.

24. Other contrasts are: the upright Temple vs. the recumbent Hills; the god on his altar entirely obscured by a multiplicity of heterogeneous objects vs. the "nothing" of the caves; the impersonal beauty and oneness of the villagers vs. the echoed identity of pathos, piety, courage, and filth; the unclean sweepers and the necessary spot of filth which makes the spirit cohere vs. the caves with "not even a bees'-nest or a bat" (p. 130); the procession advancing from Temple to tank vs. the expedition unwinding in the Hills and retracing its steps; "the friendly sun of the monsoons" vs. the Marabar sun rising "without splendour" (p. 144); the trumpeting elephants, their howdahs empty out of humility vs. the single elephant of the expedition, "a nobody," "grey and isolated, like another hill" (pp. 156, 146); and the triumphant release of the prisoner vs. the howling mob (caught up in the residue of evil from the Marabar) which storms the hospital after Aziz's release. There are also contrasts involving snakes and snake imagery: see my "Note on the Snake Imagery of *A Passage to India*," *English Literature in Transition,* IX (1966), 108–10.

25. See the program note for the 1962 production of the play adapted from the novel by Santha Rama Rau. The note is cited in Natwar-Singh, *E. M. Forster,* p. 50.

26. *E. M. Forster: A Tribute,* p. xii.

27. "The Temple," *Athenaeum,* September 26, 1919, p. 947.

28. *G. L. Dickinson,* pp. 147–48; *Appearances,* p. 9.

29. *The Ideals of Indian Art,* p. 11. Forster, in a 1915 review of Sister Nivedita's

Footfalls of Indian History, sums up her views in this way: "And to the objection 'What is India? Are there not a hundred Indias?' She replies that India once was, still essentially is, and in the future visibly shall be, One, and shall give light to those who sit in comparative darkness." See "The Mission of Hinduism," *Daily News and Leader* April 30, 1915, p. 7.

30. "A Popular Theatre," *Athenaeum,* April 18, 1919, p. 217.

31. "The Gods of India," *The New Weekly,* May 30, 1914, p. 338.

32. *A Passage to India* may be viewed as a reaction to the disappearance of God in the nineteenth century. By the time of the decadents the gulf between humanity and divinity had widened disastrously. Twentieth-century writers have symbolized this world without God as the wasteland. Part II of Forster's novel is a great wasteland image in which India expresses the absence or disappearance of God and the Marabar expresses the nonexistence of God. But not all writers have been content to stop with the wasteland. Some have set about to restore the sense of an immanent spiritual force. This is Forster's object in "Temple." But the act of restoration is at the same time a devastating critique of all orderly and institutionalized attempts to put God back in the world. God is a mystery. And the mystery is that man shall be God; indeed, that man is God. (See J. Hillis Miller, *The Disappearance of God: Five Nineteenth-Century Writers* [Cambridge, Mass., 1963], esp. pp. 14–15.)

33. Reported by Wilde, *Art and Order,* p. 151. And see Stone's excellent chapter in *The Cave and the Mountain.* Though our interpretations diverge at many points (the caves as a womb symbol, for example), we frequently reach similar conclusions as we approach from different angles. In part this is the result of our essential agreement that "Caves" and "Temple" are starkly contrasted and that "Temple" signifies reconciliation.

Index

The Index includes themes and symbols. Three items which relate to "The Celestial Omnibus" will illustrate how the reader may use the Index to go beyond the discussion in the text. *London:* As Mr. Bons screams "I see London," he sinks through the liquid rocks. This liquidity may be associated with London's mud and flux in *Howards End. Rainbow:* The solar and lunar rainbow bridge may be related to the rainbow arch of love in *Howards End. Sun:* The sunrise of the boy's departure and the sunset of Mr. Bons' departure are illuminated by Jung's account of the journey of the sun, quoted in connection with "The Point of It." No one of these associations is made in the text.

Abbott, Caroline, 113, 115, 116–18

Abinger Harvest, 22, 124, 260, 279 n.24, 289 n.3; quoted 30, 49, 53, 71, 145, 150, 173

Abrams, M. H., 276 n.45

Absence, and Presence, 142, 216, 223–4, 227, 228, 232, 236, 244, 247, 269, 293 n.32

Achilles ("Celestial Omnibus"), 48, 70, 71, 81, 130, 131; shield of, 70, 71, 81, 91–2, 95

Adventure, 45, 46, 67, 71, 114, 133, 134–6, 151, 191, 195

"Albergo Empedocle," 68, 72–4, 82, 281 n.6

Allegory and allegorical, 22, 36, 38, 51, 59–60, 64, 66, 68, 70, 94–5, 280 n.32, 283 n.2

Allen, Glen O., 289 n.1

Allen, Walter, 16

" 'Amis and Amiles' at Weybridge," 278 n.12

Andrews, Mr., 58

Anglo-Indians, 16, 49, 221, 290 n.6, n.10

Anima, 46, 192, 193

Annan, Noel G., 274 n.2, n.3, n.5

"Anonymity," 18, 40, 289 n.2

Ansell, Stewart, 51, 130, 135, 141–2, 143, 149–51, 155, 159, 280 n.38, 283 n.4; his circle, 142, 144, 153, 162, 284 n.17

Anthropology, 13, 26, 32–3, 253, 276 n.32

Antichrist, 84, 157

Anubis (and hyena), 207

Apostles, The, 24, 25

Arch, 152, 153, 176, 195, 227, 229

Archetype (and type), archetypal symbol, mythic symbol, 14–15, 32, 42–3, 46, 60, 88, 102, 125, 128, 134, 166–9, 170, 191–2, 201, 212, 217, 260, 281 n.44; defined, 38, 91, 94, 162–3. And see Novel as archetype; Symbol

Archetypal characters, 14, 87, 95, 102, 120, 122, 126–30, 132–3, 155, 158–9, 165–7, 215, 286 n.3, 288 n.26. And see Demeter; Great Mother; Hero; Heroine; Narrator

"Arctic Summer," 129–31

Arnold, Matthew, 251, 252

"Art of Fiction I: E. M. Forster": *Paris Review interview*. See Furbank, P. N.

Asirgarh, 234

Aspects of the Novel, 22, 97, 114, 120, 128, 146; quoted 49, 99, 100

Austen, Jane, 47–8, 49, 106

Avery, Miss, 174, 186, 187–8, 191, 287–8 n.20

Aziz, 17, 202–48 passim (esp. 215–16, 225, 239), 262–70 passim, 290 n.6, n.8, 291 n.11, 292 n.24

Bantock, G. H., 275 n.8

Bartlett, Charlotte, 101–5 passim, 108, 110–12 passim

Bast, Jackie, 176

Bast, Leonard, 16, 172–3, 174, 178–82 passim, 185, 188–9, 192, 288 n.26, n.28, 291–2 n.18

Battersea Rise, 173

Baudelaire, Charles, 259

Beast and monk, 176–7

Beaumont, Evelyn, 77–80, 166

Beauty, 71, 101–2, 164, 187, 197, 204, 210, 213, 221, 225–6, 230, 231, 238, 254, 255, 267, 272, 292 n.24

Beckett, Samuel, 106

Beebe, Rev. Arthur, 101, 103, 107–12 passim

Beer, J. B., 289 n.1

Beethoven, Ludwig van, 58, 172, 174, 186, 197–9, 248, 279 n.24

Bell, Clive, 23–4, 274 n.3, n.6

Benn, Alfred W., 274 n.4

Bevington, Merle M., 274 n.2

Blackmur, R. P., 14

Blake, William, 26

Blavatsky, Madame, 35

Bloomsbury and Bloomsbury Group, 23–6, 29, 42, 63, 274 n.5, n.6, 277 n.5, 286 n.8

Bons, Mr. Septimus, 48, 68–71

Booth, Wayne C., 282 n.16, n.21, n.22

Bowen, Elizabeth, 47, 48 (quoted), 54, 198

"Break-Up Day—New Style," 278 n.12

British Museum, 24, 141, 145

Brontë, Emily, 40, 82

Brontës, 46

Brothers, 133–40 passim, 145, 150, 151, 156, 158, 285 n.35

Brown, E. K., 282 n.25

Browne, Sir Thomas, 69

Bunyan, John, 68

Burke, Kenneth, 167

Butler, Samuel, 31–2, 40, 107

Cadbury Rings, 137–9, 142, 144, 145, 153, 162; Figsbury Rings, 54

Cadover, 136, 138, 140, 147–53 passim

Cambridge University, 24–5, 53, 64, 134, 135

Campbell, Joseph, 133

Castor and Pollux, 67, 81, 156

Cave, 137, 139, 161, 230, 237. And see Marabar caves

"Caves," 20, 201, 227, 236, 293 n.33

"Celestial Omnibus, The," 48, 68–71, 76, 82, 91, 130, 131

Cervantes, 46, 50

Chandrapore, 19, 206, 216, 222, 234, 236, 237, 240, 265
Chaos, 157, 170, 194, 196
Chase, Richard, 114, 282 n.26
Christian, art, 277 n.8; Church, 84, 87; Missionaries, 227, 245, 270; Religion, 278 n.11
Christianity, 153, 201, 225, 234, 284 n.10
"Churning of the Ocean, The," 291 n.15
Circle, 82, 113, 124, 125, 182, 203, 227, 229, 231, 232, 247, 268; in *Longest Journey*, 153, 161–2, 163; of creation, 95–7
Circle and square, 141–4, 149, 160, 162, 284 n.17
Clapham sect, 23, 274 n.5
Claudel, Paul, 96
Codrington, R. H., 160
Coleridge, S. T., 96, 253, 255
Collected Tales of E. M. Forster: "Introduction," quoted 54
Comedy, 67, 113, 140, 158, 197, 199, 247
Comradeship, 169, 175–6, 177, 179, 190–91, 193–4
Connolly, Cyril, 280 n.40
Conrad, Joseph, 15, 23, 29, 50, 96
Coomaraswamy, Ananda K., 284 n.14, 292 n.23
Cooperman, Stanley, 291 n.12
"Co-ordination," 58
Cornwell, Ethel F., 253
Cox, C. B., 20
Crawley, Ernest, 284 n.17
Creation, by artist or narrator, 40, 41, 44, 96–7, 99, 198, 262, 281 n.6; of man, 270; of world, 143–4, 145, 230
Crews, Frederick, C., 16
"Curate's Friend, The," 58, 59

Daemon, 65, 283 n.2
Dante, 69, 146, 174
"Dante," 280 n.23, 285 n.36; quoted 146
Darwin, Charles, 31, 33
Death, 82–3, 133, 138, 157, 186, 196, 203, 204, 230, 287 n.10, n.14, 288–9 n.28, 291 n.18; in "Story of the Siren," 85–8; in *Howards End:* "the idea of

death saves," 174, 179–84, 187, 188, 191; in Mrs. Moore's initiation, 232–5, 246
Death in life, death from which life comes, life and death, etc., 44, 64, 67, 74, 75, 100, 106, 108, 113, 126, 130, 132, 140, 145, 154–5, 170, 178, 192, 194, 198, 230, 243, 258
Demeter, 141, 144–6, 148, 162, 192–4, 260; of Cnidus, 145, 147, 158, 285 n.20, 288 n.21. And see Great Mother
De Morgan, William, 279 n.24
Desolation, vision of, 84, 93–4, 194–5, 217, 226, 232–3, 246–50
Dickens, Charles, 157
Dickinson, G. Lowes, 24, 40, 190, 242–3, 274 n.6, 275 n.16, 278 n.13, 284 n.10, 289 n.30, 292 n.21
Dionysus, 252
Dome, 141, 143, 241
Dostoevsky, Feodor, 98, 128
Doughty, Howard N., 284 n.18
Dragon, 130, 132, 133, 136–7, 139, 141, 151, 197, 222, 230, 285 n.27, 292 n.18
Dreams, 37, 41, 60, 61, 128, 208, 222, 254, 287 n.14; in *Longest Journey*, 136, 140, 147, 154, 281 n.3
Dry, Avis M., 276 n.32
Dunwood House, 139, 149, 150, 151–2

Eager, Rev. Cuthbert, 101, 107
Earth, Earth-Mother, 79–80, 138–9, 144–5, 147, 148, 153, 162, 171, 192–3, 280 n.44, 283 n.4, 288 n.26. And see Demeter; Great Mother
East, 53, 143, 229, 242, 246
Echo, 17, 47, 86, 198, 221–37 passim, 240–41, 250, 266–9 passim, 290 n.9, n.10, 291 n.11
Ecstasy, ecstatic experience, 64, 80, 102, 144, 203, 219, 238, 246–7, 250, 252–8, 281 n.3, n.6, 287 n.14; as source of archetypal symbols, 13, 14–15, 91–5, 99, 120–21, 164–6, 168, 171, 190, 286 n.2
Ecstatic apprehension, vision, etc., 14–15, 34, 125, 136, 197, 226, 249, 292 n.21
Eliade, Mircea, 145, 284 n.16
Eliot, George, 106, 109, 128

Eliot, T. S., 13, 14, 15, 66, 204, 273 n.5, 290 n.10
Elliot, Mr. 136, 148, 158
Elliot, Mrs., 130, 138, 141, 144–5, 147, 148, 153, 155, 158, 159, 163, 283 n.4
Elliot, Rickie, 63–4, 93, 101, 132–3, 134–58 passim, 162, 166, 280 n.31, n.38, 281 n.3, 284 n.11, 285 n.36
Ellman, Richard, 256
Emerson, George, 91, 92, 101–3, 104, 107–8, 110–13 passim, 121, 126–7
Emerson, Mr., 101, 103, 107, 112
Engelberg, Edward, 259 n.
England, 24, 29, 76, 77, 92, 121, 131, 136, 142, 151, 154, 177, 178, 194, 197, 209, 210, 234, 256, 289 n.30
Englishman, 47, 87, 216, 221, 225
Epic, 46, 119, 125–6, 283 n.2
"Esmiss Esmoor," 205, 236
Estheticism, 28, 256, 257
Eternal, 62, 65, 85, 87, 124, 175, 186, 195, 221, 236
Eternal moment, 52, 57, 68, 83, 91, 165, 166, 219, 247, 249, 255, 260, 278 n.11. And see Vision, moment of
Eternal Moment, The: Dedication, 278 n.14
"Eternal Moment, The," 56, 83, 93
Eternity, 66, 94, 193, 230, 246, 265, 291 n.13, n. 18
Ethel, 76, 77
Eustace, 75, 82, 130, 132
Evil, 46–50, 63, 66, 67, 84, 87, 88, 106, 137, 157, 174, 198; in *Passage to India,* 206, 208, 212–15, 223, 229–33 passim, 239–40, 247–8, 250, 268, 290 n.8, n.9, 292 n.24. And see Good and evil
Evolution (and evolving), 31–5, 39, 41, 254

Failing, Mrs., 135, 136–8, 140–41, 148, 149, 150, 155, 158, 285 n.27, 292 n.18
Failing, Tony, 140, 148, 149, 155–6, 157
Family, 76, 184–5
Fantasy, 278 n.9
Father, 127–8, 133, 139, 148, 158, 284 n.11
Faulkner, William, 50

Feo, 57
Fiedler, Leslie, 162–3
Fielding, Cyril, 19, 202–48 passim (esp. 224–5, 239), 263–70 passim
Fielding, Henry, 47–8, 99
Fifth Symphony (Beethoven), 172, 186, 198
Figsbury Rings, 54
Flaubert, Gustave, 98
Fletcher, Angus, 94–5, 283 n.2
Florence, Italy, 101, 103, 107, 112, 113, 282 n.28
Ford, 77–80
Fraser, J. G., 33
Freud, Sigmund, 27, 33, 35
Fry, Roger, 23–4, 274 n.6, 286 n.8, 289 n.3
Frye, Northrop, 14, 50 (quoted), 162–3, 277 n.4, 286 n.3
"Function of Literature in War-time, The," quoted 194
Furbank, P. N. and F. J. Haskell, "E. M. Forster" (Interview), drawn on or quoted, 27, 53, 55, 189, 230, 283 n.3

Garnett, Edward, 52
Gennaro, 44, 75, 79, 82, 132
Ghost, 105, 108, 112, 173, 196, 207, 235, 253, 267, 269
Gide, André, 44
Gilgamesh, 285 n.35
Gino (Carella), 79, 113, 115, 117, 127–8, 129, 165
Gissing, George, 29
Giuseppe, 84–6, 93, 214, 246
Goblins, 47, 48, 172, 180, 197–8, 248
God, 42, 62, 93, 95–7, 136, 143, 157, 168, 190, 251, 254, 285 n.27; in *Passage to India,* 201–47 and 262–72 passim, 292–3, n.21, n.24, n.32; character as a god, 80, 132, 153. And see Gods
Godbole, Professor Narayan, 19, 200, 202, 211–50 passim (esp. 211–12, 223, 237–8), 271, 290 n.8; his song, 220–21, 224, 232, 233, 244, 263, 266
Gods, 30, 48, 66, 71, 77, 136, 151, 156, 184–5, 193, 284 n.10, 285 n.35, 289 n.28

"Gods of India, The," quoted 246

Goethe, Johann Wolfgang von, 53, 157, 174

Goldsworthy Lowes Dickinson, 274 n.6; quoted, 40, 243

Good, 37, 50, 93, 213–15, 230, 232, 238, 247

Good and evil, 48–9, 50, 51, 56, 57, 100, 106, 108, 208, 213–15, 223, 247–8, 278 n.8, 290 n.8

Goodman, Paul, 282 n.21, n.24, 283 n.2

Goodness, 48, 50, 88, 107, 109, 180, 236

Graham, Mr., 76

Gransden, K. W., 25

Grant, Duncan, 23–4, 274 n.2

Grass, 75, 101, 136, 138, 170, 174, 180–82, 184, 187–8, 192, 194, 280 n.38, 288 n.26

Great Mother, Universal Bride-Mother, Universal Feminine, Goddess-Mother, etc., 85, 87, 131, 133, 134, 137, 138–9, 144, 146, 148, 158, 192, 284 n.17, 288 n.26, 290 n.6. And see Demeter; Sophia

Greece, 34, 76, 92, 95, 111, 112, 153, 260; Athens, 60; Parthenon, 242; the Greeks, 34, 37, 73, 120, 149, 151, 185

Grey, 112, 178, 181, 182, 195–7, 231, 267, 292 n.24

Haddon, Miss 58

Hamidullah, 19

Hardy, Thomas, 29

Harold ("Albergo Empedocle"), 72–4

Harold ("The Point of It"), 64, 67–8, 81, 82, 131, 156

Harris, Wendell V., 275 n.14

Harrison, Jane, 29, 33, 37, 38, 41, 84, 276 n.39

Harrison, Robert L., 261, 266, 292 n.22

Hartog, Marcus, 275 n.18

Havell, E. B., 230, 243, 288 n.24, 291 n.10

Hawthorne, Nathaniel, 46, 48, 282 n.26

Hay (*Howards End*), 14, 170, 171, 172, 174, 180–83, 187–8, 191–2, 194, 288 n.26; hay fever, 182

Hearnshaw, L. S., 276 n.32

Heaslop, Ronny, 17, 205, 206–7, 210, 220–21, 228, 229, 263

Heaven, 69, 102, 116, 146, 167, 195, 241, 245, 280 n.31, 291 n.18

Heilbrun, C. G., 278 n.13

Heilman, Robert B., 279 n.25

Hell, 64, 67, 116, 139, 151–2, 194, 195, 197, 248, 291 n.18

Hercules, 149

Hering, Eduard, 31

Hero (type of, Archetype), 46, 125–6, 133, 143, 163, 185, 283 n.2, 284 n.11, 285 n.35; in the short stories, 60, 63, 68, 70, 79, 81, 87, 260; of romance, 103, 107, 113; Forster's presentation of, 126–31, 256 n.; in *Longest Journey*, 132, 147, 219, 260; Rickie Elliot, 134–41; Stephen Wonham, 121, 130, 148–59, 165, 285 n.36; absence of in *Passage to India*, 216, 222, 290 n.6

Hero, Child or Boy, 71, 130, 131, 143, 149, 280 n.44; Divine Child, 82, 87

Heroine (type of, Archetype), 46, 63, 87, 107, 110, 216

Herriton, Harriet, 115–16

Herriton, Lilia, 113–16 passim

Herriton, Mrs., 116

Herriton, Philip, 100, 113, 115–18, 166, 256

Hill of Devi, The, 238, (quoted), 243

Hindu, Hinduism, etc., 221, 227, 243, 266, 270, 290 n.10, 292 n.21

History, 14, 26, 33, 164, 165, 245

Hollingsworth, Keith, 290 n.10

Homer, 48, 84, 207, 283 n.2

Honeychurch, Freddy, 103, 104, 107

Honeychurch, Lucy, 91, 92, 100–105, 107–8, 110–13, 121, 126, 127

Honeychurch, Mrs., 104, 105, 107, 111, 112

Hopkins, G. M., 29

Howards End, 14, 16, 27, 28, 40, 51, 101, 130, 131, 145, 162, 164, 167, 170–99, 203, 219, 247, 279 n.20, 287 n.14, 291 n.18

Howards End (place and house), 93, 130, 145, 160, 167, 171–97 passim (esp. 183–8), 288 n.20

Huxley, T. H., 31

Hyena: See Anubis

Identification, 42–3, 251–5
Identity, personal, 128–39 passim; with nature or other-than-self, 15, 42–3, 74–5, 81–3, 91–4, 120, 164–6, 246, 248, 251–5, 258, 260
India, 54, 190, 203–50 passim (esp. 242–4), 254, 262–71 passim, 290 n.9, n.10, 291 n.18, 293 n.29, n.32
Individualism, Individuality, 42, 126–7, 155, 157, 158, 178, 182, 269, 271, 285 n.36
Infinity, 53, 180, 195, 204, 265, 289 n.28, 291 n.13, n.18
Ingram, John H., 285 n.28
Inskip, Mr., 77
"Inspiration," 277 n.48
Isherwood, Christopher, 90
Isolation, 82–3, 86, 196, 221, 224, 227–8, 231, 240
Italy, 75, 103, 108, 114, 127, 143

James, Henry, 29, 48, 69, 98–9, 108, 109, 114, 256
James, William, 35
Jefferies, Richard, 92
Jehovah, suburban, 209, 216
Johnson, Lionel, 257
Johnstone, J. Keith, 25, 154, 286 n.7
Journey or Quest, of hero, 69, 71, 132–6, 139–40, 148, 151–2, 222. And see Adventure
Joyce, James, 13–14, 15, 96–7, 256
Jung, C. G., 15, 27–8, 42, 46, 65, 251, 277 n.54, 284 n.9, 285 n.27, n.28, 288 n.26

Kafka, Franz, 14
Keats, John, 37
Kerenyi, C., 281 n.44, 284 n.15
Kermode, Frank, 256, 258
Keynes, J. M., 23, 274 n.6, 277 n.5
Kindness, 223–4, 268
Kipling, Rudyard, 29
Krishna, 131, 220–21, 237, 292 n.21; servant, 221
Kuno, 61–3

Lampedusa, Giuseppe di, 85
Lang, Andrew, 32, 34, 37, 207 (quoted)
Lang, Bebel, 274 n.6
Langer, Suzanne, 97 (quoted), 98
Laski, Marghanita, 92–4, 281 n.3, n.6
Lavish, Eleanor, 101, 105, 110
Lawrence, D. H., 15, 90, 96, 279 n.20
Lawrence, T. E., 278–9 n.14
Laycock, Thomas, 31
Leavis, F. R., 16, 19–20
Leggett, H. W., 282 n.21
Lehmann, A. G., 255
Levy, G. R., 276 n.39
Leyland, Colonel, 57
Life, spirit of, 88, 140, 141, 147, 155
Light and darkness, 111, 112–3, 115, 152–3, 197
"Literary Eccentrics," quoted 53
London, 24–5, 60, 70, 136, 148, 152, 173, 194–7, 248, 287 n.28
Longest Journey, 18, 51, 54, 63, 67, 72, 79, 92, 101, 118, 121, 126, 129, 131, 132–3, 134–59, 161–2, 167, 219, 260, 280 n.31, n.38, 281 n.3, 285 n.36, 292 n.18; "Introduction" to, 279 n.16, n.19; quoted, 135, 148
Love, 58, 66, 83, 87, 90, 113, 117, 127, 154, 156, 200, 274 n.6, 285 n.17, 287 n.10; in *Howards End,* 172, 175–80, 182, 190–91, 193–4, 196; in *Passage to India,* 19, 205–8, 224–38 passim, 246, 264–5, 271. And see Truth
Lucas, Mr., 53, 74, 75–7, 82, 91–2, 93, 95
Lucia di Lammermoor, 282 n.28
Lyall, Alfred C., 243, 275 n.27, 291 n.10
Lyell, Charles, 31
Lynskey, Winifred, 280 n.26

McBryde, Mr., 205
MacCarthy, Desmond and Molly, 23, 25
McConkey, James, 284 n.12
MacDonald, George, 280 n.28
Machen, Arthur, 276 n.47
"Machine Stops, The," 47, 59, 61–3, 76, 78, 81 (quoted), 82, 247
MacKinnon, Stuart, 282 n.22
McTaggart, J. M. E., 274 n.6

Madingley, dell near, 134–5, 138, 143, 145, 280 n.31

Maharaja of Chhatarpur, 238

Marabar, The, and Marabar Hills, 20, 47, 93, 202–40 passim, 247–8, 262–72 passim, 290 n.6, 291 n.11, n.18, 292 n.24, 293 n.32

Marabar caves, 86, 94, 205–47 passim (esp. 230–32), 263–9 passim, 289 n.3, 290 n.6, n.9, 291–2 n.11, n.13, n.18, n.24, 293 n.33

Marianne Thornton, 287 n.19; quoted 190

Masood, Syed Ross, 190, 215

Mau, 203, 239–40, 242, 269–70

Mau festival, Gokul Ashtami, Religious festival, etc., 19, 20, 164, 203–48 passim (esp. 236–41), 262, 266, 271–2

Mauron, Charles, 22

Meadow, 170, 174, 179, 181, 182–3, 187–8, 190, 192

Mediterranean, 113, 145, 242, 244

Melodrama, 114, 115, 282 n.27

Melville, Herman, 22, 40, 46, 50, 82, 282 n.26

Mephistopheles, 58, 157

Meredith, George, 29, 146

Mesmer, Friedrich, 34

Michelangelo, 174

Micky (Sir Michael), 47, 64, 66–7, 156, 214

Midas, 78

Mill, John Stuart, 38

Miller, J. Hillis, 293 n.32

Milton, John, 280 n.44

"Mission of Hinduism, The," 293 n.29

"Mr. Andrews," 58

Monteriano, 115–18, 121

Moon, 192, 195, 231, 234–6, 242, 244, 291 n.18; moonlight, 70, 191, 280 n.28; lunar rainbow, 69

Moore, G. E., 24, 26, 274 n.6, 277 n.5

Moore, George, 29

Moore, Mrs., 17, 19, 94, 159, 201–48 passim (esp. 232–6), 265–7 passim, 290 n.6 n.10, 291 n.18

Moore, Ralph, 227, 236, 240, 290 n.8

Moore, Stella (married Fielding), 227, 236

Moorman, Charles, 13

Morgan, Charles, 119

Mosque, 201–2, 225, 227, 235, 241–2; arcades of, 201, 225

"Mosque," 201, 242

Muddle, Muddledom, 47, 175, 196, 204, 224, 233, 240–46 passim, 266, 269

Munt, Mrs. (Aunt Juley), 170

"My First Opera," 283 n.28

Myers, Frederick W. H., 35–41 passim, 258

Mystery, Mysteries, 164, 224, 241, 243, 246, 250, 266, 293 n.32

Mystical Hymns of Orpheus, 146

Mysticism, 200, 281 n.3

Mystics, 47, 92, 175, 245

Myth, and mythical method, 13–16; and Jung, 27–8; and the unconscious, 39–40; and epic, 46; and allegory, 94; order and unity of, 95, 99, 162, 260; hero of, 125–6; other references, 84, 145, 155, 197, 230, 279 n.20, 284 n.11

Myth, critics and criticism, 13–16

Myth, students of, 33–4, 36–8, 168, 258–9, 276 n.29; Forster's agreement with, 41–3, 202–3, 206, 208, 212

Mythology, 26, 30, 32–3, 243, 253

Nameless Indian, Punkah Wallah, 209–12, 215, 216, 218, 248, 263–4

Napoleon, 58

Narrator (author-narrator), 97–121, 125, 162, 165, 166, 198, 215, 217–19, 248, 282 n.20, n.21; as archetype, 95, 99, 120–21, 286 n.2

Nature, universal (human), 37, 39–41, 62, 68, 82, 126, 155, 158, 202, 208–9, 210, 212, 258, 259, 284 n.11

Nature, universal (non-human), 37, 39, 41–3, 62, 73, 75, 76, 80–83, 113, 146, 179, 188, 193, 197, 202–4, 209, 226, 251–5, 258–60, 285 n.36. And see Identity

Natwar-Singh, K., 241, 289 n.4, 292 n.25

Nawab Bahadur, 204, 206, 207, 235, 236

Negation, 47, 108; in *Passage to India,* 20, 224, 228, 231, 232, 239–41, 245, 246, 250, 262, 266–9, 271, 291 n.18

Nerval, Gérard de, 255–6

Neumann, Erich, 168, 170, 284 n.11, 288 n.26

Newton, C. T., 288 n.21

Nietzsche, Friedrich, 90

Nineties, 28–29, 35, 39, 42, 252, 257, 287 n.14

Nonexistence, 86, 223, 228, 230, 232, 247, 267, 268, 293 n.32

Novel as archetype, 201, 212, 219, 247–8

Nureddin, 204

Oedipus, 75–6, 81

Old wise man, 110, 155

Oniton, 178, 179, 180, 196

"Only connect," 174, 176, 177

Order, in relation to myth, 13, 15, 260; in relation to narrator, 99, 120–21, 215, 247, 282 n.22; in relation to India and muddle, 204, 220, 233, 241–6, 267, 269

Orion, 62, 66, 81, 141, 147, 152, 153, 162

Ortega y Gasset, José, 46, 97, 98, 200, 277 n.4

"Other Kingdom," 47, 68, 77–80, 82, 134, 166

"Other Side of the Hedge, The," 59–61, 76

Pan, 85, 135, 146; in "Story of a Panic," 44, 75, 76, 81, 132

Panic and emptiness, 172, 176, 196, 198

Pantheism, pantheistic awareness, etc., 43, 251–2, 254, 260

Passage, 56, 239, 246, 250, 271; rite of, 18, 207, 233, 266

Passage to India, 16, 19–20, 28, 41, 86, 100, 121, 131, 142, 164, 201–50, 261–72, 278 n.11, 279 n.14, n.20

Past, 73–4, 80–82, 138, 143–4, 145, 153, 162, 171, 174, 178, 183–8 passim, 191, 193, 245

Pater, Walter, 145, 149, 252, 255, 259

Patterne, Sir Willoughby, 78, 103

Peaslake, Mildred, 72–4

Peaslake, Sir Edwin and Lady, 72-3

Pembroke, Agnes, 51, 72, 93, 135–40 passim, 149, 151

Pembroke, Herbert, 139

Personal relations, 23, 24, 45, 176, 227, 274 n.6, 279 n.23

Peter Grimes, 282 n.27

Petronius, 273 n.5

Philoctetes, 137

Pigs' teeth, 189

Plato, 36–8, 95, 143, 146, 167, 168, 175, 259, 280 n.44, 284 n.10

Plot, 110–11, 114, 173, 206, 262, 266, 282 n.21

Plotinus, 100, 220

Poetry, 36, 38, 172, 176, 204, 242, 255

"Point of It, The," 47, 53, 63–8, 82, 83, 131, 156, 214, 248

Pope, Alexander, 106

"Popular Theatre, A," quoted 245

Poulet, George, 44

Presence: See Absence

"Presidential Address, A," 277 n.8, 278 n.11

Proclus, 146

Prometheus, 149

Proportion, 175–8, 194, 222, 244, 288, n.26

Psychical research, 35, 276 n.32; Society, 35, 40

Psychology, 26, 27, 32, 34, 36, 40, 253

Puddle, 111, 203, 240

Punkah Wallah: See Nameless Indian

Quest: See Journey

Quested, Adela, 17, 202, 203, 205–11, 213–48 passim, 262–9 passim, 289 n.3 290 n.6, 291 n.11

Quinton, Anthony, 274 n.6

Rabelais, François, 46

Raby, Miss, 56–7, 83, 279 n.23

Raglan, Lord, 42, 168

Rahv, Philip, 98

Railway, 140, 195, 222, 237

Rainbow, 69, 81, 176

"Raison d'Être of Criticism in the Arts, The," 41

Rank, Otto, 156

Raphael, 58

Rationalism, Rationality, 137, 210, 229,

245, 277 n.5, 291–2 n.18; rationalist, 208, 226, 244

Rau, Santha Rama, 292 n.25

Realism, Reality, etc., 16–20, 28, 29, 45–6, 52, 114, 120, 125, 278 n.12

Rebirth (and reborn), 60–61, 74, 86, 138, 142–4, 151, 153, 162, 234. And see Self

"Recollectionism," 287 n.17

Reid, Forrest, 53

Rhea, 146

Richards, I. A., 185

Rimbaud, Arthur, 44

Ritual, 33, 37, 79, 81, 137, 164, 204, 257

River, 69, 76, 81, 101, 113, 146, 151–2, 153–4, 162, 180

"Road from Colonus, The," 54, 68, 74, 75–7, 81 (quoted), 91, 166. And see Tree

Robbe-Grillet, Alain, 106

Robert (father of Stephen Wonham), 148

Rohde, Erwin, 144, 153, 184–5, 252

Rolland, Romain, 245

Romance, 29, 46, 94, 125–6, 163, 282 n.26, 283 n.2; characters, 18, 87, 103, 106–9, 113, 212–13, 215; fiction, 13, 16, 46–51, 61, 68–9, 100, 113–14, 121, 126, 127, 157, 165, 201, 212, 247; pattern, 52, 55, 56, 57; Italian romances, 95, 99, 121, 219

Romantic, 28, 29, 42, 43, 110, 254–8 passim; hero, heroine, 107, 113, 125

Romanticism, Romantics, 26, 28, 29, 95, 252–6 passim

Room with a View, A, 91, 92, 93, 95, 100–13, 119, 121–2, 126, 127, 165, 166

Rose, mystic, 144, 152–4, 158, 163, 284 n. 17; roses, 267

Rubin, Louis D., Jr., 283 n.29

Sacred Lake, 103, 108, 111, 112

Salisbury, 136, 148–54 passim

Salvation, 62, 278 n.11; in Forster's fiction, 64, 67, 83, 86, 130, 156, 184, 187–8, 191; in *Passage to India,* 19, 227, 233, 236–40 passim, 271

Sanders, C. R., 274 n.2, n.3

Santa Deodata, 117–18

Satire and satirical, 49–50, 68, 104, 115

Sawston, 114–17, 135, 139, 151–2, 154

Schlegel, Helen, 130, 166, 167, 170–95 passim (esp. 177–8, 189), 286 n.7, 288 n.20, n.26, n.28, 291 n.18

Schlegel, Margaret, 40, 101, 166, 167, 170–97 passim, 248, 288 n.20, n.26

Schlegel, Mr., 288 n.20

Scholes, Robert, 282 n.21

Schroeder, E., quoted 143

Schwob, Marcel, 44

Sea, 64–5, 84–7, 93, 148, 151, 153–4, 197, 209–10, 221–2, 234, 236, 280 n.28, 291 n.11

Self: higher, lower, deeper, 36, 41, 73, 116, 153, 202, 206, 208, 211–12, 271; new, reborn, etc., 73, 81–2, 132, 134, 256 n.

Senior, John, 276 n.30

Serpent, 66, 136–7, 230, 246, 285 n.27, 291 n.18

Shakespeare, William, 40, 53, 124

Shelley, P. B., 238, 252, 253–4

Short Stories, 43, 49, 51–2, 55, 56, 79, 82–3, 87, 91, 120–21, 126, 131, 165, 166, 213, 219, 260, 278 n.11

Shri Krishna: See Krishna

Sidgwick, Henry, 35

Silence, 61, 75, 81, 85–6, 93, 136, 151, 155, 158, 220, 229–30, 240–41, 257

Siren, 84–7, 130, 280 n.44

Sirens, 53, 84, 280 n.44

Six Hills, The, 180, 184, 185

Snake, 136–7, 232, 240, 268, 291–2 n.18, n.24. And see Serpent

"Songs of Loveliness," quoted 230

Sophia, 192–3, 194

Stace, W. T., 281 n.3

Stars, 53, 62, 64, 66, 207, 208, 221, 231, 234–5, 237; in *The Longest Journey,* 141, 145–8, 152, 158, 162, 285 n.36

Stephen, Adrian, 23–4

Stephen, J. Fitzjames, 56

Stephen, James, 274 n.2

Stephen, Leslie, 24

Stephen, Thoby, 23, 24

Stephen, Vanessa (married Clive Bell), 23, 24

Stephen, Virginia: See Woolf

Stevenson, R. L., 29

Stewart, J. A., 37–8, 41, 43, 168, 258, 259–60

Stone, Stones, 42, 143, 160, 165; in *Passage to India*, 19, 224, 238

Stone, Wilfred, 18, 279 n.14, n.20, 293 n.33

Stonehenge, 148, 154

"Story of a Panic, The," 44, 54, 68, 74–5, 76, 86, 93, 130, 131–2, 157

"Story of the Siren, The," 47, 84–8, 93, 130, 214, 246, 248

Strachey, Lytton, 23, 274 n.6

Stream, 70, 75, 77, 93, 101, 140, 144, 145, 151, 152–4, 182, 191. And see River

Subconscious: See Unconscious

Subliminal and Supraliminal, 36, 37, 39, 82, 212

Sun, 42, 64–5, 78, 79, 80, 116, 158, 168, 197, 203, 204, 206, 221, 222, 236, 240, 243, 263, 267, 292 n.24; sunlight, 149, 150; sunrise, 69, 183, 263; sunset, 65, 69; sunshine, 112, 136, 177, 195

Swinburne, Algernon, 43, 156

Sydney-Turner, Saxon, 23

Symbol, Symbols, 15, 22, 27–8, 32–42 passim, 93, 161, 162, 191–5; defined, 161; in Forster's fiction, 13, 28, 49, 59, 61, 63, 93, 95, 114, 116, 125, 155, 158, 163–4, 171–2, 190, 206, 216, 249, 258, 260. And see Archetype

Symbolists, 30, 256–9, 287 n.14

Symonds, J. A., 29, 33, 35–6, 38, 41, 43, 168, 258–9, 286 n.10

Symons, Arthur, 255, 256–7, 287 n.14

Tank, 203, 234–5, 239, 292 n.24

Taylor, Jeremy, 20

Temple, 73, 143, 242; in *Passage to India*, 202, 212, 239, 247, 248, 292 n.24

"Temple," 20, 201, 202, 203, 217, 236, 247, 269, 271, 293 n.32, n.33

"Temple, The," quoted 242

Tennyson, Alfred, 65

Terrible Mother, 139, 230–31, 285 n.27. And see Dragon

Tetrazzini, Luisa, 282 n.28

Thomas, Dylan, 15, 127

Thornton Family, 173, 274 n.1; Henry, 23

Thornton, Marianne, 287 n.19

Time, 38, 44, 65, 144, 164, 165, 188, 194, 245–6, 271, 291 n.18

Tolstoy, Leo, 48, 127–8

Totality, 99, 120, 154, 156, 167–8, 170, 171, 201, 219, 247, 249, 254; and mythic unity, 122, 164, 169, 219; sense of, 92, 94, 99, 120, 128, 162, 190, 192

Tragedy, 158, 162, 180, 198

Transformation, 77, 80, 133, 153, 170, 177, 196; ecstatic, 91–2, 164, 166; feminine figure of, 192, 193, 288 n.26

Tree, 42, 84, 161, 165, 167–8, 190; in Forster's fiction, 77–9 passim, 101, 134, 145, 179, 184, 195, 203, 233, 266–70 passim; on road from Colonus, 76, 81, 91–2, 93, 95; at center of Rings, 137–46 passim; at Howards End (wych-elm) 93, 145, 160–86 passim, 188–94

Trilling, Lionel, 16, 20; quoted 45

Truth, 68, 175, 242, 283 n.4; Adela's vision of, 206, 210, 213, 217, 234; Love and, 67–8, 175–6, 194, 223, 234, 288 n.20; Reality and, 134, 135, 142–4

Tunnel, 152, 207, 231, 235

Turtons and Burtons, 224, 249

Twilight, 139, 222, 233, 248

Twins, 67, 156–7. And see Brothers

Two Cheers for Democracy, 275 n.12, 282 n.27; quoted 18, 22, 40, 41, 45, 96, 177, 198, 200, 215

Tylor, Edward, 276 n.29

Tyndall, John, 32

Unattainable, 142, 202, 218, 221, 237, 241, 245–6, 271

Unconscious and Subconscious, 27, 28, 31, 39–43, 155, 157, 253, 254, 258, 277 n.47, n.48, 279 n.20, 289 n.3; in Forster's fiction, 60, 73–4, 81–2, 85, 87, 130, 137, 140, 196, 256 n.; in *Passage to In-*

dia, 209–12, 231, 246, 264, 291 n.11.
And see Identity, with nature
Universe, 35, 36, 66, 92, 94, 142, 144,
146, 162, 190; in *Passage to India,* 203–
6 passim, 214–15, 219–50 passim, 265–
71 passim, 290 n.8, n.10. And see
Achilles, shield of; Goblins
Universe, oneness with, 205, 206, 246–7,
269–71; and Mrs. Moore, 201–2, 234–7,
248
Unseen, the, 173–83 passim, 195

Vashti, 61
Velasquez, 22
Vickery, John B., 275 n.26
Vine, 183
Virgil, 190
Vision and anti-vision, 59, 73, 75, 165
Vision, artist of, 52–5, 249–50
Vision, moment of, 50, 76, 120, 136,
165, 206, 213, 217, 281 n.6. And see
Eternal moment
Vision, Visionary experience, 17, 43, 48–
51, 100, 109, 113, 114, 121, 124, 215,
219, 220, 254, 255–6, 281 n.6, 286
n.2; ecstatic, 92–5, 164–6; in the short
stories, 56–88 passim, 91, 95, 130;
Rickie Elliot, 144, 147, 154, 281 n.3;
Margaret Schlegel, 167, 179, 183, 187,
191, 195, 196–7; Adella Quested, 206–
8, 213, 217, 225–6, 263; Fielding, 226;
Mrs. Moore, 226, 227, 232–3, 246–8
Vyse, Cecil, 103–7 passim, 111, 112

Wagner, Richard, 90, 190, 285 n.27
Waite, Arthur, 34
Warren, Robert Penn, 18
Wasp, 19, 238, 248
Wasteland, 17, 46, 201–2, 204, 227–8,
236, 240, 262, 265–9 passim, 290 n.10,
293 n.32
Wellek, René, 254–5
Wells, H. G., 29
Werry, Richard R., 289 n.1
West, 60, 176, 227, 229, 242
Westbury
Westcott, B. F., 37, 38, 41, 95, 168, 212,
258, 259–60, 276 n.39

Westburg, Barry R., 286 n.7
Western, 220, 226, 244, 246
Where Angels Fear to Tread, 54, 79, 95,
101, 113–19, 121–2, 127–8, 130, 165,
166
Whewell, William, 134, 283 n.1
"White Devil at Cambridge, *The,"* 278
n.12
Whitman, Walt, 174
Whyte, L. L., 275 n.19, 276 n.46
Wickham Place, 174, 183, 186–8, 194, 195
Wilcox, Charles, 170–71, 174, 183, 184
Wilcox, Dolly, 287 n.15
Wilcox, Henry, 48, 173–8 passim, 184,
187, 194, 196, 275 n.13, 288 n.28
Wilcox, Paul, 170–71, 172, 178, 188–9,
288 n.26
Wilcox, Ruth (Mrs.), 27, 93, 130, 145,
159, 167, 170–71, 172–88 passim, 192–
5, 196, 216, 287 n.20, 288 n.26
Wilcox, Stewart C., 280 n.32
Wilcoxes, the, 16, 49, 172, 173, 175, 178,
182, 186, 196, 289 n.30
Wilde, Alan, 279 n.23, 289 n.1, 293 n.33
Wilde, Oscar, 29, 35
Williams, Basil, 274 n.6
Willowes, Lolly, 58
Wiltshire, 93, 121, 135–6, 139, 140, 142,
143, 149, 151–2, 162, 163
Wimsatt, W. K., 286 n.1
Windy Corner, 103, 108, 111–12
Wonham, Stephen, 54, 79, 92, 121, 126,
130, 131–3, 135–45 passim, 147–59,
162, 163, 165, 191, 283 n.4, 285 n.27,
n.28, n.36
Woolf, Leonard, 23–5
Woolf, Virginia, 16–18, 23, 24, 45, 99,
278 n.13
Wordsworth, William, 43, 252
Worters, Harcourt, 47, 77–80
Wych-elm: See Tree

Yeats, W. B., 29, 98, 256–9 passim
Youth, 64–8, 75, 80, 85, 87, 102, 127,
149, 179, 183, 198. And see Vision,
artist of

Zeus, 85, 289 n.28